IN TWO
COUNTRIES
WHERE THEY TURN
BACK TIME

IN TWO COUNTRIES WHERE THEY TURN BACK TIME

GROUNDHOG DAYS IN EGYPT AND BULGARIA

PETER PAUL O'CALLAGHAN

CONTENTS

Contents

JUST A QUICK WORD

I was going to call this section "Preface" like everyone else does but if I did that, I knew that you, the reader, would skip over it and I'd rather you didn't as there are one or two things you should know. I started to write this particular account in October 1998 and by March the following year having realized that I had produced enough material for three books, I undertook a series of re-writes, revisions, updates and overhauls for many years, during which time I changed the running order from chronological to geographical and back again. There were also a number of titles, many of which were discarded, as soon as they were considered. In the end I opted for "*On a Morning from a Bogart Movie,*" the first line of Al Stewart's song *"Year of the Cat,"* as it was set in North Africa, only to find that I'd been beaten to it by one Richard Russell who had used it for a detective novel. Undeterred, I cannibalised the second line of the same song and continued with that.

So, why did I take so long to complete this book? The main reason was a problem every first time author has, that is, where to place it and who to approach. I gave up at this stage and for a long time took things no further. I was advised to buy the "Writers and Artists Yearbook" which, I was told, contained some good advice and an exhaustive list of contacts but, if anything, I was discouraged by what I read there. For instance, they advised every new writer to get an agent which appeared to be good advice, until they added that no agent would touch a new author unless he/she had first been published – a typical "Catch 22" situation, which I chose to ignore. However, after having had several manuscripts returned, I became disheartened and remained so until I contacted Kindle.

It would be untrue if I were to say that I spent the whole time from October 1998 until now writing and editing this book. Indeed, I spent most of that time not writing it at all in the near certainty that I would never see it in print due to the reluctance of the British publishing industry to entertain unknown writers. From a commercial point of view, I can understand their approach. After all, they are in business to make money for their shareholders rather than to launch the tentative careers of unpublished authors and I was suitably discouraged, so much so that I selected certain edited passages from the text for inclusion on the "Gates of Vienna" website in essay form, while retaining the copyright.

When I first started to write this book, it was intended to be a simple travelogue but other stories found their way in. For instance, the section on Hungary is really about labour relations in the UK during the 1960s and 1970s and the failure of the various politicians in office at the time to take control of a deteriorating situation. This opened the way for the hard line policies of Margaret Thatcher from 1978 onwards. I was an active trade unionist from the mid-1960s onwards and lived through it while it was happening around me. It was the time of the Cold War and there was Communist inspired disruption around the world as Communists, their sympathisers and fellow travellers created mayhem all over Europe, Asia and the USA. A modified version of the chapter on Hungary appeared on the *"Gates of Vienna"* and *"Vlad Tepes"* websites in April 2017.

When I was much younger, I worked with two older colleagues, one of whom served in the Long Range Desert Group during the Second World War, while the other served in the RAF during the 1950 – 1954 Suez Canal Zone Emergency. Most of what they told me never made it to these pages, indeed the story of the Emergency itself and the young national servicemen who served, has been effectively suppressed by successive, self-serving British Governments, but not completely. Accounts of events that occurred are included in a web site called *"Britain's Small Wars"* along with details of many other global military engagements instigated by our politicians which our armed forces had to clean up. In writing this section, I should like to thank John Marrs, webmaster of the Canal Zone section of the Britain's Small Wars website for the assistance and encouragement he gave me, for fact checking the content and for suggesting amendments which I gratefully included. The website is currently down but I have hard copies of the articles I have used and credited them accordingly. I should also like to thank John Middleton, author of *"Sweetwater Blues"* for his advice and encouragement.

In passing, I recall making one or two unkind comments about the USA initially in the context of the 1994 World Cup but, they accorded with my observations at the time and as such should stand. I might not have made them today, either in part, or, indeed, at all as my view of that great country has changed over the years. Anyone seeking legal redress should be warned that I have no possessions and anyone wishing to indulge in lawfare should save themselves the trouble for this same reason.

Finally, a belated thank you to Dorian Hayes for lending me his computer on which to write the first draft and to David Thompson for printing it out.

Peter

GROUNDHOG DAY

With a population of just under 6000, Punxatawney, Pennsylvania sounds as though it was named by a committee and it is more than likely that this peaceful little backwater would have whiled away its tranquil existence in pastoral obscurity had it not been for two episodes that between them propelled it onto the world's stage. The first of these was Groundhog Day, a public holiday in rural Punxatawney and the second, the 1993 film of the same name produced by Harold Ramis.

The origins of Groundhog Day, a bizarre celebration, date back to the early Christian festival of Candlemas, when clear skies on Candlemas Day were interpreted as being a sign that winter would last for another six weeks or so. The introduction of furry rodents into the process came about far later in Germany when local people took to observing the post hibernation activities of badgers on Candlemas day. If, after emerging from their sets, the badgers were to catch sight of their own shadows, they were reputed to go back to sleep for another six weeks leading people to assume that the winter was not yet over, a strange tale since Badgers are supposed to be nocturnal. No matter.

The Punxatawney variation originated in 1887 after German settlers had come to Pennsylvania but instead of the badger it was the Woodchuck or Groundhog whose end of season awakening came under scrutiny. Nowadays, there is but a single such rodent, popularly known as "Punxatawney

Phil." This furry quadruped has been installed in a purpose-built shelter on a wooded hill curiously named "Gobblers Nob," which, if nothing else, confirms my suspicion that Americans have no comprehension of English colloquialism. On 2nd February annually, revellers gather at Gobblers Knob in their tens of thousands to see whether or not the beast would remain outside its winter quarters after waking from hibernation.

The film is set against the background of these festivities and features Bill Murray as a television journalist sent to cover the event who finds himself being forced to re-live the same day over and over again until he becomes a better person and is allowed to move on with his life. Since the film was released, the term "Groundhog Day" has found its way into modern folklore where it has come to mean doing the same thing over and over again, hoping for a different outcome.

Although I was never forced to re-live the worst day of my life as was the character in the film, I have, nevertheless, associated the term Groundhog Day with my visits to Egypt and Bulgaria because every time I went to either country, something unpleasant happened to me or to somebody I was with. Indeed, my first visits to Egypt and Bulgaria turned out to be such complete disasters that I forced myself to go back having deluded myself that nothing quite so bad could ever happen again but, of course, it did.

Whether I have become a better person as the result of my experiences, I'd rather not say but every time I have seen posters or film clips promoting holidays in either country, I swear I've heard the menacing voice of Clint Eastwood's Dirty Harry invading my subconscious to ask me whether I felt lucky, "*Well, do yuh?... Punk.*"

Up until now, I never have.

BULGARIA 1991

WHY DIDN'T THEY GO CHRISTMAS SHOPPING LIKE EVERYBODY ELSE?

I had never considered Bulgaria as somewhere I really wanted to go. That is not to say I was never going to go there but I was going to go to a lot of other places first and if I dropped dead before I got around to Bulgaria, then so be it. Not surprisingly, my first visit was pure accident. I'd booked up to go on one of those so-called adventure holidays to Egypt over Christmas and New Year 1991/92. The idea was that by judicious use of bank holidays and recess days I could take three weeks holiday while only using two weeks of my annual leave. There was, of course, a down side to this. I was due to fly on 21st December which was the last Saturday before Christmas and the people arranging my package tour found out at the last minute that they could not book flights for all of us with Egypt Air. I was one of the unlucky ones and, after scouring all the bucket shops in and around the Earls Court Road, I found I was faced with two choices and, frankly, I didn't like either of them. Firstly there was a Balkan Air flight via Sofia. The alternative was a Tarom flight via Bucharest and I really couldn't choose between them. Balkan Air, the Bulgarian State Airline, used Russian aircraft and the word was, while the Russians could provide a reliable plane if they wanted to drop a nuclear bomb on you, they weren't quite so diligent when it came to reliability and passenger safety. As for Tarom, the Romanian state carrier, they used Russian aircraft, too, which left me very little choice. So I opted for Balkan Air and set in motion a chain of events, which made life extremely interesting while they unfolded.

I arrived at Heathrow Terminal Three about an hour early for check-in but I needn't have bothered. I could have turned up three hours late for all the difference it made. Half the population of the British Isles had arrived in front of me and none of us was going anywhere. Flights were being delayed, diverted, cancelled and probably forgotten in the chaos and confusion. I must have stood in the check-in queue for the best part of five hours and then taken another two to clear customs and pass-port control. Check-in time of 12.30 came and went as did the 2.30 flight time, while those of us going to Sofia stood aside to let those travelling to places like Athens and Salonika check in ahead of us. Then, when we finally made it through to the departure lounge, there was still no flight time and we were left to lay siege to the British Airways service desk along with all the other lost souls who had been left by their tour companies to fend for themselves.

They gave us a few £1 vouchers ostensibly to buy a meal, but over the previous ten years the prices at Heathrow had been jacked up to such an extent that all my precious vouchers would run to was a cup of black coffee and a sticky pastry both of which I had to consume standing up. I have never seen a departure lounge at Heathrow so crowded. In a scene reminiscent of one of those Costa Del Rip-off airports through which we were herded in the early seventies, there wasn't a seat to be had. It was the last Saturday before Christmas for God's sake, so how come all these people weren't out Christmas shopping? Then things started to improve and by eight thirty we were in the air. While we had the service desk under a virtual blockade we elicited the promise from a stewardess that our connecting flight to Cairo would be held for us.

She lied.

After all the waiting around, once we were airborne our progress was quite swift. I put this down to the strong tail wind, the congenial company and the endless supply of free alcohol poured into us by the cabin staff. By the time we landed with a bone-crunching jolt on Sofia Airport's ice-encrusted runway, followed instantly by another and then another after that, we were so full of beer and benevolence we never considered that we might have been in any sort of danger. The post flight alcoholic glow stayed with us while we scuttled uncertainly across the frozen runway in sub zero temperatures but the reception we encountered upon entering the terminal soon sobered us up. There were armed soldiers everywhere as we ascended the stairway sign posted "Transit Passengers." I'm not sure what sort of trouble they were expecting or from what source but when I reached the growing throng around the reception desk and heard what they were being told, I surmised that it might have been us.

There was a very young woman, certainly no more than eighteen, dressed in an ill-fitting blue uniform that made her look frumpy. She stood alone and vulnerable behind a long table top, that extended from one wall to another, completely blocking off one end of the hall and the lines she delivered were so well rehearsed, I had a strong suspicion that it might have been the only English she knew.

"You were late. Plane has gone. You will go to hotel two days. Plane will come Monday. You go. OK!"

"No, it's not OK as it happens" I said to her. "What happened to our connecting flight?"

"You were late" she started again.

"But we were promised that ... '

"Plane has gone. You will go to Hotel ... ."

It was no use. I moved away and, as there were no seats, I leaned against the wall and others took my place as the woman continued to recite her party piece. They were red in the face, they were shouting but she stumbled on through her monologue regardless. Occasionally, I could see her strained expression through gaps in the mob. Tears were rolling down both cheeks now as she kept on with her message. She was nothing more than an animated voicemail but the crowd would not relent. Why did nobody come to help her? In the last century they put miscreants in the stocks so that people could throw missiles at them. Now, they put them behind a desk in an Eastern European airport so people can yell abuse at them. They didn't need to be miscreants either, just young girls out late at night in the wrong place at the wrong time. I was angry, too but shouting at her wasn't going to change anything.

To take my mind off this scene out of bedlam, I took out my camera and loaded a film but this attracted the attention of one of the goons with a gun and I put it away quickly before he came over and smashed it or something. I'd lost my tour. The others had been met at Cairo Airport that afternoon and were probably tucking into a first class meal at a hotel and here I was watching a lynch mob baying for the blood of a teenage receptionist. She, in turn, was reciting an incantation over and over again, hoping that it would placate them but it only made matters worse. It was like a scene from a Hammer Horror film. All we needed was Christopher Lee to appear in his Dracula suit and the sequence would have been complete. At least the location was right.

I felt like I was the only one there, who realised what was happening. There had never been any question of a connecting flight. That had left hours ago and it had been full. The authorities were well aware of this and the girl had been put there to bear the brunt of our wrath. Presumably, when we had shouted ourselves out, we would be more amenable to reason and we would be taken to a hotel, but for the present, we hadn't yet reached that stage. After another fifteen minutes, the men with the guns decided we had been suitably softened up and marched us through to immigration where our passports were stamped with temporary entry visas and we were pushed and shoved into a vast warehouse of a place where we were to await our baggage. Some of us needn't have bothered.

The baggage reclaim area could best be described as a single storey building, three storeys high with a hollow lofty ceiling area that had no discernible use and would have been extremely expensive to heat if anyone had ever felt the need to do so. The floor space was so extensive that it could have staged an eleven a side football game were it not for the presence of three luggage carousels. We were gathering around carousel number one as instructed by our armed warders when carousel number three sprung into action and a trail of suitcases, bags and backpacks emerged from a hole in the wall and collapsed onto the moving belt in a series of untidy heaps. Some minutes after it had started, it stopped abruptly and without explanation, leaving about two thirds of the assembled company without their luggage. This happened again on a number of occasions until there were only seven of us left without bags. Those who had claimed their belongings were marched off, presumably to somewhere warm with a bed for what remained of the night, all except for us, who some wag ultimately named "The Sofia Seven".

We had been thrown together at Heathrow and, with a shared feeling of impending doom we kept close to each other for safety. There was Andy, a stout Londoner from Barnes and Louise, his French fiancee. Matt, an Irish lawyer based in North London, who was off to Cairo for a second honeymoon with his Australian wife Lisa. Mick, a big teddy bear of a man in his late forties, who had dropped out a decade ago to a farm cottage in North Wales where, if he was to be believed, he lived in quiet seclusion, broken only by occasional visits from his children. Maria came from Brazil, way down south from a place I couldn't pronounce. She was a small, attractive woman in her thirties who was currently doing a PHD in nutritional studies at the University of Reading. She was a member of the university choral society, which was currently rehearsing "Aida" and she said she was doing some extra curricular research. As for me, I was supposed to be on a package tour but somebody had lost the package.

We were shuffling around trying to keep warm when Andy produced a small, plastic American football from his hand luggage so we picked up sides and started to play, taking care not to run into any of the luggage carousels. I don't think any of us knew the rules but we'd all seen it on television, it didn't look as rough as rugby and if it was played by Americans, it couldn't be too difficult to pick up. The two remaining armed guards were nonplussed. What we were doing was clearly unauthorised behaviour but we weren't damaging anything and we were not unruly in any sense of the word. I think what saved us in the end was that we had organised ourselves and that had struck a chord with our military escorts, that and Matt giving each of them a packet of Bensons and a hefty swig of his duty free Scotch.

All the running around had certainly warmed me up and taken my mind off the fact that when I'd packed my bag, I'd done so for the sunny haze of Cairo rather than the arctic bitterness of Sofia but in a few minutes, that was likely to be academic. Our game was terminated in the time-honoured fashion – someone blew a whistle but it wasn't a referee. It was a uniformed customs official complete with peaked cap and nightstick. His English wasn't brilliant but it was a good deal better than my Bulgarian. After a couple of attempts, he managed to explain that there was no more luggage left on the plane and ours had gone missing – probably to Nairobi.

We started to protest but thought better of it when our minders who we assumed were friendly, started to unsling their weapons, and, fearing with some degree of justification that any act of dissent on our behalf was likely to be suppressed with the butt of a rifle, we meekly acquiesced and allowed ourselves to be taken to a minibus and driven to a hotel. I didn't really notice where we were going but, thankfully, it did not take long to get there. We were unloaded outside what looked like a modern hotel and, surprisingly for that time of night – it must have been after three a.m. by then – the reception area was crowded with people who looked like locals but none of us was particularly interested in them or what they might have been doing there at that time of the night. It took another fifteen minutes while they found rooms for us but the whole charade merely confirmed my suspicion that they had been expecting us all along even before we had left Heathrow. Right then I didn't care. I'd had a hell of a day. I had little more than the clothes I stood up in. It was freezing cold outside. It was three thirty in the morning local time and I was all in. Anything else that wanted to happen would just have to wait until after breakfast.

I managed about two and a half hours sleep and arrived downstairs for breakfast at nine thirty. My uncharacteristic act of early rising could be put down to my unfamiliar surroundings, the inclement weather and the notice in my room to the effect that anyone arriving for breakfast after nine thirty wouldn't be served. I joined Mick and Maria who said they had been there for some time. It looked as though the others were going to give it a miss and I didn't blame them. There was a buffet type table from which Mick and Maria told me the waiters had been serving guests earlier. Curiously, they had been ignored. I got up and spoke to one of the waiters and he made it clear that if he served us, then we would have to pay him ten US dollars each. I explained this to the others and Maria jumped to her feet angrily and stormed downstairs to reception. I had been under the impression that we were getting full board and neither Mick nor I was going to part with any cash.

Ten minutes later, Maria reappeared with an official looking man in a black suit. After a few brusque words with our waiter, which drew a surly response, he started to shout at him, which prompted the waiter to shout back. Reinforcements then arrived in the form of a dozen more waiters and they started shouting at the man, too, stopping every so often to glower in our direction. Suddenly, the shouting stopped and the man from reception calmly issued instructions to his staff before coming to our table. He politely informed us that breakfast would be served immediately and he apologised for any misunderstanding. We thanked him for his trouble and this, we thought, was the end of it but something similar happened at lunch and again at dinner. I was to learn later that all sorts of shenanigans went on at Bulgarian tourist hotels and what had happened to us at breakfast had been a pretty common occurrence. After another delay, we were served with bread, cheese, a couple of slices of cold salami, a hard-boiled egg and thick black coffee. It wasn't the best breakfast I'd ever had but it might well have been the best they had to offer and we accepted it gratefully.

After breakfast we went down to reception and found Matt and Lisa at the desk, joined almost immediately by Andy and Louise. Apparently, a young couple in our group had just gone off skiing on the slopes of Mount Vitosha, overlooking the city. Given our situation, it seemed like an interesting way to spend the day and about as far removed from meandering around the pyramids at Giza as we could get but it was not to be. It appeared that the transport had just left and while the hotel staff assured us that they would have been happy to arrange for another bus, there wasn't one to be had so that seemed to be that. The good news was that the tram for the city centre stopped just outside the hotel so we changed up some currency and went out into the cold to see what we would find.

The buildings in the street outside were formal, grey and Gothic, the way all Eastern European capital cities are supposed to look. There was snow and slush on the ground but the sky was crystal clear and the sun was shining. The tram stop was on the opposite side of the road and we had to negotiate our way under a subway to reach it. The dimly lit underpass doubled as a subterranean market and was full of traders selling a variety of items such as foreign cigarettes, plastic lighters, food and cheap household goods in a scene reminiscent of the underground galleries either side of the Galata Bridge in Istanbul, but this one was smaller and less crowded. The people, too, would not have looked out of place in Istanbul being dark and swarthy, the women wearing brightly coloured scarves while the men were scruffy and unshaven. I guessed that Gillette didn't have much of a market in this part of the world. A few of the people wore overcoats to protect themselves from the cold but the majority just wore several layers of normal street clothes that did not look anything like sufficient. They must have been very resilient people.

The tram service was frequent and ours contained a fair number of English speaking locals who were able to tell us when we arrived at the Eagle Bridge at the end of the Boulevard Lenin, which was where the hotel reception staff had advised us to get off. Following the collapse of communism, the new Government had decided to change all the names of the streets and buildings but they hadn't yet completed the exercise. It was going to be very confusing until they did but fortunately that wasn't my problem.

Having left the tram, we set off along what we later learned was Boulevard Ruski, past the imposing facade of Sofia University until we saw a small park where, despite the freezing weather, there was an open air art exhibition and a small market. It was here that I became detached from the others. As we moved from picture to picture and from stall to stall I noticed breaking through the trees a little distance away, a magnificent Byzantine church, with numerous golden domes like a cluster of gilded bubbles glinting in the late morning sun. I felt a powerful, almost gravitational urge to get closer and, only slowing down long enough to take the occasional photograph, I pressed on until I stood outside its wooden gates. While I had seen disused Byzantine churches in Turkey, particularly the Hagia Sophia in Istanbul, which had started its life as a Byzantine cathedral, I had not seen such a church in use nor had I seen one as outstanding as this. Unfortunately, its darkened interior proved to be a disappointment after the splendour of its domes and I was unable to take any photographs. Even if it had been light enough, there was this woman with a face like a bull mastiff and built like something out of WWE strutting around barking "No Photo!" every time she saw a camera. I was in the middle of telling her what I thought she should do before stopping myself. What was the point? It was bad enough having to be here at all without getting involved in a slanging match with a woman who had more bristles than Desperate Dan.

As I left the church, I noticed through the trees an emerald green spire supporting what looked like a small gold sphere. However, I was feeling a bit peckish and my watch said it was mid-day so I retraced my steps to the Eagle Bridge and caught the first tram back. I'd written down the name of the hotel – the Hotel Pliska – on a piece of paper I'd found on the writing desk in my room. As I boarded the tram, I recalled that I hadn't paid last time and no-one appeared to be collecting fares this time either. I put it down to a hangover from the failed Marxist miracle, which had probably provided all public transport free of charge. A nice idea, but considering all the repression and human rights violations that went with it – I'd sooner have paid the tram fare.

I arrived in the hotel restaurant at about twelve thirty. Lunch was in full swing and appeared to consist of a mutton goulash with vegetables but as with breakfast, it didn't look as though I was going to get any. Every time I tried to attract the attention of a waiter, he either looked the other way or lit up a cigarette – it seemed that chain smoking was a national pastime here – so in the end, I went over to where the waiters were congregating, only to be told that I would be served lunch if I parted with twenty US dollars. I was about to go to reception to complain when I felt a tug at my arm. When I turned around, I found that a portly, middle-aged man of eastern appearance had hold of my sleeve.

"Why don't you go back to your table and I'll have a word with the waiter" he said with a smile.

"Do you think it will do any good?' I asked.

"Wait and see" he replied, still smiling.

I went and sat down and in a few moments he joined me, having first spoken to the waiter who had just asked me for money. Sure enough, two plates of lamb goulash arrived at our table. My new companion's name was Nico, a Greek businessman from Salonika. He was on his way home from a trip to London and a regular visitor to this hotel. He confirmed my earlier suspicions that we had been booked in for a two-day stopover in Sofia as soon as we had bought our tickets. He always travelled with Balkan Airways because it was cheaper and he enjoyed his two-day freebie here. When I asked him about the waiters hustling for bribes he told me it was part of the culture. The Communists had been so corrupt that the only way people could get anything done was by bribing the relevant official. Now that Communism had been officially abandoned in this Country, everybody had got in on the act. The waiters, like most other employees in Bulgaria were very badly paid. Since prices had shot up in recent years, they had no option but to try to make ends meet by squeezing the customers at work. Normally, I would have sympathised but being on the receiving end of their kleptocratic activities had coloured my perception.

Nico was an entertaining companion and he knew Sofia well. Apparently the Byzantine church with the golden domes I'd just visited was the Alexander Nevski Memorial Church which, he said, had been built to honour the Russian soldiers who fell in the 1877 war against the Turks. Building had started in 1882 and took over 40 years to complete. Curiously enough, the gold leaf, which coated its many splendid domes, was a later feature having been donated by the Soviet Union in 1960. I thought it was odd for an atheistic regime like the Soviet Union to give gold to decorate a church in a subservient satellite state. When I mentioned this, Nico explained that in spite of the repressive government during the communist era, the churches remained open and services, especially at the

Alexander Nevski Memorial Church, were very well attended. This was a tribute to the faith of the congregation and, indeed their courage, for in those days, Bulgarian security had been controlled directly from Moscow and the KGB were at the Church doors after every service to note who was there, presumably so they could gather evidence of counter revolutionary activity for use at a later date.

The green spire I had seen through the trees was part of the Russian Church, or to give it its correct title, the Church of St. Nicholas the Blessed. According to Nico, I was unlikely to find it open but he encouraged me to go there anyway, just in case. Nico had to telephone his wife immediately after lunch so I took a tram back to the Eagle Bridge to continue my sightseeing. When I reached the Russian church, it was closed. This did not prevent me from admiring its exterior, which, although small, was spectacular with yellow tiled walls and five golden domes. The domes did not seem as bright as those of the Nevski church, leaving me to conclude that the benevolence of the former Soviet comrades did not extend to this side of the street.

I carried on walking in no particular direction until in the distance I saw a small Ottoman Mosque. As I drew closer, I could see that the doors and windows had been bricked up, giving the impression that some sort of restoration work had been started and then abandoned. Later, I learned from Nico that this was the former Banya Bashi Mosque, which had been built by Mimar Sinan. Sinan had been a Turkish engineer, acclaimed for the creation of many classic Ottoman mosques including the Mosque of Sultan Suleiman the Magnificent, deemed by those who know to be the greatest mosque in Istanbul. I thought for a moment that the Banya Bashi Mosque might have been the greatest mosque in Sofia, but somehow I doubted it, standing forlornly at the roadside, a diminutive replica of Sinan's Turkish masterpieces, a treasure reluctantly discarded by the Ottoman's as their crumbling empire finally fell. The mosque had been closed throughout the Soviet era and had reopened sometime after my subsequent visit. Curiously enough, I have not felt the need to return to Sofia for a third time to see it again.

Earlier I had passed a great featureless pile that could have been lifted straight from the set of Citizen Kane. It resembled a cross between a block of offices and a department store and I went back for a closer look. It turned out to be the TsUM , pronounced as it looks, the central department store in Sofia. It had the usual recognisable departments such as menswear, ladies fashion, furniture, kitchenware etc, except that there wasn't much of anything to buy. I'd read about places like this in mainstream newspapers and magazines all over the English speaking world. Several years later I would find out for myself that it had all been true. As for Tsum, there were huge spaces all over the place, which could have been used for goods had there been any. I headed for the menswear hoping to pick up a few bargains. After all, I'd just lost most of my luggage and I was in desperate need of socks and underwear but there was nothing to be had, at least, nothing that might fit me. Most of what was there looked as though it had come from a charity shop and, as far as fashion was concerned, I'd seen better in Tesco's.

I had been walking around for some time and I was beginning to feel the need of a cup of tea and a quick snack. There was a cafeteria on the top floor so I joined the queue and shuffled along until I got to where tea, coffee and cakes were being dispensed but if there had been a choice at all, it was take it or leave it. There were a few ordinary-looking cakes and a plate of what looked like stale bread. I took a cake and, when they didn't have tea, I asked for coffee which turned out to be a tepid, weak, watery liquid with a strange, oily aftertaste. The cake had been stale a week ago. I was glad I didn't have to live here.

Nico joined us for dinner and we put two tables together while the waiters served us with modest quantities of goulash that had clearly been left over from lunch and re-heated. Whether it was because of this, or perhaps Nico's presence at the table, the waiter made only a cursory attempt to extort money from us before serving our food. We responded to this uncharacteristically good service with a whip round for him, which resulted in a ten-dollar tip. He thought we were mad but took the money anyway. By then, vast quantities of beer had been consumed and our resentment at losing our luggage and having to be in a freezing, post-soviet mausoleum like Sofia had temporarily diminished. I was very aware that I had missed the chance of seeing the pyramids and was still feeling a sense of anger and loss but I felt more sympathy for Matt and Lisa. They had paid a great deal of money to book the bridal suite for one night at Shepheard's hotel in Cairo. Unfortunately, it was for the previous night and they'd lost their money. I decided that, if they could take their loss with a good grace then so could I and I would make the most of my unscheduled stop in Sofia no matter how dreary it turned out to be.

Bulgarian beer is strong. According to the labels on the bottles, the beer we had been drinking was for export only and had a specific gravity of 14 degrees by volume. Strangely enough, it was not soupy like most Western European beers of that strength. Indeed, it was quite thin by comparison but the hangover with which I awoke the following morning bore testimony to the potency of the brew. By the time I presented myself in the restaurant, it was ten thirty and I'd have done anything for a cup of coffee. I went straight up to the waiter we'd tipped the night before.

"Breakfast feeneeshed!" he said as he saw me coming.

"What about coffee?' I asked

"Coffee feeneeshed!' he said but I knew the drill by then.

"How much for a pot of coffee?' I asked

"Ten dollar' he replied without stopping to think. He probably didn't rate his chances of getting twenty and five wasn't enough for him.

"Ten dollars – two pots of coffee" I countered

"OK" he answered.

"No milk, lots of sugar, OK?"

"OK".

I spent the rest of the morning drinking coffee trying to mitigate the effects of last night's binge and by lunchtime I had come close to succeeding. I didn't feel much like eating lunch and went back to the town centre instead. TsUM was closed for some reason. I did not know whether this was a recent thing or whether the communists, too, had kept some kind of Sabbath. Maybe they just thought their labouring poor needed one day off a week and Monday was as good a day as any. There were plenty of people around, though. Right outside the main entrance to TsUM, there was a street market, which extended down to a sunken plaza where a variety of goods and services were being offered but nothing I needed. I carried on walking.

A VIOLENT FAREWELL TO SOFIA

I returned to the hotel halfway through the afternoon and thought I saw Maria sitting across the lounge from me. I waved, she acknowledged me and I went over to find it wasn't her at all.

"You want madam for night?" she asked, "Thirty dollar".

Considering I'd paid ten dollars for two pots of coffee that morning, it was probably a good deal for anyone who might have been interested but, in the classic mode of Sunday newspaper reporters, I made an excuse and left. As usual, the foyer was full of people but up until now, I hadn't taken much notice of them. There were a number of women who were obviously hookers, under dressed with too much make up and a number of dubious looking characters who could have been pimps or dealers.

"Hey, you wanna score?" asked a stubbly-faced scruff of about thirty who had sidled up to me. His attempt at an American accent was passable. "I got dope, speed, anything you want." Just then I wanted a cup of tea but had already despaired of getting one.

"I'm sure you have" I said and went upstairs to the bar. It was just as bad there. More scantily clad women with matchstick limbs draped over swarthy looking men in the sort of sharp western suits they didn't sell at TsUM. We were due to leave for the airport sometime that evening but nobody knew when.

Gradually people started to assemble in reception at about five o'clock. The bus finally came for us at about six-thirty and took us straight to the check in, although we seven had nothing left with which to check in. We did ask for a loss report but nobody knew what we were talking about. In the end, they took us to a man at the Balkan Airlines office, and after failing to make him understand what we wanted, Matt sat down at the word processor, typed out a statement, printed off seven copies on Balkan headed paper and was handing them round when the man from Balkan Airways went into a blind panic and threw us out. Matt's statement wasn't worth the paper it was printed on but at least we felt better for having it.

We shuffled through customs and passport control into a spacious but dilapidated departure area – it could not possibly have been described as a lounge. There were several rows of wooden benches and two refreshment kiosks but it was two hours before either of them opened. At nine o'clock one of them started to serve beer but there was no indication of when we would be leaving. Apparently there were two planeloads of people, both going to Cairo and we were in the later party. By this time, the departure area had become extremely crowded and, with very few seats, those who couldn't get to them had to sit on their luggage and those who didn't have luggage had to stand.

We'd been stuck in here for about four and a half hours when a group of German students who'd clearly consumed a few beers started to make a noise. They were protesting at the way we were being treated and who could blame them? Four uniformed Policemen appeared and rapidly headed in the direction of the noise, manhandling aside anyone who happened to be in their way. Having located the source of the disturbance, they then proceeded to set about the German boys with what looked like metal truncheons. There was blood everywhere. It is difficult to know how long the beating would have lasted had it not been for the flash of a camera from somewhere close behind me. The Police immediately left their bloody victims and went looking for the photographer. Unfortunately, they came straight to me.

"Camera!" the senior one barked.

"No." I said shrugging my shoulders. Mine was at the bottom of my shoulder bag and it was staying there.

"Camera!" he screamed, malevolently, waving his metal stick in my face. There were a lot of things I wanted to say to him right then, none of them very pleasant and a lot of suggestions I wanted to make as to what he could do with his metal truncheon but I thought better of it. He was clearly in a mood to shed more blood so I did not reply. Instead, I pointed over my left shoulder in the direction from which the flash had come. All four of them galloped off to brutalise someone else but they didn't need to go far. I heard them gruffly repeat their demand for a camera and when I turned, I saw what must have been the Obergruppenfuhrer or whatever they call uniformed thugs in Bulgaria, snatch one from a young fair haired man, coldly rip off the back, tear out the film and expose it before slamming what looked like an expensive compact Nikon onto the concrete floor where it shattered into tiny fragments. All four of them slowly stared around the hall slapping their metal truncheons into the palms of their hands as they did so, defying anyone to protest. When nobody moved, the Policemen slouched off emanating an ill-concealed air of displeasure leaving the passengers to observe their exit in stunned silence. Thank God we were leaving.

EGYPT 1991

FOLLOW THAT TOUR

It must have been five am by the time we'd disembarked from the battered old Balkan Airways Tupelev and stumbled across the pitch-black runway towards the airport terminal known as the "Old Airport." The condition of our aircraft did not inspire confidence as one or two of the light switches did not work and there was a constant and disturbing dripping of water from the light bulb in the aisle adjacent to my seat. Additional terminals would be added to the Old Airport a few years later but this particular building was a dirty dismal place, a sort of study in sand blasted concrete and had originally been used as a military air terminal by the Americans in World War ll.

Getting through the formalities should have been straightforward – at least for us. Balkan Airways had already lost our luggage so there was no need for us to hang around in baggage reclaim. Also, at that time of the morning, there was very little activity and even fewer passengers – in fact there was no-one around at all apart from a couple of young men wearing smart suits and badges. These were representatives from independent tour companies who were waiting to pounce on us once we had cleared passport control. Unfortunately, there was nobody at the passport control desk either which meant we were stuck there until somebody turned up. Mick suggested that we should head straight to Giza so that we could watch the sun rise over the pyramids. I'd planned to contact my tour company as soon as I could but it would be some time yet before their office opened so I said I'd go along. But first, we had to clear passport control.

It was obvious that the immigration officers were expecting passengers to be held up for some time in baggage reclaim and they were probably enjoying a quiet break until they were needed. One of the tour touts who was wearing a badge, which bore the legend "Ginger Tours" went to find somebody and returned almost immediately with two uniformed officials in tow. One of them armed himself with an official stamp and manned the desk while the other stood and watched. The man with the stamp processed the others very quickly but something seemed to bother him about my passport. He showed it to his colleague and then he went into an adjoining office, taking my passport with him.

"What's happening?" I asked the man from Ginger Tours, who said his name was Ali

"He says the serial number is wrong" he replied

I was not in the mood for this.

"Bollocks!' I shouted, "How can a bloody serial number be wrong? He's taking the bloody piss!" I headed off to the office to sort it out with Ali in hot pursuit.

'Relax' he said, 'No problem, but do not get angry, you will just upset them'.

Upset them? Right then, I was in the mood to hospitalise them but I knew this approach would get me nowhere. We found our official with two of his colleagues in a small grubby office with a desk, two chairs and a computer that did not appear to be working. My passport was on the desk and when I came in, the two newcomers appeared to be taking great interest in it. They were very convincing. They might even have convinced me that there was something irregular had I not been to the Passport Office in Petty France to renew it personally.

"Ask them what's happening' I asked Ali. There was some brief discussion in Arabic between the four of them before my companion turned to me.

"He says the serial number on your passport is incorrect" said Ali glancing uncertainly at the nearest official. Then, moving a little closer and speaking more softly he said 'Maybe a little money might help them to change their minds.' It had been a long and tiring night. I'd had no sleep and the last thing I wanted was a crude shakedown by Egyptian immigration. I took a very deep breath.

'Who's in charge here?' I asked calmly. Ali repeated the question and they looked at each other blankly before one of them said something in Arabic to Ali.

'Boss no come until nine' said Ali, 'maybe he not come before ten, maybe ten thirty'. I'd heard that one before, so I sat down in one of the chairs, reached over, retrieved my passport and made a great show of getting comfortable.

"I want the Police here now." I said slowly in an assumed officious tone. I fixed the three miscreants with what I hoped would pass for a chilling stare and continued

"Nobody is leaving this room until the Police arrive so pick up the phone and call them at once." Ali told them what I'd said which started off a heated discussion between the three crooked officials. Clearly, this wasn't in their script.

"They want to know why you want Police' Ali told me after they'd all stopped talking.

"I want these three to be arrested and thrown into jail" I said in a matter of fact way, "I am being delayed here for no good reason. There is nothing wrong with my passport. I know it. They know it. They are just trying to extort money from me. Presumably extortion is a criminal offence in this country and I want action taken." Ali stood there with his mouth open, seemingly unable to speak. "Tell them what I said" I told him and he did so. He was hesitant and the others were hanging on his every word. After he had finished there was stone cold silence for about ten seconds. Nobody moved. Nobody spoke.

Then Pandemonium broke out.

The two new officials turned on their colleague and started yelling at him. I don't know what they were saying but it didn't sound like they were offering to buy him a drink. For his part, he was shouting back, but his riposte was less assured. While all this was going on, I leaned over and asked Ali what all the shouting was about.

"They say he bring trouble on them. Maybe they lose jobs. Maybe go to prison." I shrugged.

"Tell them if they stamp my passport now, I'll forget all about what just happened'. I nearly asked for money to keep quiet but I thought I'd better not push my luck. The original official who had caused all the trouble produced a stamp and an inkpad from the desk drawer and I gave him my passport. He stamped it grudgingly and slid it back across the desk at me. I smiled, thanked him ironically and got out of there before he changed his mind.

I hurriedly left the immigration area behind me and, with Ali in tow, went off in search of the others. I didn't have to look far. Ali led me to a left turn just past the immigration barrier where there were numerous kiosks, most of which were closed and shuttered but all bearing the names in English of various local tour operators. In the middle of it all, I could see Matt and Mick in earnest discussion with an aging rotund Egyptian while the others gathered round.

"They can't take us to the pyramids" Mick said on seeing me, "He said they don't open until nine. He can take us to a cheap hotel, though. Maybe we can get our heads down for a few hours".

'Suits me' I said, 'What's everybody else doing?'

Matt and Lisa wanted to go to Shepheards to see if they could salvage anything from their lost booking and Maria decided to go with them. Andy and Louise said they'd come with us. Aziz, the portly Egyptian, with whom Mick was bargaining, had a car and he finally agreed to take us to a hotel, while Matt, Lisa and Maria took their chances on the taxi rank outside. Our car, when we saw it, was a bit of a surprise. It was very old and very, very small – a Fiat 127, I think the model was. At first sight, I doubted whether Mick could fit into it on his own, never mind the rest of us but our lost luggage once more proved to be a blessing because there was no way anything but a few items of hand baggage could have fitted into the minuscule boot. Mick managed to squeeze himself into the front passenger seat after the three of us, by some miracle, made room for ourselves in the back. Aziz then set off as though he was piloting a re-entry capsule and we soon left the airport far behind us.

Although it was still dark, the street lighting showed us a good deal of our immediate surroundings which were not very inspiring, all tall square concrete buildings. The romantic illusions portrayed in the travel brochures were nowhere to be seen. City of Gold it was not, although my vision was impaired by the fact that Louise was sitting on me but Andy was much worse off. I was sitting on him.

We were taken down a labyrinth of narrow side streets flanked by more tall characterless buildings until we stopped outside the hotel. We knew it was a hotel because there was a sign in English to that effect over the entrance. Had it not been for that, it would have been no different from any of the other buildings in the street. Maybe they were all hotels. I was relieved to see that at least it looked like a hotel inside. The foyer was full of cigarette smoke and there was a reception desk with a few battered chairs and tables that had seen better days though not in my lifetime. There was an eerie looking man behind the reception desk negotiating room rates. His angular features were distorted in the twilight of the dimly lit room and he bore a startling resemblance to Boris Karloff but by then, the whole weekend had started to catch up with me and I was feeling desperately tired. We took two twin rooms for the equivalent of one pound sterling a head but unfortunately they were on the eighth floor and there was no lift.

The porter led the way as we trudged up flight after flight of bare concrete steps in an enclosed cement-rendered stair well. I suspected that part of the building was still in the course of erection – and indeed might never be completed – but in my state of fatigue, I really didn't care. The room looked passable. Mick took the bed farthest from the door while I tore off my shoes, socks and clothes and climbed into the other one.

When I awoke, it was daylight and I groped around on the floor for my watch. It was 11.30 A.M. but whether that was local time I couldn't say as I couldn't remember whether or not I'd adjusted my timepiece when we landed. It didn't matter. I had to get moving. I picked up my shoulder bag and went outside to find the bathroom.

There was no hot water in the taps or the shower but for a pound a head, I was lucky to get water at all so I made the most of what there was. Fortunately, the hotel had provided clean towels so I was able to have a shower. For all I knew, my own towel had arrived in Nairobi by now, along with the rest of my clothes. When I got back to the room, Mick was awake but did not seem inclined to get up. I didn't really blame him. As I was putting on my shoes, I explained that I was going to try to catch up with my tour, which, according to my calculations had now reached Aswan. We were booked on the same flight out, so I wished him a good trip and would see him in a couple of weeks.

The reception area looked just as unwelcoming in the morning as it did when I arrived. There were no windows so any daylight there might have been outside failed to penetrate and the same dim lamp we saw earlier was still attempting to illuminate the area. Apart from the man at reception, who didn't look a bit like Boris Karloff by now, there were two other Egyptians sitting at a table, smoking with empty coffee cups in front of them. I paid my bill and showed him the address of my tour company, which I shall call Sinai Desert Tours. He said I would need a taxi and he wrote down the address in Arabic for me to give to the taxi driver. We went outside and he hailed a battered Fiat parked a little way down the narrow street, which looked as dismal in daylight as it had the night before. There was some dialogue in Arabic and the receptionist told me it would cost twenty Egyptian pounds – at that time there were six of these to one pound sterling so it sounded like a good deal.

The taxi driver said his name was Ali and he came from a village near Luxor. This worried me. He probably knew his village very well, but how well did he know Cairo? My fears were well founded. The Sinai Desert Tours office was in Heliopolis, a smart commercial and residential suburb away from the downtown area. He said he knew the district but he did not know the address, although he told me he would ask someone when we got closer. Twenty minutes later he had asked four people already and we were no nearer our destination. I could tell he was getting desperate when he started to ask me where it was but I hadn't a clue. At least I was honest enough to admit it. Once, he took me to a block of flats in a residential street and tried to tell me that this was the place but it couldn't have been. I could see he was getting fed up. The time this journey was taking was eating into his profit margin and preventing him from picking up anybody else. Inevitably, he started to ask for more money but I ignored him.

We had to be very close as we had been up and down the same road about four times but had been unable to locate the exact address. Every time Ali asked someone for directions, we found ourselves being sent back the way we had just come no matter which way we happened to be facing at the time. Finally, we stopped outside this bright multi storey office block. We'd stopped there twice already and each time we were sent first one way and then another. We asked an elderly man where he thought the place might be and he turned round, pointing to what looked like the eighth floor of the building in front of us … and he was right. I gave Ali another five pounds on top of his fare and, after a few more words with the elderly gentleman, presumably to ask the way to the place from which he'd started, he roared off in his Fiat, leaving me staring into a black cloud of exhaust fumes.

There was a uniformed commissionaire on the door and a lift so I had no trouble finding my way. Sinai Desert Tours was buzzing with activity and, at the height of the tourist season this was hardly surprising. There was a collection of smartly-dressed, dark haired young women working away at desk top computers, occasionally interrupted by sporadic bursts of telephonic interference from the various appliances scattered around the office. Egypt had not yet succumbed to the curse of the mobile phone but I guessed that, even as I stood there, someone, somewhere was working on it.

A beautiful olive skinned young woman with brown eyes and severely tied back hair greeted me. I told her who I was and she showed me to a comfortable chair in the reception area, ordered coffee for me and proceeded to make a series of phone calls on my behalf – one of which was to Aswan to warn them to expect me. In the meantime, she organised someone else to type me a statement for my insurance company to the effect that I'd missed three days of my tour and my luggage had gone missing, adding at the end that none of the above was the fault of Sinai Desert Tours.

I spent about half an hour sitting comfortably in the reception area watching people coming and going when a smartly dressed young man aged about twenty-five came up to me, introduced himself as Ali and said he would take me to the airport and put me on a plane to Aswan. I thanked the lady in reception for her kindness and followed Ali to the lift. His car, another Fiat, had more lumps and scrapes than a relief map of China. In an earlier existence it could have been the sole survivor of a demolition derby or maybe a mini cab in Southall. While I was at the Sinai Desert Tours offices there had been an unseasonal cloudburst that had only lasted about fifteen minutes but it was enough to leave several large pools in the road, and, once we were travelling on the various flyovers and underpasses, we found the low lying areas to be flooded causing vehicles to crawl through water up to their wheel arches. Ali told me that there was no drainage in the road system as, most of the time, any rainwater just evaporated in the heat. It had to be an improvement on the slush and ice in Sofia.

Once we arrived at the airport, Ali put on a badge, similar to those I had seen that morning only this one read 'Sinai Desert Tours'. This enabled him to park his car in a reserved area and to enter places marked 'out of bounds' or 'Staff and Authorised persons only'. I'd never been behind the scenes at a major airport before and I was curious to know what went on. Unfortunately, Ali was leading me through a warren of dirty, litter strewn corridors at such an alarming pace that I never had the time to stop and find out.

One of the corridors opened out into a public area where there were offices occupied by various air travel companies, many of which I had never heard of before. We stopped outside one displaying an 'Egyptair' sign and Ali told me to go in and buy a ticket.

"Be sure to buy an open ticket" he advised me. He seemed to know what he was doing and I did as I was told. In a matter of minutes, the transaction was completed. The ticket cost me about a hundred US dollars and I went outside, handed it to Ali and we were off again at a pace that only the Durham Light Infantry or an Olympic class road walker would have found comfortable. After another series of twists and turns we came to a huge check-in area about half the size of the main terminal at Gatwick but with twice as many people, many of whom looked as if they were emigrating and taking with them every single possession they had ever owned. They would have needed a Hercules transport plane for the luggage alone. I noticed there was one particular queue, much longer than any of the others that went around the perimeter of the hall and out of a door at the far end. There was no way they were going to get all these people on one plane. My fears were not alleviated when Ali told me that this was the queue for the Egyptair flight to Aswan and steered me straight towards the check-in past a few hundred very disgruntled Egyptians.

"Don't worry" he said reassuringly, "the man on the desk is my uncle. He will make sure you get on the plane."

When we got to the desk, Ali explained my predicament to his purported relative. Before I knew what was going on, I was instantly handed a boarding card and we were off again, avoiding all the various formalities until we arrived at the departure lounge.

"I leave you here' said Ali, 'but first you must give me twenty pounds'. He did not explain whether this was a fee for the services of Sinai Desert Tours, money to cover his expenses or just baksheesh, but whatever it was for, it was cheap. Without his help, I could have been at the back of that queue for the check-in, or worse, I could have been outside trying to buy a ticket. I gave him thirty pounds and was happy to do so.

I slept through most of the flight and nearly got off at Luxor by mistake as no one had explained to me that we would be stopping there first. Immediately I went into a very deep sleep only to be awoken by a sharp bump, which announced that we'd landed in Aswan and I was soon in a taxi heading for the Hotel Cleopatra where, hopefully, the rest of the tour party were staying. I presented myself at the hotel reception desk where I was confronted by two surly men in their forties, who clearly didn't want to be there, but, as they were, they were going to be as unhelpful as possible. They looked at me as though I'd come to empty the dustbins and had entered through the wrong door. Maybe they didn't like my Marks and Spencer Shetland wool sweater. They said the hotel was full and they tried to turn me away twice. I told them I was with the Sinai Desert Tours group but they did not believe me. In a fit of exasperation, I told the man nearest to me to fetch the manager but this did me no good. He was the manager. Finally, I persuaded them to produce the list of Sinai Desert Tours clients and when they did so, I pointed to my name, which had been crossed through in pencil.

"He not come" said the manager.

"Yes he has. It's me and I'm here" I said

"No," retorted the manager emphatically, "It says here he not come so he not here. Hotel full. You go now."

I felt like Doc Daneeka in Catch 22 after the aircraft he should have been on had crashed and he had been declared dead by his comrades because his name had been on the flight roster. The hotel paperwork said I hadn't arrived so I wasn't here, and that was the end of it. I took out my passport and showed it to the manager to prove that I was his missing guest but if I thought this would bring about a change in his mood, I was only partially correct. He became even more surly. He had set his heart on showing me the door and it was looking less and less likely that he'd be justified in doing so. In the end, he accepted the situation albeit reluctantly.

"You wait for Mr. Saleh," he growled unpleasantly. "He boss of Sinai. OK?"

"OK." I said. It was all I could do. I had not eaten since breakfast in Sofia the day before and was beginning to feel hungry but I did not want to have anything further to do with these two jobsworths. I could smell food being prepared somewhere and it was bothering me. In the end I gave in and asked the manager where I could get something to eat.

"No!" he snarled angrily, "you wait there for Mr. Saleh."

I went back to my seat and stayed there for a while watching people come and go. After about ten minutes, I was joined by three elderly German ladies, and, after a brief conversation, they said they were going to the hotel restaurant on the first floor so I accepted their invitation to join them. As we got up, I saw the manager glowering at me. I gave him the middle finger and followed the ladies up the stairs.

Forty-five minutes, a shish kebab salad and a pot of coffee later, I took my leave of the three ladies, thanked them for their company and prepared myself for another confrontation with the manager, but to my relief, the two old miseries had gone and there was a different man at the reception desk. I went up to him, explained who I was and asked whether Mr.Saleh had appeared yet.

"Not yet' he said in flawless English, "if you would like to sit down over here' he said indicating a table close to his desk, "I will tell you when Mr.Saleh comes."

I thanked him for his trouble. It was not an ideal situation. I would have liked the opportunity to look around the town for a while, as I knew I would be leaving in the morning but at least I was finally in the right place.

"Can I get you a beer?' asked the man in reception. It sounded like a good idea and I accepted gratefully. He summoned a waiter who went away and brought me a glass from the refrigerator and a litre bottle of beer labelled 'Stella Export'. Sadly, it was not Stella Artois but it was cold, wet and fizzy and I was happy at last. As the beer went down, I felt the tension drain out of me. I was about to order another when the receptionist called out to me.

"Mr. Saleh's coming now' he said and waved to catch his attention.

He was smaller than I'd imagined, about five feet five inches tall, in his late twenties or early thirties with fierce brown eyes, a small moustache and straight black hair that was receding prematurely.

"Call me Saleh" he said as he shook my hand. "They told me you were coming this afternoon. Come, we must talk." He promptly ordered two beers, sat down and went into tour guide mode. He took me through the history of Upper Egypt and Aswan and then told me what he planned for me the following morning while the others were relaxing. I had a lot of time to make up and it appeared that I was going to be busy. I told him about the reception I'd had when I arrived at the hotel and the trouble I'd had getting the manager to believe me. When I told him how rude they had been, he was genuinely surprised and pointed in disbelief to the man currently on duty.

"No. Not him" I said, "He's been great. It was the other two."

"I will talk to them" said Saleh "but first I must get you a room."

And he did. I sat there for another hour and another two beers talking to Saleh when I looked at my watch. It was eleven thirty, I was tired and a little drunk and, as I was going to be called at six thirty next morning, it was time I turned in. My room was beautiful with pale pink walls soft bedding and nothing like the cheap flop-house I'd left that morning. As I undressed, I realised I only had one other shirt, two pairs of underpants and three pairs of socks, all crushed up in my shoulder bag. Somehow, I had to make time in the morning to buy some more.

CRUISING THE NILE ON THE AFRICAN QUEEN

There was a knock at my door at a quarter to seven, which did not disturb me as I was already in the bathroom shaving. I stuck my foam-covered face outside the door, thanked the man who called me and stepped under the shower. By seven fifteen I was in reception where Saleh was waiting for me with a younger man called Michael, who would be my driver that morning. Formalities having been concluded, we went straight outside to Michael's car and he took me on a whistle stop tour of Aswan leaving the Hotel, Saleh and a cloud of dust somewhere in his wake. Our first stop was a huge stone pillar, some twenty metres long, lying on its side in a rock bed. Whoever had been working on it all those years ago had given up on it when it cracked, leaving a huge fissure running down a considerable portion of its length. Known as the Unfinished Obelisk, had this colossal venture been completed as had many others before and since, it would have been manhandled down to the river by a cast of thousands, lowered onto a series of pontoons and floated down the Nile to the place where it was required. The logistics, materials and manpower needed to carry out such an enterprise were breathtaking. In true tourist fashion, I walked around the obelisk and climbed all over it, before finally taking a few photographs and returning to where Michael had left the car. We then sped off towards the river. It was still early and there were plenty of boats

Tourists visiting the Unfinished Oblisque on Christmas Morning.

moored at the water's edge but very few tourists. They were probably having a lie in and I'd just remembered why.

Today was Christmas day.

The river frontage or Corniche was little more than a collection of bazaars, souvenir and carpet shops that had once been painted white but where this had not been obliterated by dust, sand and time, it had been covered over by awnings and advertisements for cigarettes and fizzy drinks. The riverside was lined with Palm trees and floating restaurants, although none of the latter was open at this time of the morning, not even for breakfast. Most of the vessels I could see on the river were high-masted felucca's with white canvass sails. There were a few multi-storey tour boats moored there as well and I wondered which one would be ours. I followed Michael to the riverbank where he introduced me to a wizened man in a faded Bob Marley t-shirt standing by a felucca. We shook hands and Michael told me that he spoke only Arabic.

"Don't forget to tip him afterwards" Michael said as I climbed into the boat.

"How much should I give him?" I asked

Felucca on the Nile outside the Winter Palace Hotel, Luxor.

"Ten pounds for him, five pounds for the boy. I will see you later" he said and was gone. I was about to ask 'what boy?' when a young dark-skinned child apparently wrapped in a sheet emerged from behind a sail.

The sun had not yet risen fully and a slight breeze caused a mild ripple on the otherwise calm river as our felucca eased away from the shore and out into open water. We headed past the main islands towards the opposite bank where I could see a white marble shrine. Saleh had told me that this was the tomb of the late Aga Khan III, spiritual leader of the Ismailis, a Shia Muslim sect. He had died in 1957 and had formerly lived in a villa close to his final resting place. By all accounts, he lived in a lot of other places, too, but this had been his favourite. From the boat, the shrine looked impressive on top of its sandy peak but, when I disembarked, I found that it was still quite a way off to the left and I had a good ten minutes walk up a curved and sloping path before I reached it. Close to the landing there was a tented bazaar and a collection of tribesmen offering camel rides to the early-morning tourists. I wanted to stop and ride a camel but I thought I'd better visit the shrine first. On reaching the gate, I removed my shoes and signed the visitors' book, noting that I was the first visitor that day but I knew there would be many more before

Sailing on the Nile towards the Aga Khan's Tomb, Aswan.

Tomb of the Agha Khan, Aswan.

nightfall. This was a simple Islamic shrine in white marble with a single dome. While it wasn't the Taj Mahal, it was clearly a monument to a man of distinction, albeit a surprisingly modest one bearing in mind that he had allowed himself to be weighed in diamonds in 1945 to mark the occasion of his diamond jubilee.

The mausoleum was not at all spacious, containing a minute, unpretentious courtyard and the great man's sarcophagus. I was aware that the site was a holy place for Shia Muslims so I did not remain there long before heading back down the path pausing at intervals to take photographs as the shimmering white monument gradually receded from view. More boats were beginning to arrive and the area around the landing had become quite congested. I was about to go to the camel enclosure but I caught sight of my boatman. He was gesticulating at me and clearly wanted to be away while he still had a clear exit.

As a single grey heron wheeled overhead we glided effortlessly in the direction of the nearest island, which even from a distance appeared to be rich in flora, trees and other vegetation. This was the Plantation or Botanical Island. As I disembarked from the boat, I found myself overwhelmed by a blinding explosion of colour, from the brilliant scarlet of flame trees, dazzling purple, white and crimson of bougainvillaea to the pink and white blooms of toxic evergreen oleanders.

I spent much of the morning strolling along pathways shaded by palm and acacia trees interspersed with vivid red Poinciana's, hibiscus and wine-red flowers, while sparrows, egrets and the occasional parakeet fluttered in the branches above me. It was a truly breathtaking experience and I was a little surprised by my reaction as I have never been much of a gardener. In the spring, I intended to give my own garden a facelift with the aid of several tons of shingle, and dozens of large paving slabs under-pinned by a vast sea of ready mix concrete and nothing I was witnessing now was going to persuade me to do otherwise.

I was aware that this island was also known as Kitcheners Island as it had been given to Lord Kitchener in 1911 during his time as Con-sul – General. It was he who had been responsible for laying out the original gardens and again, I was somewhat taken aback, when con-fronted by what remained of his handiwork. All I remembered about Lord Kitchener was the severe-looking visage staring out at me from the posters they used to sell in Carnaby Street during the 1960's. Apart from that, my history teacher had described him as a stern military man who cut his teeth fighting tribesmen in the Sudan, enhanced his career by de-feating the Boers in South Africa and finally ensured his place in history by sending a generation of young British and Commonwealth soldiers to their deaths in the trenches of Flanders. However, it appeared that he had also been a keen gardener and, for all I knew, he was probably polite to old ladies and kind to his dog as well.

We set off again and headed towards a larger island, overlooked by the picturesque Old Cataract Hotel which had featured in the film of Ag-atha Christie's novel 'Death on the Nile.' I was told that there were two entire villages on this island but I never got to see them because, this time, I never got off the boat. Instead, we slowly circumnavigated this curiosity, known locally as 'Abu' or 'Elephantine' island because of grey rock formations around its coastlines said to resemble the likeness of el-ephants but they didn't look like any elephants I ever saw. It must have been approaching eleven thirty and the sun was high in the sky, reflect-ing a blinding white light from the surface of the water as we continued to sail upstream. Having passed the landing area, we began another slow, leisurely cruise around the islands, by which time the river had started to fill up with white-sailed feluccas as the tourists came out to celebrate what remained of Christmas morning on the Nile. This was the signal for me to go and the skipper gradually brought the boat about and we approached the landing. I tipped the old man as he helped me out of his boat and reached back to hand five pounds to his young assistant. I thanked them both and went to where Michael was waiting to take me back to the Hotel for an early lunch. There was still no sign of the tour group. I met Saleh in reception. He told me everyone else was eating at a restaurant down on the Corniche and I would be meeting them later.

'Don't worry, the food here is much better' he said with a grin.

After a delicious lunch consisting of lamb stew, dried semolina and unleavened bread, I hurried towards the main road to the north of the

Christmas Morning on the Nile at Aswan.

hotel where Saleh had told me there were local shops as opposed to those on the Corniche which specialised in over-priced tourist tat. I had twenty minutes before the tour bus was scheduled to arrive, which didn't give me a lot of time. This unfortunate situation was compounded by the fact that I had some difficulty in finding a shop that sold what I needed and when I did, there wasn't much to choose from. In fact the choice was the same as it had been in the cafeteria in Sofia, take it or leave it. I hurriedly bought six pairs of socks, three pairs of regulation white Egyptian cotton baggy underpants and three cotton t – shirts and, not having time to haggle in the time-honoured fashion, I probably paid far more for them than they were worth. Calvin Klein they were not, but they only had to last for a couple of weeks.

When I arrived back at the Cleopatra, Saleh was standing in the doorway waiting for me. If he was annoyed that I was late he didn't show it. Initially, he didn't show anything at all because a massive, 52 seater Volvo coach had been parked in front of the hotel entrance completely obscuring him from view. When I managed to negotiate my way through the narrow gap between the side of the coach and the wall, Saleh handed me my shoulder bag, which I'd left with him for safe keeping and indicated that this was our tour coach. I went up the steps and found myself a seat with ease as there were only 16 of us on the tour. Several of them gathered around me to find out what had happened and how I had contrived to get myself lost. There was a pleasant Australian lady in her twenties called Julie, Lesley, an older Essex woman now domiciled in Weirside, Julian a teacher from Luton and John, originally from Sheffield but now living in London. I briefly related the tale of my unscheduled stop in Sofia and my mad dash to Aswan, which provided them with much amusement, heaven knows why. Maybe it was the way I told them.

Apart from heavy breathing, there was little sound at all from the seat in front of me where a young Australian couple who were either in love or in lust, had eyes only for each other. From what I could see, they weren't doing too badly with their hands either – fast work considering they'd met for the first time four days ago in the check-in queue at Heathrow airport. The cursory greeting I received from the remaining members of the group, all of whom were female between the ages of thirty-five and forty-five, belied their true nature, which only started to unravel as the tour progressed. I did not know what the female equivalent of "nerd" or "numpty" would be but whatever it was, it suited the witches

Loading produce onto a Nile Felucca.

I subsequently christened the Sisters of Mercy, three middle-aged school-teachers from somewhere in the far north of Scotland. For the whole trip, they never stopped complaining and for reasons they never disclosed, probably because I never asked them, they took an instant dislike to me.

No sooner had I put those three harridans out of my mind than I started to wonder why on earth we needed a coach at all. We were just round the corner from the market in Sharia Al-Souk and about five minutes walk from the Corniche where the tour boats were moored. Things became even stranger when the coach started up and whisked us away northwards out of town. After we had been travelling along the palm and vegetation-laden river bank for about twenty minutes, we pulled into a clearing and were told we would be getting on the boat here but there was no sign of a tour boat. These were huge, square, shallow-bottomed, cruisers which rise some four to five storeys out of the river and if one had been anywhere around we would have seen it from a long way off. What we did see was a small wooden steamer with two Egyptians loading provisions and crates of beer into the stern. The engine, controls, galley and storage areas were also at the rear end, while the best part of the remainder was taken up by a wide, flat, shaded area over which cushions had been spread.

This was the steamer Sobek, our home for the next three days. It looked more like the African Queen. There were two small dormitories consisting of bunk beds, one in the stern and one in the bow section. Accommodation was apparently unisex and clearly nobody envisaged taking off much in the way of clothing during the trip. I didn't have too much to begin with so it wasn't really a problem. I ended up in the stern with Lesley, John and Julian – and a few other people I never really got to know.

There was one more surprise in store for us, too. There had been a cool breeze in evidence all day but because the weather had been warm, it had been refreshing. However, once the boat had got under way and had built up a bit of speed, our close proximity to the water had turned this pleasant breeze into a cold, biting wind. The first thing most of us did was put on sweaters but this proved to be only a temporary solution. In the end, we had to return to our dormitories, take the blankets from our beds and wrap ourselves up in those. As we went on our way, I regretted having had so little time to spend in Aswan. Apart from missing out on visits to Abu Simbel, the temple on Philae Island and the Aswan High Dam, I would have liked to spend a week just being there, hanging out, having a few beers and meeting the locals. One way or another I was going to go back but that would be some time in the future. Right now I was sitting on deck wrapped in a blanket and listening to my teeth chattering. The Australian couple were clearly concerned for each other's welfare and were quietly giving each other the kiss of life while some other people had already buried their heads in books and lost interest in their surroundings, strange people. They could have stayed home, read the same books and saved themselves a lot of money.

I went down towards the bow where there were two small sets of steps either side of the shaded deck. I sat on a tarpaulin, pulled my thick woolly blanket tightly around me and watched the village life, the fields and the vegetation come and go like tableaux in a vast theme park, only this was real. Late in the afternoon, we drew into Kom Ombo. The temple of Haroeris and Sobek was visible from some way off just before a bend in the river. There were a number of craft already moored including two multi-decked tour boats and if the Gulf war had had a detrimental effect on the Egyptian tourist industry then I did not want to be around when it got back into gear. In spite of the crowds, Saleh fixed us up with a qualified guide who took us around the vestibules and sanctuaries, while explaining the meaning of the various hieroglyphics and the gods they depicted.

He explained what pylons were – vast towering frontages – and why Kom Ombo didn't have one. Apparently it had been washed away by centuries of Nile flooding. He told us that the principal feature of the temple at Kom Ombo was its bi symmetry, which meant it had two of everything other temples only had one of, apart from a pylon, in honour of both Haroeris and Sobek. He was just getting into the historical – or mythological – narrative of exactly who Haroeris and Sobek were when we were whisked off back to the boat to continue our journey. This was unfortunate since, while we were on shore, the weather was pleasantly warm but now, with the sun going down, the temperature was reminiscent of the day before yesterday in Sofia. Only the two Australians seemed pleased about this as they wrapped themselves together in two blankets and sprawled out along one side of the covered deck leaving everyone else to huddle up opposite them. I went back to the tarpaulin and waited for the sun to go down and we tied up for the night.

They served supper at around seven thirty and it was delicious. As far as I could make out, it was a sort of vegetable stew on grain with brown pitta-type bread and salad. There was plenty of beer on board and the idea was that we helped ourselves to whatever we wanted and entered what we'd had taken in a book to be settled up when we got to Luxor. Everybody was a lot more comfortable after they'd eaten and drunk a few bottles of beer. The Australians were staring longingly into each others eyes while the sisters of mercy were glowering at them disapprovingly. Lesley had joined me on the tarpaulin with a bottle of southern comfort and as we passed the bottle back and forth, she explained to me how she'd started her working life as a bank clerk in Essex and was now employed in the Nissan factory on Weirside. She was extolling the virtue of Japanese management techniques and non-union agreements but she was wasting her breath on me. I remembered one Sunday afternoon in Portsmouth when I met Ray Stubbs, a bright eyed senior citizen who had also worked on a Japanese – run project in Thailand many years ago and had just written a book about his experiences. There were no union agreements then, either. There were no agreements of any kind, and, because of the "superior" production techniques employed by the Japanese many of his friends and colleagues did not survive the experience.

It was quiet along the bank now and the moon was up leaving a trail of silver ripples across the river. Lesley decided she would have an early night and as she got up to leave, she kissed me, pushing her tongue firmly between my teeth as she did so. Next minute, she had gone.

I got up next morning a little later than everyone else in the dormitory. I'd heard them all moving around and defining all sorts of territorial issues, like who was going to use the miniature bathroom next, so I turned over and would have gone back to sleep had I not smelled cooking. I waited until everyone had gone on deck and then threw on my clothes. I was aware that I needed to wash and I had a face like a brillo pad but I wasn't going to miss breakfast for anything – especially if it was as good as last night's meal – and it was. There was a village the other side of the clearing and somebody had been to market early. There was fresh fruit, crusty loaves of bread like baguettes, cheese, tomatoes and a limitless supply of thick black coffee with plenty of sugar. As I climbed the steps to the sun-deck, Lesley made a space next to her for me to sit down.

"Do I owe you an apology for last night?" she whispered. I shook my head. We had breakfast and during the general conversation, we learned that we were going to stop at Edfu that day and visit the temple of Horus. Saleh was explaining to everyone what we would see when we got there and he warned us that there would be a market we would have to go through before we reached the temple. The traders had a reputation for driving hard bargains and he warned us to be on our guard. As far as I was concerned he could have saved himself the trouble. I'd been ripped off by experts. I'd been to Morocco.

Our arrival in Edfu was a bit of an anti climax. We had to walk for about half a mile from the river past what they called the tourist bazaar, a now-familiar collection of stalls, tents and kiosks selling handicrafts, metal trays and textiles. We walked through unmolested as the stall-holders just stood there and watched us go past. There were one or two half-hearted attempts to gain our attention but they weren't really interested in us. They wanted the people from the large tour boats – and their money. We obviously didn't look very prosperous and they probably thought we weren't worth the effort. They must have been having a good season in spite of all the publicity to the contrary.

The temple of Horus was in an excavated compound and our new guide met us outside the huge pylon. It was the first pylon I had ever seen and I was impressed. Once again, our guide took us through the temple explaining the numerous hieroglyphics and reliefs. Horus, to whom the temple had been dedicated, was the Egyptian Falcon Deity, complete with Falcon's head and the temple was said to have been constructed on the site of a mythical dual in which Horus defeated his wicked uncle Seth for the throne of Upper Egypt. By all accounts it was a bit of a rough house with both combatants suffering appalling injuries. We were told a lot of other things too, for example; Haroeris – remember him? He was another falcon headed deity, a sort of Horus the elder and Sobek was the crocodile god, except that most crocodiles from this stretch of the river had now been transformed into shoes and handbags. There was so much information to absorb at once that most of it went over my head, which was a pity. One thing I did remember though was that, before the excavation in the 1860's there had been a number of small houses on the roof of the hypostyle hall but these had been demolished. The original construction had been started during the reign of Ptolemy VII, known as 'Fatty' to his friends. He died at the age of 29, proving that, even then, being overweight was an unhealthy state of affairs. However, more light has been shed on his condition by Dr. Gillian Vogelsang Eastwood, the curator of the Ethnological Museum in Leiden, Holland who has suggested that many of ancient Egypt's crowned heads could well have suffered from the same hereditary ailment, the symptoms of which were corpulence, especially around the hips and lower body. It was understood that she had reached this conclusion by carrying out forensic tests on the burial garments worn by Tutankhamun. "We did not think he had a common shape," said Doctor Eastwood, "but not enough medical research has been done in this area." I can spot an unfeasibly large backside at sixty paces so what did they need medical research for?

The site started to fill up with tourists again as we assumed, rightly, that the tour boats had caught up with us and we had to break off and return to the Sobek. It had been quite warm in Edfu and we did not relish going back to that freezing sundeck and our woolly blankets. After the Sobek had been moored up for the night, we were served supper on deck and then the crew took us ashore and built a bonfire. There was beer, bonhomie and music. One crew member, inevitably called Ali had a drum, not unlike a Celtic bodhran, while Ahmed, the Cook, had a deep sonorous bass drum. Together they beat out pulsating rhythms on their instruments while the other Egyptians in our company sang traditional folk songs. I don't know whether it was the beer or not, but the entire lyrical content sounded like "Willie, Willie, Willie, lah, lah,lah, lah, lah" to a tune very similar to Springsteen's "Born in the USA." It's rhythmic repetition became addictive, so much so that on my last day in Egypt, after I'd seen the Pyramids, the citadel and the El Khalili Bazaar, I embarked on a whistle stop tour of the music shops in downtown Cairo asking if they had a tape of a song that went "Willie,Willie, Willie, lah,lah,lah,lah,lah.." They probably thought I was mad, but were too polite to say so. I never found what I was looking for and I will regret for ever that I never brought my recording Walkman with me.

Lesley was a little more amorous that evening and, thanks to an overdose of alcohol, I did nothing to discourage her but at bed time everyone went back to their respective bunks like good little girls and boys or so we all thought. It was three am. It was dark outside and the crickets were chirping like there was no tomorrow only it was tomorrow already. There were also loud noises coming from on deck followed by irregular thumps and bangs. Then the noises got louder. There were moans and groans, too. It sounded as though somebody was being hurt. I jumped out of my top bunk, pulled on my jeans and groped around for my shoes. John and Julian were ahead of me, which didn't stop one of them from stamping on my bare foot in the confusion. By the time I'd found my shoes and put them on, the noise had stopped. I staggered towards the deck, tripping over a similarly disorientated Ahmed on the way, only to be stopped by John.

"It's OK' he said, red-faced before explaining to me that it had been the Australian couple up on deck ... shagging!

By the time breakfast arrived, so had Esna. It was a comparatively short walk from the river, through a market to the centre of town where we were confronted by a deep pit in which lay the remains of the Temple of Khnum, already gift-wrapped for Christmas in a case of wire mesh. The temple had been completely buried and built over, and, to avoid the complete destruction of the various houses, only part of the site had been excavated. All that was there was the hypostele hall which had been fenced off at ground level by a metal screen, presumably to stop people from getting in without paying, and covered with wire mesh to discourage the birds from nesting. All in all, it was a pretty inhospitable place and what was visible was disappointing but the visit was not entirely wasted. We did see the Esna Barrage, a vast barrier constructed by the British in 1906 straddling the Nile from bank to bank. We had plenty of time to look at it, too as we had to let the cruise boats go through the lock ahead of us. This was particularly galling as, for the last two days, whenever one of these multi-storey, gin palaces went past we nearly turned over in their wash, which caused us untold grief. Beer was spilled, people fell over each other and one of the sisters of mercy nearly went over the side, saved only by a timely lunge from Ahmed, the chef. She rewarded him with a kiss. Later on, after he had recovered from the shock of her extravagant display of gratitude, he asked me what I had done to make her so mad at me so he could do it too.

We could see Luxor from a long way off and a buzz of excitement went round the boat. Even the Sisters of Mercy looked happy. Maybe they were planning to kill me. We parted company with the Sobek here, said fond farewells to the crew and settled our bar bills. A Sinai Desert Tours coach then transferred us to the Windsor Hotel, a respectable but nondescript establishment in a cul de sac just off the Corniche where I was lucky enough to get a room to myself while everyone else had to share. After dinner, I went down to the Old Winter Palace with John and Julian for a beer.

A beer on the terrace of the Old Winter Palace was considered to be one of the 'must do's' while visiting Luxor. It was an old colonial building with a sweeping staircase up to the entrance and it was still considered by many to be the best hotel in town. Long ago it might well have been but the advent of the ultra modern New Winter Palace next door had relegated it to a secondary, supporting role. It was due to close for refurbishment but nobody had any idea when, if ever, this was likely to happen. We had rather more beers than the one we originally went in for but I heeded Saleh's warning that tomorrow would be a long and tiring day and headed back for an early night, leaving the other two with one for the road. My early departure was just as well as I wasn't going to get another chance to relax for some time.

FROM LUXOR TO HURGHADA WITH
AN ASSHOLE FOR A GUIDE

When visiting Greece, tourists are told that patience is a virtue. In Egypt it is a necessity. This was a particular feature of the Windsor Hotel restaurant where we were waiting to have breakfast. Unfortunately, the people who were arranging our tour around Luxor took no account of this. Saleh explained that, while he was going to remain with us throughout our stay in Luxor, regulations decreed that package tourists had to be guided around the historical sites by specially accredited guides and ours turned out to be a total asshole.

Just as some of us were being served breakfast and the rest of us were still waiting, this officious little cretin came roaring through the restaurant telling us that the bus was leaving and he wanted us on it – now. I waited until I had drunk my coffee before I joined the others but some of them had allowed themselves to be bullied onto the coach without having had anything at all. As is quite common in cases like this, no-one had told the driver we were going and we had to wait forty-five minutes for him to turn up. Apparently, he had been in a restaurant down the road having breakfast.

When we got close to the Temple of Karnak there were hundreds of horse drawn caleches, taxi's and motorcycles, all picking up, dropping off or waiting for people. There were also long queues of luxury tourist

47

coaches looking for a place to stop. Our driver realised that his temporary halt was likely to be a permanent one and, not being able to move any further in any direction, he set us down where we were, about ten minutes walk from the site entrance. The temple itself was a breath-taking monument to human endeavour but the sheer volume of visitors ruined our enjoyment. Taking photographs was virtually impossible. As soon as I lined something up, I was shoved sideways by hordes of other tourists who slowly shuffled by and got in my way. I took no comfort from the fact that I had probably got in their way, too. There were guided tours from all over the world and so many guides addressing their respective clients and anyone else within earshot, either through battery driven megaphones or by shouting through cupped hands while waving their arms around maniacally that the result sounded like an audition for a re-run of the day of Pentecost.

After a couple of hours of taking in the sights without knowing what the hell I was looking at, and, at the same time trying to avoid being trampled to death, it was time to go. After what was to become a customary half hour delay while the driver was persuaded to stop gossiping with his friends and get on the coach, we drove down the busy Corniche to the Windsor for lunch. After the fiasco at breakfast, which very few of us had been given the opportunity to consume, people were generally hungry and bad tempered, so, when the tour guide made an entrance again and tried to move us out just as lunch had started to appear on the tables, he received a rude response. Saleh had a quick word with us, taking the company line but the consensus view was that we were going to eat and the guide and the coach would have to wait. This did not go down very well and in the end, I asked Saleh to explain to the guide just who was paying whom. If the guide had a problem, then we would dispense with his services and ask for a refund. That seemed to be that and we were about to continue with our lunch when the sisters of mercy started to whinge. They said that they had paid for a guided tour and they felt that they should have it, which was the same way the rest of us felt about lunch, so we stayed put.

Luxor Temple was just ten minutes walk down the road so we elected to go on foot, largely because the driver had taken umbrage at having to wait for us and had gone home. For all I cared, he could have taken cyanide as long as he shared it with the guide who was still sulking over his lunchtime rebuke. He was lucky. Several of the women had been very close to smacking him in the mouth for his rudeness and I suspect Saleh had told him as much. When we arrived, we found that this temple was considerably smaller than the one at Karnak but there were still as many people tramping through it. It seemed as though the people we'd encountered this morning had followed us here or maybe it was us who had followed them. Either way, there wasn't much pleasure in being there. There was a beautiful avenue of sphinx's on the way to the entrance but I was unable to get a decent photograph because of the crowds. In the end, Saleh took control of the situation, told us we could go off on our own if we wanted and that he'd meet us in the Hotel reception at seven that evening for the Son et Lumiere at Karnak

Luckily, our guide had been given the evening off and we left for Karnak four at a time in a cavalcade of horse drawn caleches. If it had been chaotic during the day, the evening proved to be considerably worse. There seemed to be just as many people as there had been that morning but, as the commentary was due to be in English, at least there would be no Germans so that the risk of getting an elbow in the face was considerably reduced. There were no tour guides either. People were getting lost and the risk of being trampled in the dark became far greater. One of the Egyptian staff made a favourable remark about Margaret Thatcher while saying something detrimental about President Mubarak so I told him he was welcome to her. This didn't go down very well with Lynn, a plumb in the mouth Sloane Ranger from our group, who'd had everything but plastic surgery and a lobotomy to make herself look like the Princess of Wales, so I told the Egyptian that the British people would willingly change Thatcher for Anwar Sadat if they were given the choice.

"But Sadat is dead" said the man in genuine confusion.

"It's still an improvement on Thatcher" I told him.

"Better than Kinnock," sniffed Lynn.

"Wouldn't shag either of 'em," retorted Andy, the male half of the loved-up Australian duo in a statement that begged more questions than it answered while killing any further discussion stone dead.

We moved on to the Sacred Lake, which looked surreal and lunar under the ever-changing floodlights and all the time people were taking photographs with their mini-automatic cameras. What they expected to achieve remained to be seen. I suspect only Julian emerged with any pictures worth keeping as he had a tripod with him and a very expensive

Nikon SLR, which he seemed to know how to use. It was very tempting to take pictures though, just in case one of them did come out. Even I took a few with my bottom of the range Riva, although I was certain that nothing would come of it – and nothing did.

Next day, we were due to take a public ferry across the river to see the Valley of the Kings and later the valley of the Queens. Predictably, the landing stage was crowded and none of us could make out which ferry was going where. Somehow, in the confusion Julie and I managed to board a boat that was heading back in the direction of Esna. As soon as we realised our mistake, we found the nearest crew member and explained our plight. Immediately, he took us to the wheelhouse and told the captain, a craggy, ageing man who looked like a captain. In a trice, he had put the boat about and headed towards the far shore and the Valley of the Kings. Just as we were leaving, we remembered our manners and gave the Captain twenty pounds each and he grinned broadly revealing a mouth full of tobacco stained teeth. We re-joined the rest of the party on the west bank. The sisters of mercy were scowling at us both. I'm not sure what they had against Julie but neither of us cared.

We were taken first to the Temple of Hatshepsut, an imposing colonnaded, terrace that was still in the process of restoration. It will probably stay that way for the remainder of my lifetime, and, I suspect, for a number of other lifetimes as well. We had a new guide and like his predecessor, he seemed to be in an almighty hurry but today I could understand why. This was high season and there were crowds of people everywhere. If we did not maintain brisk progress, we would become lost in a sea of bodies and see very little.

There are all sorts of ways that you can approach the Valley of the Kings. Most tourists go straight there and take in Hatshepsut's Tomb on their way back but our guide decided to do things the other way round in the hope that we would miss the crowds. He nearly got it right, too, but there were so many people it didn't make a lot of difference. Adventurous souls can now soar above it all in a hot air balloon while those with a surfeit of energy can hire bicycles and explore this spectacular landscape by pedal power. The cheapest way is to do it on foot and many people still prefer to do this but it can be exhausting and time consuming. Being taken around by air conditioned coach has its advantages but, with the hordes of people that were there that day, even a hot air balloon would have been of little help. You can't get into many tombs from up there. We couldn't get into many tombs anyway because most of them were closed and those that were open were under siege. At first, it appeared unlikely that we would ever get into any of them. Then, by some dubious device, I suspect that our guide bribed a colleague who's group was better placed in a queue, we finally did get to see the inside of a tomb, that of Ramses III, I think it was. When it was our turn to go in, we tip toed tentatively through the gloom into this dry, musty tunnel. There were hieroglyphics on the walls but they had been desecrated and the result was disappointing. It was also very claustrophobic down there and I felt like I was trapped down a coalmine with the entire congregation of my local church. Obviously we were unable to spend much time there because of the number of people waiting outside but it was long enough. When they told us that the Tomb of Tutankhamun was closed, many of us lost interest but they did manage to get us into two more before we boarded the coach and headed for the village of Qurna.

There are many stories about what goes on in Qurna. Some say the locals do a roaring trade in grave robbing, forgery and making fake antiquities. Maybe they're right. All I could see being made was money, oodles of it, especially in the carpet showrooms and alabaster workshops where plates and vases were being hand ground, traditionally and sold like hot cakes. I found it fascinating and I bought a couple of miniature busts of Nefertiti as presents. Others with more money or higher credit limits bought Egyptian hand-woven carpets with their plastic while the guide kept in the background with a wry smile on his face.

He was making money, too.

All in all, it had been a tiring and frustrating day and once again, I promised myself that I'd go back off-season, when there were less people and things were not so frantic. Our departure from Luxor, the following day started out just like every other day we'd spent in Luxor. We'd got our old guide back and, right on cue, he rampaged into the restaurant cajoling and agitating just as breakfast was being served. It was the same old line. The bus was leaving immediately and we should board now. I was for telling him he could go if he wanted to but I was waiting for breakfast and if I were to be left behind, I would make my own way to Cairo and sue the company when I returned to London. Unfortunately, no-one supported me and we filed out to the coach obediently only to endure the mandatory half hour wait while the driver finished his breakfast in a small cafe round the corner. One or two people complained to Saleh but there was little he could do. We had to get to Hurghada that day but before we did, we were due to visit the temples of Abydos and Dendera.

The journey to Abydos seemed comparatively short but it wasn't really. I just fell asleep. The Temple of Seti was very much as I had expected it to be, except that the pylon had been worn away with time and no longer existed. The guide once more took us around the site and pointed out the various items of interest, which, in this particular case were the reliefs. Unfortunately, for most of us, this was one temple too many and by the time we arrived at Dendera, only about three people stayed with the guide while the rest of us wondered off. The majority went straight to the stairway from the Hall of Offerings and climbed up to the roof, which afforded clear views of the nearby village and the desert beyond.

Flash photography was forbidden here and I spent some time watching a very elderly Japanese tourist, who was a real De Mille. Not content with using a huge tripod to take his pictures, he had brought with him a small set of scaffolding, which, when erected, stood some ten feet above the ground. With the aid of some battery-powered arc lights, which he produced from his hand baggage, he began taking photographs of the reliefs in the shadows higher up the walls. All this expensive equipment fascinated me and I wanted to talk to him about it but I couldn't think of anything to say. I suppose I could have asked him if he'd ever met Ray Stubbs.

We left Dendera in the middle of the afternoon and sped across the rocky wasteland of the Eastern Desert towards Hurghada, which proved to be a disappointment. For a start, it didn't look much like the description in Lesley's guidebook, which said that Hurghada was a small fishing town, which had recently begun to expand to meet the demands of tourism. It must have been an old guidebook as the beach area proved to be one mass of tourist hotels, many of them low budget flop-houses for backpackers. There did not seem to be much to see here, either, which was just as well because we were due to catch the ferry to Sharm el Sheikh the following morning.

We stopped at a high-rise hotel, with what looked like an expensive restaurant staring out impressively from its first floor. Saleh confirmed that we would be staying here. Unfortunately, nobody had told the proprietors. We had been waiting around in reception for about fifteen minutes when Saleh appeared looking as though he was barely controlling his temper. Another man was following him looking highly embarrassed.

"The manager has something to say to you," announced Saleh tersely. The man stepped forward and started to whisper something to John, who took a pace back and said loudly,

"Don't just tell me. Everybody else wants to know as well." The manager looked stunned as well he might.

"The person who took the phone call to book the rooms...." he stopped apprehensively looking around for help but there was none, so he continued," The person who took the phone call did not tell anybody and we have no rooms for you." There was a general gasp of disbelief and a few of the women made passable impersonations of "disgusted of Tonbridge Wells" and said they were going to complain when they got home but it wasn't going to change anything. Saleh said they were going to give us dinner later at no charge but since we'd booked full board, we'd already paid for it anyway so that wasn't much in the way of compensation. The manager said he knew of another hotel and he gave our driver directions. We went outside and got back on the coach, which took us about a mile along the corniche and stopped outside a cream coloured building that smelled strongly of fresh paint and looked about three months short of completion. Saleh asked Lesley and I to go in with him to check it out. The corridors had only recently been emulsioned and all the rooms had stained hardwood doors, beds and cupboards but there was dust everywhere, electric wiring was hanging out of the walls and the whole place looked more like a building site than a Hotel. We shook our heads and went back to the coach.

They took us back the way we'd come and we parked outside a run down looking hotel opposite the establishment at which we should have stayed. All of us went in and looked at a few rooms. The place was lively with young backpackers from all over the world sitting at tables in the lounge drinking beer and swapping stories. It was a bit cheap and cheerful but it was only for one night and it certainly looked clean and comfortable. John, Julian and Julie agreed with me but the sisters of mercy once more switched into whingeing mode. They felt that as we had all paid for three star accommodation we should have something better than this. They had a point but it was getting late, it was high season and we could be wandering around this busy resort all night if we weren't careful. We went across the road for dinner with our accommodation problems still unresolved.

It was a self-service restaurant, which would have been ideal were it not for a large party of European package tourists who insisted on having six helpings of everything in sight. As a result, the catering staff kept running out of food causing long delays and even longer queues. After about an hour, we had more or less finished eating when Saleh came back with two other Egyptians and asked for a volunteer to help with the accommodation. Somehow, and even now I don't know how because I did not volunteer, I ended up going with them. The first thing Saleh did was to hand me a badge bearing the legend "Atlas Travel-Tour Director" and told me to put it on.

"Does this mean I get paid?" I asked but no-one answered. My wearing the badge seemed to affect my status within our group and even Saleh started to defer to me. Suddenly, I wasn't a tourist any more. I really was "Atlas Travel-Tour Director." First of all, I made a list of the entire tour party and, with Saleh's help, I paired them off so that everyone was sharing with the same person they shared with in Aswan. That was good because it meant that I would have a room to myself but it didn't work out that way. We jumped into a Land Rover and after one of the other Egyptians handed me a clipboard for my list, I was taken on a whistle-stop tour of hotels accepting any halfway decent room I could find, bearing in mind that some people were going to be more particular than others and, if the second night on the Sobek was anything to go by, the Australian couple were likely to be very noisy.

TO SHARM-EL-SHEIKH ON THE GOSPORT FERRY

Next morning I was waiting in the restaurant with John and Julian when a man I'd never seen before came in and told us that the bus was leaving and that we should get on it now. I sighed deeply. Enough was enough. I was sick and tired of being rushed away from the breakfast table only to wait in the bus until the driver had condescended to put in an appearance. The man became angry which didn't make any difference to the way I felt. I told him what I should have told the other chap the day before and he stormed out in a rage. John and Julian sat down again and the waiters brought us bread, cheese, hard-boiled eggs and thick black coffee. Just then, Saleh came in to look for us. He told us we had to go but he had no wish for a confrontation. I was glad about that. I pulled up a chair for him and ordered him a cup of coffee. It transpired that he had stayed at the back packers hotel and he'd been very comfortable, which was more than could be said for me. I'd ended up on a lumpy camp bed in a corner of John and Julian's room with my head wedged underneath a washbasin with a dripping tap and the waste pipe against my right ear.

Saleh told us glumly that the guides were paid by the hour and they complained to the company if they were kept waiting. He would get into trouble if there were too many complaints. I told him not to worry because a few of us would be complaining about the guides. This seemed to cheer him up a little and he ordered another cup of coffee.

Eventually, we got on the bus and proceeded to round up the rest of our party from the various temporary addresses, in which I'd billetted them the night before. Inevitably, the Australians caused us a slight delay after they'd been interrupted while practising the Karma Sutra in the shower and they were still wet when they got on the coach. Luckily, we arrived at the landing for the ferry to Sharm-el-Sheikh in good time, so much so that we were the only people there. I guessed that the guide was in a hurry to get rid of us because he had to deliver the coach back to Luxor to pick up another tour. We were told to wait in a queue next to the ticket office by a man in uniform. I noticed that there were many small boats in the harbour and one of them had a familiar look about it. It was a small, two-tier ferry with steel superstructure. Those who regularly crossed Portsmouth Harbour to Gosport by ferry would have recognised it immediately, even though it had been painted in different colours. I spoke to Saleh and he confirmed my fears. When the Children of Israel crossed the Red Sea, the waters divided and they were able to do it on foot.

We would be crossing on the Gosport Ferry.

I decided that the people at home had to see this and I left the queue to take some photographs. I had plenty of film and took a series of pictures of the ferry, the harbour and various small boats. I was on my way back to the others when the man in uniform came over and started to badger me.

"Get back over there" he ordered, an error of judgement on his part. Apart from all the hassle over breakfast and accommodation, for the last three days I'd been ordered about, pushed, shoved, pestered and abused and I'd had enough. I suggested to him in a manner that was rather less than polite that he should go away, and, when he failed to do so the first time, I became considerably more graphic and insisted that if he did not leave me alone I would beat him to a pulp and throw his mangled remains into the harbour.

He glowered at me as though he was going to turn nasty but that didn't matter because I was nasty already. Nothing happened for a number of minutes. It was like one of those long menacing pauses from a spaghetti western only it didn't have an Ennio Morricone sound track throbbing away in the background. I slowly let go of the strap from my shoulder bag, allowing it to fall gently on the ground at my feet, leaving both hands free. Luckily, that was all I needed to do. The official must have decided against taking matters any further and walked slowly away. I picked up my shoulder bag as I watched him go.

It was another forty-five minutes before we were allowed onto the ferry and even then, there were problems. By that time, the queue had grown considerably with the arrival of a party of backpackers. There had been some middle aged Germans, too, who had gone to the head of the queue but had been forced to re-join it at a more appropriate place after remonstrations from the people they had tried to displace. We were stopped at the gangplank and the man in the uniform went down the queue, apparently at random, picking out people and escorting them onto the ferry, including the party of Germans. I suspected at the time that baksheesh had previously changed hands and he was delivering his end of the transaction. At this stage, Saleh had a word with him, and presumably more baksheesh changed hands as we were suddenly waved forward up the gangplank. The boarding ritual took another fifteen minutes before we cast off, and, by the time we'd arrived at Sharm-el-Sheikh, most of us wished we'd taken a bus and gone round the long way.

About five minutes out of port, we hit a swell and waves seemed to tower over our tiny ferry, something that never happened to its counterpart while crossing Portsmouth Harbour. We might not have known all the people on the boat when we started, but, after twenty minutes or so, we knew exactly what they'd had for breakfast, at least those of them who had been fortunate enough to have had breakfast. Julie sat opposite me looking as though she might be tempted to join in the movement currently afoot to convert our ferry into some sort of maritime vomitarium. I suggested she shut her eyes and try to sleep. I did the same and stayed that way until I felt Saleh nudging me to let me know we'd arrived.

Our hotel, the Ghazala Gardens was a short bus ride away in nearby Naama Bay on a strip of curved beach next door to the antisceptically clean Mowenpick with the slightly more salubrious Hilton just around the corner. The Ghazala Gardens had spacious, immaculately coiffured grounds with chalets tastefully located in leafy glades adorned with fountains and flowers. Some of the women were lucky enough to be allocated chalets but I found myself in the main block in a luxurious double I had to share with Saleh. This proved to be useful when dealing with Lesley who had been trying to get into my room for the last three days.

It was New Years Eve and we'd all bought tickets for the hotel's party, which was being held in the vast restaurant complex near the beach. We had been allocated two tables and food was being served from a generously stocked buffet. As the restaurant started to fill up, I noticed the Germans we had encountered earlier occupying three tables some distance away from us. As soon as the buffet was pronounced open, two of them elbowed their way to the front of the queue and loaded up their trays with everything they could lay their hands on. From where I was standing, I saw them return to their respective tables, quickly remove the plates of food and hand their empty trays to two other members of their party who headed back to the buffet while their compatriots tucked into the feast that had been brought for them. Ten years earlier, I'd seen a folk club in Chiswick drunk dry inside two hours by revellers using the same principle but for tonight's festivities, there seemed to be plenty of everything to go around and no need at all for this sort of activity. Nevertheless, two more Germans made straight for the front of the queue where one was persuaded to go to the rear by a member of the staff while his more rotund companion was being helped unsteadily to his feet after appearing to injure his groin. There was a pretty cosmopolitan collection of revellers there that evening and it was refreshing to see that we were not the only people who had been upset by the oafish behaviour of the Germans. I was also relieved to observe that it had not been a member of our group, who had kneed fatso in the nuts.

As the evening wore on and the alcohol continued to flow, one of the women in our group, a right-on, raving, chip-on-the-shoulder, feminazi called Pandora draped herself around me and offered to open her box. I'd made a particular point of avoiding her since the first night on the boat when she'd had an almighty argument with Ahmed the cook, who had maintained that the Nile flowed from south to north. While she did not attempt to diminish Ahmed or his argument on the grounds he was Egyptian, she took great pleasure in doing both because he was a man. Of course, he had been quite correct in his assertion but he couldn't convince mouth-almighty who did not appear to think it flowed in any particular direction at all. Unfortunately, the flow of her current thinking was only too clear.

"Let's go somewhere quiet," she cooed drunkenly as her hand started to move south of my Mason-Dixon line with all the subtlety of an Exocet missile. I cringed and told her I had a headache.

... AND BACK AGAIN TO CAIRO

After spending the next couple of days discovering the various hotels and shops that hugged the line of Naama bay, we were taken by bus through the Sinai desert back to Cairo. Before we left, Saleh was very solicitous, taking pains to ensure that everyone who wanted breakfast had it and was not put under any pressure to hurry. We stopped at the Suez Canal just before the entrance to the Ahmed Hamdi Tunnel and filed out of the tour bus for a final photo call. Most of us had only seen the canal in the film "Lawrence of Arabia" and the sight of ocean going tankers appearing from behind sand dunes was awe-inspiring. When we were back on the bus, Saleh told us that the canal still carried fourteen percent of the world's maritime trade. He also drew our attention to the huge gaps in the sand ramparts, which had been made by Egyptian forces using high-pressure hoses prior to the surprise attack on the Israelis, which heralded the start of the 1973 Arab-Israeli war. He did not mention the counter attack, which drove the Egyptians back across the Suez Canal but I couldn't blame him for that.

Several things bothered me about those wars. First of all, why call them Arab-Israeli wars when for most of the time the only Arabs who did any serious fighting were the Egyptians? The other thing that bothered me was, having defeated the Egyptian army and occupied the East bank of the Suez Canal, with nothing between them and Cairo but a goodly number

Tanker navigating the Suez Canal close to the Ahmed Hamdi Tunnel.

of white flags and sixty kilometres of desert, why didn't the Israelis just go ahead and take the city? I have a theory about that . As soon as the swiftest tanks of the Israeli advance party had sped into the outskirts of Heliopolis, they would have been swallowed up in an almighty traffic jam and forced to remain there until they were arrested for causing an obstruction by the Cairo Traffic Police.

Having installed us at the Marwa Palace Hotel in Dokki, Saleh gave us the following day to ourselves. I shared a taxi with Julie and Lesley while they visited the old churches in Coptic Cairo, the Cairo Tower and

Muhammed Ali's Mosque, The Citadel, Cairo.

the Mohammed Ali Mosque in the Citadel before spending what remained of their Egyptian currency at the bustling El Khalili market. At
about eleven thirty back at the hotel, I said goodbye to everyone who was
still talking to me, relieved that they would be flying off without me in the
early hours of the morning.

Seeing the churches in Coptic Cairo reminded me that Christianity
had first been brought to Egypt by St Mark the Apostle in 48 AD when
he established a Church in Alexandria and became its Patriarch. A large
number of native Egyptians embraced the faith, which within fifty years

had spread throughout the country. Egypt was still part of the declining Roman Empire and Christians continued to face persecution by their Roman rulers until the end of the 4th century AD, by which time most Egyptians had converted to Christianity as had many of the Romans, too. St Mark, himself, was martyred in 68 AD when pagans seized him and dragged him behind a horse for two days through the streets of Alexandria until he expired and his body was dismembered.

The Arab Muslim conquest of Egypt took place in 639 AD when *Amr ibn al-'As*, a contemporary of the Islamic prophet Mohammed and one of the Sahaba (companions) led an army through the Sinai and, after a two month siege, overran the incumbent Roman garrison at Pelusium, an important settlement to the East of the Nile Delta. His reinforced army then continued its conquest, offering those they captured the usual three choices, conversion to Islam, Dhimmitude or death. Many opted for life as a second class citizen or Dhimmi, paying jizya or protection money to their captors, which explains why Egypt did not become a Muslim majority country until the end of the 12th century.

The word *Copt* was adopted into the English Language in the 17th century, from the Latin word *Coptus,*or *Cophtus.* By June, 2015, the population of Egypt was estimated to be in the region of 86.28 million, of which 10 to 15% were Coptic Christians, the largest Christian minority in the Middle East. In spite of this, they have been systematically persecuted throughout their history both by the state and by the Islamic mob. Even today, the Egyptian government does not officially recognize conversions from Islam to Christianity and prevents marriages between Christian converts and those born into the faith. In addition, permits are required from the government to repair churches or to construct new ones, and these are often withheld in the face of violent protests by Muslims. No permits have ever been required for the repair or construction of Mosques. Since the removal of Mohammed Morsi in July 2013, restrictions on the repair and construction of churches appear to have been eased.

One recurring problem has been the abduction and rape of Coptic women and girls by Muslim men. The women are then forcibly converted to Islam and compelled to marry their abductors. The girls' families experience great difficulty in getting their daughters back due to the reluctance of the civil authorities to act against those responsible. To be fair, this problem is not exclusive to Egypt and is prevalent in many Muslim majority countries, particularly Pakistan.

Violence against Coptic Christians had been on the rise in Egypt for decades before reaching its bloody climax during the overthrow of President Hosni Mubarak and the election and subsequent ouster of Muslim Brotherhood Prime Minister Mohammed Morsi. During this period, the worst in living memory, Copts were murdered and churches burned, plundered and pillaged by Muslim mobs in attacks of unprecedented ferocity. Over 40 Christian churches were destroyed and looted up and down the country in what was interpreted as revenge for the overthrow of Egypt's first Islamist president.

When I went down to breakfast next morning, I had the whole restaurant to myself so I took my time and consumed two pots of coffee before the people at reception arranged a taxi to take me to the pyramids.

The route was quite straightforward, almost a straight line for eleven kilometres down the Sharia al Ahram past endless rows of tourist hotels and night clubs. Although the road is usually busy, there was little traffic that morning. We arrived outside one of the entrances and I could see the great pyramid of Cheops looming over us. Ali, my taxi driver, directed me to the ticket booth and showed me where he would be waiting with the taxi. No sooner had I purchased a ticket than it was snatched from my hand by a fat official looking Egyptian wearing a badge.

"Give me your ticket." he bellowed, which I thought was a little strange as he had already grabbed it from me and was walking away with it at a rate of knots. "Come with me." He ordered, and took off towards the entrance gate.

"Hey, get back here," I shouted at him and when he faltered I asked him what was going on.

"I am your guide." He declared earnestly

"Nice Try" I told him "Give me back my ticket."

He did so reluctantly and, if he'd been a dog he would have put his tail between his legs, whimpered and slunk off but it was all part of the act. I left him outside the enclosure and after getting my ticket torn in half by a genuine attendant, I was drawn towards the great pyramid taking photographs as I went. While the place was crowded, it was big enough to absorb everybody. There were all sorts of fake guides, hustlers, people selling rides on horses and camels but, because of all the space, I could see them from a long way off and I waved them away before they had the opportunity to come close and invade my privacy. This was something I had saved up and I wasn't going to share it with anybody – except maybe a few thousand other tourists but I wasn't going to bother them if they did not bother me. I visited everything there was to see in the complex, from the Great Pyramid of Cheops, the one that looks as though it has a hat on, to the smaller Pyramid of Chephren and then to the Pyramid of Mycerinus, which was smaller still. I then walked around both sets of Queens Pyramids before heading towards the Sphynx.

So much has been written about this splendid monument, which is strange since erosion has worn away much of its face and left it with no nose at all. Maybe that was the inscrutability they all talked about. I heard

The Sphinx.

a guide say something to the effect that "Sphinx" was a name given by the Ancient Greeks to the creature that put riddles to passers by and killed those who gave incorrect answers. Just think of all the misery the British people would have been saved if, in 1979 they had hired one of those to interview Margaret Thatcher.

As the mid-day sun rose in the sky, I decided that I'd seen as much of Egypt as I could absorb in one visit, but I would be back.

BULGARIA 1993

GIVE WAR A CHANCE AND WE'LL ALL
HAVE A PEACE OF VERSAILLES

At this stage one might be forgiven for wondering why, in view of my previous bad experiences in Bulgaria, I should want to return not once but twice to this shell-shocked, post-communist state, teetering as it was on the verge of post-traumatic stress disorder after 44 years of communist misrule. It also had a brutal and unaccountable police force which appeared to serve no purpose other than to provide an effective barrier between a corrupt and oppressive government and those they cheated and oppressed. Organised crime was in the ascendancy and violent street robbery and other similar offences had reached epidemic proportions. Why on earth would I want to go back?

Towards the end of 1992, I was in a branch of Thomas Cooke's travel agency in Hammersmith to book a week-long break in Prague for the following April. Having completed my transaction, I casually picked up a brochure for Bulgaria and was struck by the spectacular photographs it displayed, particularly galling as my own had not come out for some reason. I took the brochure home with me and when I flicked through it, I found a segment on the history of the country, and, my interest aroused, I went into my local library in Uxbridge where they loaned me a copy of *"A Short History of Modern Bulgaria" by R.J. Crampton.* I found the contents to be compelling. From the late 1800s until the end of World War ll

Bulgaria had been involved in a series of wars and intrigues which only ended after the Communist takeover in 1944. However, I had booked to go to Prague and that was where I was going, or so I thought.

Unfortunately, I had to change my plans at the last minute due to a family bereavement, and, as I was unable to arrange an alternative date to visit Prague I went into my local travel agency during my lunch hour and by the time I left, I had booked a week-long all-inclusive package tour to Bulgaria. At just over £500 it seemed a trifle expensive when compared to what else was on offer and the low commodity prices in Bulgaria but suddenly, possibly due to Mr Crampton's gripping account of the labyrinthine conspiracies and rip-roaring battles, I developed an urge to go back. I felt that the most significant period in Bulgaria's re-mergence to nationhood occurred in the late 1800s and its participation in the war against the Ottomans. If possible, I wanted to see where some of the action had taken place.

The 1877/8 Russo-Turkish war between the Ottoman Empire and the Russian Empire and its eastern allies including Bulgaria, Romania,Serbia and Montenegro enabled Russia to recover territorial losses it suffered in the Crimean War while supporting the Balkan states in their efforts to break free of declining Islamic domination. Bulgarian Militia played a major part in this campaign, which drove the Turks back to the gates of Constantinople. Under the Treaty of Berlin, which finally concluded hostilities, Bulgaria was given a level of Independence unknown since before the fall of Constantinople in 1453. A new state of Bulgaria was proclaimed, with Sofia as its capital, to be ruled by a prince whose only major constraints were that he should not be a member of any Major European dynasty and that he had to acknowledge suzerainty, a sort of loose sovereignty, to Turkey, while retaining autonomy in all other matters. It meant that Bulgaria had achieved self-determination by force of arms and it was probably this fact more than any other that led it to participate in the Balkan Wars in 1912.

During the First Balkan War in 1912-13, the Balkan League, consisting of Bulgaria, Greece, Montenegro and Serbia once more took arms against the Ottomans. The Bulgarian army was a formidable force consisting of 592,000 soldiers plus another 15,000 volunteers from the Macedonia – Adrianopolis Militia. In a short sharp series of battles lasting no more than two weeks, the Turks were routed at Lule Burgas and again at Bunar Hissar from which they were forced to make a rapid retreat to the Tchatalja Lines, a massive fortification some forty kilometres west of Constantinople. Here, they dug in while their leaders frantically tried to sue for peace.

As things turned out, this would have been to the mutual advantage of both parties. The Bulgarian army was well aware of the redoubtable obstacle facing it in the form of the Tchatalja Lines. Worse, having covered a considerable distance and fought a number of battles in a very short period of time, the army was showing signs of fatigue and, most disturbing of all, cholera had broken out amongst the troops. Unfortunately, there was some division within the Bulgarian leadership as to whether to accept the Turkish offer of peace or to press on to Constantinople. By now, Bulgaria had a king, Ferdinand, to whom the idea of a triumphal entry into Constantinople was particularly appealing. He had even ordered new clothes and carriages for the occasion. Bulgarian politicians, too, were well aware of the bargaining power they could gain from the occupation of Constantinople but it was not to be.

The attack on the Tchatalja lines started early in November 1912 and proved to be an abysmal failure, so much so that it was the Bulgarians rather than the Turks who finally sued for peace. From the terms of the treaty, Bulgaria made substantial territorial gains but the peace proved to be a fragile one and fighting broke out again and continued until a second armistice was brokered in April 1913 and concluded in London a month later. Again the peace proved to be only temporary. The treaty required the victorious allies to divide amongst themselves the territories they had gained, from Enos on the Aegean to Midia on the Black Sea but no agreement could be reached. The Bulgarians wanted the land to be divided on the basis of proportionality, that is, the proportion of the military effort and sacrifice made by each of the allies. The Serbs and Greeks countered this assertion by stating that the division of former Turkish territories in Europe should be undertaken in such a way as to prevent any single Balkan state, particularly Bulgaria, from becoming too powerful. After much disagreement, which grew increasingly acrimonious and hostile, as well as a last ditch effort by the Russians to avert a resumption of hostilities, the Bulgarian army returned to battle and moved westwards to confront the Serbs. Initially this ploy was successful, but it left the rest of the country virtually defenceless and tempted Romania to join the fray. The Romanian army crossed the Danube and entered Sofia virtually unopposed while the Turkish forces regained Adrianopolis in the South. Danev, the

Bulgarian Minister President promptly resigned and Radoslavov, his successor, immediately sought a cease-fire leading first to the humiliating treaty of Bucharest and subsequently to the Treaty of Constantinople in October 1913, which finally brought the Balkan wars to an end.

The second Balkan war had been little short of a catastrophe for Bulgaria both economically and in loss of life. All the territorial gains of the First Balkan war had been lost, save for a small part of the Struma Valley and an even smaller part of Thrace, while the remainder of the country had been divided, leading to the loss of its profitable agricultural region and the dubious acquisition of barren, rural areas, which would have needed a great deal of investment to make them in any way viable. After all that had happened, one might have assumed that the Bulgarian leadership had become so heartily sickened by war that they would never consider embarking on such a course again but by 1915, the unthinkable had happened and they allowed themselves to become embroiled in the First World War.

In November 1913, Minister President Radoslavov held a general election but when this failed to produce a working majority, he went to the people again in April 1914 and this time achieved the required result. Having secured victory, Radoslavov now needed to raise a foreign loan to pay for the cost of the wars and for the improvement of the various backward and arid regions that had been foisted upon Bulgaria as part of the Constantinople settlement. As the great European powers converged upon the cataclysmic path to war, it became clear that the source of any loan would depend on which of the potential antagonists the Bulgarians chose to support. The French announced that they might be prepared to advance the necessary funds providing Bulgaria supported the entente, Britain, France and Russia, but this would have necessitated a further general election since Radoslavov's party was pro Austria and Germany. It was finally agreed to accept a German loan though the Parliamentary majority in favour of this proved to be wafer thin.

The loan was for five hundred million gold Leva at a rate of 5% for fifty years, the repayment to be guaranteed by the ring-fencing of specified Government revenues. In addition, Bulgaria was compelled to buy its military hardware from Austria, to award the highly lucrative contract for the construction of a new railway line to Port Lagos to a German consortium and finally, to allow another German company to participate in the running of its state mines. Negotiations for the loan were completed in July 1914 and the First World War broke out a month later.

Initially, there were no strongly pro-war factions within Bulgaria, although the powers on both sides of the conflict vied fiercely for its support, recognising Bulgaria's strategic importance in the Balkans. The Bulgarian leadership maintained a position of neutrality, while they observed the course of the fighting and weighed what each side was offering in the way of territorial gain. Initially, Germany and the central powers offered that area of Macedonia, to which Bulgaria felt it had a legitimate claim and, after it joined the war, any more of Macedonia that it might take by force. The entente offered Thrace up to the Enos-Midia line from the Black Sea Coast to the Aegean but stressed that any part of Macedonia that might subsequently fall to Bulgaria would depend on what Serbia was willing to sacrifice. Neither offer was in the least bit tempting leaving Ferdinand and Radoslavov to bide their time. However, the only questions were when rather than whether Bulgaria would join the war and on which side. The latter would depend on the degree of inducement presented by each of the antagonists. In 1915, events seemed to favour the entente as first Przemsl fell to the Russians and immediately afterwards Anglo-French troops landed in Gallipoli. Italy then joined the entente and voices were raised in the Subranie, the Bulgarian Assembly, encouraging the Bulgarian leadership to do likewise.

During the period of horse-trading that followed, the entente nations were contacted again but once more, their terms, though improved, fell short of expectations. The same area of Thrace was on offer as well as a larger part of Macedonia but this was dependent upon compensation being agreed with Greece and Serbia and then, only after victory had been achieved. By the middle of 1915, Bulgaria had received a far more tempting proposal from the central powers, which also appeared to be gaining the upper hand on the battle field. The Anglo-French landing in Gallipoli remained stranded on the beaches, sustaining heavy losses in the face of fanatical Turkish resistance, while in the north, the Russians having been driven back through Warsaw, Vilna and Kovno were in full retreat. This persuaded Bulgaria to throw in its lot with the central powers and by October 1915, it was officially at war with Russia, France and Great Britain.

Initially, Bulgaria's campaign was successful and the army occupied most of Macedonia. In 1916, Bulgarian and German forces moved against Greece and steadily advanced through Drama, Seres and Kavalla. When the Romanians entered the war on the side of the entente, the Third Bulgarian army crossed the Danube and thrust deep into central Romania, where it remained until the end of the war. In Macedonia during the latter part of 1916, the Bulgarian army suffered its first serious reverse, when the Serbian army emerged victorious from a ferocious encounter for Mount Kaimakchalan and went on to regain control of Bitoyla.

While most of the news from the battlefield was favourable, the situation at home was not so encouraging. In March 1915, the Government had enacted the Public Welfare Bill, which introduced price controls and the rationing of scarce commodities. A year later, bread became one of these as shortages of supplies became increasingly acute. The mobilisation of able-bodied men for military service in 1915 had disrupted the harvest that year and a disproportionate amount of the grain crop that had been produced was subsequently requisitioned and handed over to the military. This state of affairs was made worse by the activities of Austrian and German forces, which bought up vast amounts of Bulgarian-produced food, both legitimately and on the black markets, and sent it to their families back home. Allied food purchasing agencies and corrupt Bulgarian officials also played their part so that, by 1917, three-quarters of the country's fertile soil lay fallow, due to lack of seed.

Deaths from malnutrition and deteriorating quality of life finally led to protest and civil unrest. If the country's leaders had not yet had their fill of war, then the population most certainly had. There were popular demands for a peace settlement with Russia, traditional allies of Bulgaria, and the pressure for peace became more intense following the Russian revolution in 1917. The latter had repercussions in the army, too, when Bulgarian troops facing Russian forces in the north were reportedly setting up councils or soviets within their ranks resulting in the arrests of several hundred soldiers for seditious activities. Radoslavov repeatedly ignored the growing calls for peace, even in December 1917 when over 10,000 people took part in a public demonstration in Sofia, followed a month later by protests in Gabrovo and riots in Stanimaka and Samokov. In the summer came the news that long awaited food supplies from the Ukraine would only be moderate, while the Bulgarian harvest was likely to fail.

By now, the Americans had entered the war and the tide had turned in favour of the entente. Soldiers who were home on leave saw for themselves the privations of the people in the towns and villages and this affected the already dwindling morale in the armed forces. They, themselves, were short of food and equipment and in no condition to give any sort of account of themselves against the Anglo-French force that confronted them at Dobro-Pole on 15 September 1918. By 17th September, the Bulgarian army had been routed and had to endure heavy losses due to aerial attack as it retreated through the Kresna Gorge. A week later, The British and French had entered Bulgaria in force and what remained of the army offered no further resistance. On 29th September 1918, a cease-fire was agreed in Salonika and Bulgaria, which had been the last country to join the Central Powers became the first to withdraw from the coalition.

The Treaty of Versailles, which formally brought to an end the First World War, was described at the time by Archibald Wavell – later Field Marshall Earl Wavell – as the "peace to end all peace." These proved to be prophetic words for less than twenty years later most of the participants in the first war were at each others throats again, though not necessarily on the same side as they had been in the previous conflict. Bulgaria's participation in the Second World War bore many similarities to its role in the first one except that for a very short period of time during September 1944, it contrived to be the only country in the history of the planet to be at war, simultaneously with Germany, Great Britain, the United States and the Soviet Union. Its fate at the conclusion of the Second World War was far less favourable, too, as, along with the rest of Eastern Europe, it passed into the shadow of communism, where it remained in thrall for over forty years.

In 1940, Bulgaria, now ruled by King Boris III, strove to maintain its independence and to stay out of the war in spite of internal and external pressure to do the opposite. Indeed, Boris went to great lengths, both to maintain neutrality and to avoid taking any action that might be interpreted by either side as tacit support or partiality. In October 1939, he had already resisted a pact with Russia for mutual assistance and in 1940 he declined an offer to join the Balkan Entente as he felt this would have aligned his country too closely with the western powers, which in turn would have brought down the wrath of Hitler, Stalin and Mussolini upon him. For the same reason, Boris also rejected an offer from Turkey and Yugoslavia for a joint defensive alliance but the pressure to take sides was becoming more intense.

A month after the Turkish offer, Boris received an approach from Mussolini to assist with an attack on Greece, offering Bulgarian access to the Aegean as an inducement. In November, 1940, the Soviets turned up the heat, when the Deputy Commissar for Foreign Affairs, Sobolev, proposed a mutual assistance pact which would have allowed the Soviet Union to use the Black Sea naval bases for a joint Soviet-Bulgarian attack on Turkey, which had already declared its own neutrality and had sought a defensive alliance to protect this status. In the face of this diplomatic insistence, Boris remained steadfast in his refusal to enter the war or to take any action that might appear to favour one side or the other but his hand was about to be forced.

Throughout the 1930's Bulgaria had forged close trade and cultural ties with Nazi Germany, and, although its traditional links with Russia were still very strong, there was an equally robust pro-German feeling in the country. Bulgarian exports to Germany had increased from 48% in 1934 to 68% by 1939, while over the same period the volume of Bulgarian imports from Germany had grown from 44% in 1934 to 66% in 1939. However, King Boris and the rest of the Bulgarian leadership were equally aware of Germany's military might and, after their spectacular successes in 1940 Bulgaria was under increasing pressure to join the Axis powers. As events unfolded, it was not military power in the end that was instrumental in persuading them, rather the lack of it.

While the Italian military might have had many attributes in World War II, dexterity on the field of battle was not considered one of the most prominent. By December 1940, the Italian army was being routed and pursued across the North African desert by its allied counterparts and was close to defeat in Albania. A similar disaster in Greece had prompted Mussolini to seek help from Germany whose forces had occupied Romania during the summer but Bulgaria's strict neutrality raised logistical difficulties.

Hitler had already decided to transfer troops from Romania to assist the beleaguered Italians in Greece and he opened negotiations with Bulgaria's Minister President, Filov, to secure their passage through his country. Before any agreement could be reached, however, a party of forty German staff officers appeared in Bulgaria disguised as businessmen, to be followed at regular intervals by large numbers of unaccompanied German males posing as tourists. A similar subterfuge was used by the Japanese throughout 1941, prior to their invasion of British Malaya.

In spite of a last ditch effort by the Americans to persuade him that Great Britain, backed by the United States would ultimately achieve victory, Filov went to Germany to finalise an agreement with Hitler. By now, Boris and Filov had come to realise that further attempts to keep Bulgaria neutral were useless and they decided to co-operate with the Nazis rather than oppose them and be crushed. In February 1941, Filov consented to the construction of a temporary bridge over the Danube and a month later, German troops started to move across Bulgaria en route to Greece. Simultaneously, Filov signed the tri-partite agreement in Vienna thereby making Bulgaria a de-facto member of the Axis.

Upon entering the war, Bulgaria immediately occupied Macedonia and Thrace, but was dismayed by Hitler's attack on the Soviet Union in June 1941, which destroyed at a stroke Bulgaria's cordial relationship with that country. In January 1942, a series of mass internments was instigated and by September of that year, 15,000 people had been detained, 11,000 in labour camps while the others went to various prisons and concentration camps. Many communists were interned at this time and those who survived would return to seek their revenge when Bulgaria's involvement in hostilities finally came to an end.

Although Boris had failed to keep Bulgaria out of the war, there were two areas of Nazi activity that he was determined to resist. Firstly, there were demands both from the Bulgarian right as well as from their German allies for a Bulgarian force to be sent to the Russian front. Boris resisted the Nazis, skilfully arguing that the entire Bulgarian army needed to remain in the Balkans to counter three likely threats, an attack by Turkey, an assault by the Soviets on the Black Sea Coast and an allied landing in the Balkans. In addition, Boris pointed to the likelihood of guerrilla warfare being instigated by partisans and the fact that the Bulgarian army was not equipped to fight anywhere but in the Balkans and could not be expected to perform effectively in any other theatre of war – particularly the Russian front.

The second Nazi initiative that Boris resolved to defy was the threat hanging over 50,000 Bulgarian Jews. By January 1941, various decrees had been issued, including an order for all Jews to wear yellow stars. For various reasons, this edict was never wholly complied with. Two years later, plans were being drawn up for mass deportations of Jews to death camps. When these became known, the whole of Bulgarian society rose up in protest thereby saving Bulgarian Jews from wholesale liquidation. Unfortunately, Boris's triumph was short-lived and two weeks later, he died in mysterious circumstances after visiting Hitler in Berlin. It was believed at the time that Boris had been poisoned for opposing the Nazis on the Russian and Jewish issues but this was not the case. Officially, he died from Coronary Thrombosis and there is no reason to doubt this.

Before his death, Boris and many other prominent Bulgarians were beginning to waver in their support for the German war effort. In 1940, history started to repeat itself with a disproportionate amount of Bulgarian grain being exported to Germany. In 1941, more than the required quantity of grain was requisitioned by the Bulgarian army and in the following year, food production was crippled by a severe drought. What food there was soared in price because farmers preferred to sell their products on the black market and because, as in the 1914-1918 war, German soldiers were sending home vast quantities of Bulgarian-produced foodstuffs that should have been made available to the Bulgarian people. Inflation was also rampant as the Government sought to cover its inability to raise foreign loans by printing an excessive volume of paper money.

The German defeat at Stalingrad coupled with partisan activity in the east prompted Boris to open clandestine negotiations with the allies but they offered him no comfort. Their demands were simple and blunt, unconditional surrender, complete withdrawal from the occupied territories and immediate allied occupation of Bulgaria. Boris was unable to accept these terms and on 28 August 1943, at the age of forty-nine, he died.

Boris was succeeded by six-year old Simeon, for whom Filov, Boris's brother Prince Kiril and General Mihov were jointly created Regents. In reality, Filov alone acted as Regent and he appointed the docile Dobri Bozhilov to succeed him as Minister President to ensure that he retained all vestiges of power.

Up until now, Bulgaria had succeeded in keeping the war away from its borders but on 19 November, 1943, disaster struck in the form of the first major air attack on Sofia followed in quick succession by two more. On 19 January, 1944, Sofia suffered a massive heavy artillery barrage followed by a series of incendiary attacks and, finally, on 30th March, a devastating bombing raid, which reduced much of the city to rubble.

The air raids had demonstrated to disillusioned Bulgarian citizens that their German allies were unable to protect them and, for this reason, blame for the air attacks was attributed to the Germans rather than to allied pilots who had carried them out. There was an emergent anti-German movement in the country coupled with the growing belief that Bulgaria should avert impending disaster by changing sides and supporting the allies. Further clandestine approaches were made during February and March 1944 but the allied terms remained the same. This put Filov and Bozhilov in a quandary. The presence of German forces in Bulgaria meant that unconditional surrender was not yet an option, especially as the allies were too far away to intervene. However, the real threat came from the Soviet Union, something of which Filov and Bozhilov were only too aware.

They really missed the wily diplomacy and low animal cunning of Boris as they tried to keep the Soviet menace at bay until an agreement could be concluded with the allies. They nearly succeeded, too, but for a fatal error of judgement later in the year. In the meantime, pressure from the Soviets was increasing in its intensity. They had refused Filov's request to mediate with the allies to end the air raids and instead, persisted with their own demands for Bulgaria to clear the Black Sea area of all German forces and shipping, to formally declare its neutrality and to break off diplomatic relations with Germany. In a diplomatic note delivered on 18th May, 1944, the Soviets spelt out these conditions, hinting that failure to carry out all or any of these might well result in attack by the Red Army which was about to invade neighbouring Romania. Two weeks later, Bozhilov resigned to be replaced as Minister President by the pro-western Ivan Bagrianov.

Bagrianov immediately re-opened negotiations with the allies, who intimated that they might not take such a hard line on sovereignty over the occupied territories but they insisted on unconditional surrender and immediate allied occupation of Bulgaria. Bagrianov opted to take time to consider his position in the hope of achieving better terms and, in so doing, sealed Bulgaria's fate for the next forty-five years. Bulgaria's strategic position was weakened on 2nd August when Turkey broke off diplomatic relations with Germany but Bagrianov insisted that he could not reach a settlement with the allies until after the harvest had been collected. He reasoned that if he acted any earlier, the Germans might either commandeer or destroy the crops as a reprisal but time was running out. On 20th August, three days after he had informed the allies of his decision, the Red Army invaded Romania and the Soviet Union was now demanding that Bulgaria declared war on its former ally, compelling Bagrianov to resume his negotiations with the allies with renewed urgency. He knew that refusal to comply with the Soviet demand for war with Germany would lead to an attack by the Red Army but if he managed to negotiate terms with the allies before this happened, the Soviet Union would have no say in post-war Bulgaria. Unfortunately, Bagrianov was no Boris and, at the end of his tether, he offered his resignation, to be replaced by Konstantin Muraviev. On 8th September, Muraviev declared war on Germany but by then it was of no use. The Soviet Union had declared war on Bulgaria the previous day, so that the latter was now officially at war with Germany, Great Britain, the USA and the Soviet Union.

Matters then moved speedily to a conclusion. Filov formally re-signed as Regent on 8th September while Soviet troops were entering Sofia unopposed. Far from being regarded as an army of occupation, they were greeted as liberators and were being hailed and applauded everywhere they went. In the meantime, a partisan-inspired coup had toppled the Muraviev Government and replaced it with representatives from the left wing opposition coalition, the Fatherland Front. It took another three years of intrigue, conspiracy and blood-letting before the communists fi-nally took control but with the Red Army in occupation, a communist takeover of Bulgaria was now inevitable.

IN SEARCH OF SPARTACUS

Like my previous visit, my second stay in Bulgaria was not exactly planned but one way or another, it was quite an eye-opener and, at times, quite enjoyable. They called it the "Spartacus Tour" after the slave who originated from Thrace in Southern Bulgaria and led a revolt against the Romans in the first century BC thereby inspiring a Hollywood epic in the sixties starring Kirk Douglas, Tony Curtis and a load of other people I can't remember. The tour started off in Burgas on the Black Sea coast, then back-tracked to Sofia before heading eastwards again to Plovdiv, south to Sandanski and back to Burgas for the flight home. Due to work commitments, I was only free for the second week in May but for that week there was no package leaving from London. The only tour they could offer me left from Manchester at 7 A.M. so I decided to take the shuttle from Heathrow and stay overnight in an airport hotel.

I spent the evening in the hotel lounge in front of the television with a large brandy watching Chris Eubank slap and shuffle his way through twelve boring rounds against Irishman Ray Close. Eubank thought he'd won but I disagreed with him. So did the officials who declared the fight a draw. I decided Close had been robbed, got myself another brandy and took it to bed with me.

I asked for a call at 5.30 but I was already showered and dressed by the time the phone rang. My taxi got me to the airport at 6.30 for a 7 A.M.

check in but once again, I could have taken my time, slept late and eaten a hearty three-course breakfast. There was fog at Burgas and all flights to the Black sea coast were delayed until further notice. Although it is an international airport, Manchester tends to fill up rather quickly so it only needs a couple of flights to be delayed for the place to become unbearably crowded.

It was 11 A.M. by the time we took off and by then, I had become totally stressed out but I was not alone. Children were becoming petulant and screaming. Agitated parents were trying unsuccessfully to placate them. Non parents and fellow travellers irritated by the noise, the over-crowded conditions and the delay were becoming belligerent, fractious and impatient, each and every one of them contributing in their own small way to an all too familiar witches brew of cacophonous, bad tempered chaos.

So-called departure lounges are little more than shopping malls designed to separate travellers from their hard-earned cash before being herded onto aircraft and strapped into cramped seats where they are required to sit forlornly like Lilliputian galley slaves.

We landed in Burgas at about 3 P.M. local time and it took us another two hours before we cleared the various formalities. Burgas airport was a desolate, grey, concrete building, the age of which was difficult to determine because it appeared to be so neglected. A thorough clean up might have improved the look of the place but it would have brought about a total disaster as I surmised it was only the decades of compacted grime that held the structure together. As we entered the outskirts of the city in our battered, Russian-built tour coach, we passed streets of crumbling concrete tower blocks, which, if they had been maintained at all, had been maintained badly. I lost count of the missing window-panes that had been replaced by plastic sheeting and of the balcony railings, which had disappeared altogether leaving no defence against a sheer drop from a great height. Our hotel, the imaginatively named Hotel Balgaria, was at the southern end of town in a square some ten minutes walk from the sea. It was a tall grey box in the familiar post-Kruschev modernist style that could have been borrowed from the set of a Batman movie. Inside was wall-to-wall sleaze, a cathedral-like reception and lounge area, which looked more like the giant waiting room of some mythical railway station. It was a study in brown stained wood and polished stone and would have taken a great deal of effort to keep clean if anyone had ever bothered to try. There was a thick haze of cigarette smoke caused by a large number of unkempt middle-aged men who sprawled across upholstered plastic arm-chairs, chain smoking at lounge tables and hawking up unceremoniously onto the floor. In their shapeless black leather jackets they reminded me of the elderly Athenians, who used to haunt the ouzo bars in Ommonia Square twenty years before.

Dinner was an elaborate six-course affair, three of which I didn't dare touch, and was conducted in a covered court yard on the ground floor, well away from the main restaurant. There were less of us here than there had been on the plane and it turned out that I was the only one who had booked for one week. The other people on this tour would be going to a place called Slanchev Bryag or "Sunny Beach" for the second week, while the other passengers on the plane had been taken straight there for the whole two sun – filled weeks. Slanchev Bryag sounds like Bulgarian for cess-pit so I can understand why even the Bulgarian Tourist Board always refers to the place by its anglicised name. Can you really see people spending good money to come to a place that sounds like "Slurry Pit by Sea?"

The parts of the meal I managed to eat were tasty but the early start, the delay and the journey had left me with a splitting headache and, having grown bored with the meal-table small talk, I slipped away to explore the hotel before they served coffee. A sweeping spiral staircase led me from the reception lounge to a dimly-lit bar with a wide overhanging balcony that served no useful purpose other than to defy anyone sitting down to see over the top. Black plastic upholstered chairs surrounded low wooden tables that were lined up in regimented ranks like supplicants before a long sunken bar illuminated by concealed fluorescent strip lights. The subdued lighting was not so much atmospheric as a convenient disguise for the same degree of dirt and grime that passed for décor in the lounge below. I ordered a brandy in a glass that was surprisingly clean and looked around me.

There were a number of unattended young women sitting at various tables. They might have been hookers but it was difficult to tell. In the preceding two years, I had visited Poland, Hungary and Romania and I had seen a lot of young women who might well have been quite respectable but, in an attempt to appear westernised and modern had overdone the eye make up, wore exceedingly short skirts, and instead of looking trendy, they ended up looking extremely tarty. As an unfortunate consequence of this, whenever these ladies appeared in the street, they often became the focus of the unsolicited and unwelcome attention of a large number of unshaven, malodorous male pedestrians, with the occasional Lada driver thrown in for appearances sake, who passed for kerb crawlers in this part of the world. At the other end of the scale, the real hookers looked exactly the same except that their clothes were more expensive and the only way to tell the difference was to wait until they came onto you.

I finished my brandy and was on my way down to reception when I met her on the stairs coming up. She was a petite peroxide blonde with green eyes and an infectious grin. She wore German made denims, a matching top and a pair of white, strappy, high-heels that had obviously been bought outside Bulgaria. We started our conversation in German but she switched to English when I told her where I was from. We went back to the bar and I bought her a coke, which was all she wanted, while I got myself another brandy. She said her name was Rosa and she had just returned from Germany where she had been working as a cabaret singer. She was an ethnic Greek and told me she had been making good money singing in Tavernas and Bazouki bars throughout Germany. Unfortunately, her work permit had expired and she was staying here with her parents until she could get it renewed. I'd heard similar stories before, mostly from Eastern European hookers. When I asked her if she was working, I was relieved when she said "no" as the last thing I needed right then was to be hustled.

She did want something, though. There was a nightclub and cabaret on the ground floor and they wouldn't let her in on her own, so she wanted me to go with her. At any other time it might have been a nice idea but I had to get up early next morning and of course, I still had that headache. She tried to get rid of it by massaging the back of my neck but I'd earned this one by lack of sleep and a whole lot of hassle so it was going to take a lot more than manipulation, physical or any other kind, for it to go away. In the end, she gave up and accepted the situation. We finished our drinks and I left her in reception after agreeing to meet her for dinner when I came back at the end of the week.

We arrived at the airport at 6 A.M. the following morning and it didn't look any better than it had the day before. Neither did it look any different two hours later after the sun had come up and we were still there. We were told that the plane was being checked and we could not get on board the aircraft until it had been declared safe. If that statement was meant to reassure us as to the rigorous safety standards of Balkan Air and their scrupulous regard for the welfare of its passengers, it had been wide of the mark. What was taking them so long? What was so wrong with their Russian-built aircraft that had rendered it so unsafe for us to board? Their statement was far from reassuring. Fortunately, it was also far from true.

Although I haven't smoked for ten years, I always take cigarettes on holiday with me as they tend to be better received than money in places like this. While I was wandering around the passenger lounge I struck up a conversation with one of the security guards who spoke English. Inevitably, we talked about football. He was thrilled that the Bulgarian football team was off to America the following year to play in the World Cup while I tried to steer the conversation away from the fact that England had failed to qualify. In the end, I produced a couple of packets of Benson and Hedges and gave them to him. I asked him what was causing the delay and he gave me a different story and a far more entertaining one than the official version. Apparently, we were waiting for the pilot, whose uncle had once been an influential member of the Communist Party but, since the Communist Party had now become unfashionable, he had made the logical transition to the local Mafia and he tended to be a bit protective towards his favourite nephew.

"Does that mean he can turn up for work when he wants?" I asked, harbouring the secret fear that we might still be here at lunchtime.

"Not really," replied my companion "But he is always late when this air traffic controller is working."

"Why is that?" I asked

"He's screwing the air traffic controller's wife."

An announcement in Bulgarian followed by a translation in English told us that at this particular moment he wasn't. He might have been earlier and from what I had just been told, it was possible that he would do so again later but at that precise moment, the flight to Sofia was ready to board and as I walked across the runway, I was hoping that the air traffic controller in question had no knowledge of his wife's extra marital activities and that we were not about to be directed into the flight path of an incoming jumbo jet.

We landed in Sofia slightly more than an hour later having received no in-flight services, not even a cup of coffee. As we were a domestic flight, our passage through the airport was rapid and within the space of half an hour, we'd reclaimed our baggage and were riding in a coach towards the city. I did not know where they were taking us but I was praying that we wouldn't have to stay at the Hotel Pliska with its drug dealers, hookers and pimps. Fortunately, they took us to the Rodina, a very smart hotel just outside the city centre on the Ploshad Ruski. The Rodina had a number of plush bars, several good quality restaurants, and there was a nightclub somewhere but I never went looking for it. It was advertised extensively on posters in reception and in the lifts but our sightseeing schedules proved to be so demanding, by the time I'd finished dinner, I was no longer in the mood.

Our guide introduced herself as Svetlana, a short plump dark woman in her early twenties. She had gained a degree in engineering from Sofia University but, once qualified, she had been unable to find work as an engineer and had become a tour guide instead. I don't know whether her employers thought she was a good tour guide or not but as far as I was concerned she had her priorities right. Every morning was greeted in a leisurely manner, nobody rushed about and there was no question of anyone going anywhere until Svetlana had eaten her breakfast and drunk a liberal amount of coffee, which suited me. After we had checked into the Rodina, we had the rest of the day to ourselves and I went out to rediscover the places I'd first found two Christmases ago. Apart from the disappearance of the ice and slush and the sharp rise in temperature, nothing appeared to have changed, except that the people on the streets were wearing a few less layers of clothing, but whether or not it improved their appearance, I can't really say. Shaving was just as unfashionable among the men as it had been on my last visit and the women were still hiding their heads under brightly coloured scarves.

I headed straight for the Alexander Nevsky Church, armed with a new camera and a determination to take some photographs that would not resemble a black mass in a coalmine at midnight. After I'd taken a number of pictures of the dome – clustered exterior, I went inside, fitted the flash and took a picture of the magnificent chandelier, which dominated the centre of the church. Although there was lighting, it had not been turned on so that the interior was very dark indeed, the only source of illumination coming from the chandelier itself. I was about to take a picture of some icons when she appeared.

"No Photo!" she thundered. She hadn't changed. She was just as large, just as ugly and just as loud as she had been two years ago. She didn't remember me, though, so I tried another approach.

Alexander Nevsky Memorial Church, Sofia.

Chandelier in the Nevsky Memorial Church, Sofia. It was still pitch black in there.

I took her by the hand and led her out to the foyer where there was a souvenir kiosk. Although she spoke no English and I spoke no Bulgarian, by means of a crudely improvised form of sign language, I made a deal with her. If I bought some goods from her souvenir stall, she would let me take a couple of pictures inside the church. I was hoping to persuade her to put the lights on as well but just then I was concentrating on keeping my end of the deal. I bought a box of transparencies just in case none of my photographs came out and a few postcards, too, and, just for luck, I bought a cassette of the church choir singing Gregorian plainchants. Having performed my duty, leaving her with a generous tip in the process, I went back into the church. I was just slipping the flash into the bracket on my camera when she rushed in after me.

"No!" she shouted angrily "No photo!"

To this day, I will never know whether there had been a genuine breakdown in communications or whether she was just being a good communist and welshing on the deal. Either way, I knew I wasn't going to win and reluctantly I left. Once again the Russian church had been closed so I went back to TsUM and spent the rest of the afternoon inspecting the empty shelves. To be fair, the shelves were not all empty but there was nothing on them that I considered worth buying. I went out into the street and walked briskly towards the Banya Bashi Mosque. It was still bricked up and looked as if it was going to stay that way forever. I took a few half-hearted photographs but the building was lost in a sea of people and an endless flow of passing cars. I was feeling tired, my feet were beginning to hurt and I was dying for a cup of that thick black coffee they served in Bulgaria. There was a coffee shop on the first floor of the Rodina, and, rather than risk the foul concoction they served in TsUM, I trudged down the Bulevard Georgi Dimitrov and turned into Ulitsa Alabin, where another ten minute walk took me to the Rodina and its coffee shop.

After dinner, I was pretty shattered so I decided to have an early night. Before I retired, I went into one of the Rodina's bars for a brandy. As I did so, all the hookers suddenly sat up straight, stuck out their chests, hiked their skirts up another two inches and fixed me with the standard "come up and see me sometime" look. When they realised I wasn't buying, they relaxed again, let it all hang out, lit up another cigarette and carried on with their conversations.

NICOLA PETKOV: NO STATUE FOR A DEAD PATRIOT

As I mentioned earlier, this tour had been sold to me by Balkan Holidays as the "Spartacus Tour" in honour of the Bulgarian folk hero who was born in Thrace and led a slave revolt against the Roman Empire. This was no mean feat as he and his army of gladiators held the Roman legions at bay for the best part of two years before his inevitable defeat and death. As I was wandering around the centre of Sofia that afternoon, I found myself drawing a parallel with another Bulgarian hero who had also taken on the forces of oppression against overwhelming odds and, like Spartacus, he had paid for it with his life. I knew there was a statue of Spartacus in Sandanski and I would see it for myself in a few days but just then I found myself looking for another statue, a relatively new one. It had to be new as there was no way the Communists would have honoured this man but Bulgaria had been free of communist dictatorship for more than three years and it was just possible that Nicola Petkov had finally received the recognition he deserved but if he had, I saw no tangible indication of this and certainly no statue, which was a pity.

From the surrender of Bulgaria to the Allies in 1944 until his execution in September 1947, Nicola Petkov had personified Bulgarian resistance to the orgy of lies, deceit, purges, plots, conspiracies and mass murder indulged in by the communists to gain control of the state. From the very beginning, Petkov and his supporters, like those of Spartacus, had little chance of success. Indeed few political organisations have had the odds so heavily stacked against them. Faced by a well-organised, disciplined and ruthless party machine, resourced by the world communist movement and operating in the shadow of the occupying Red Army, the significance of Petkov's opposition was without equal anywhere in central or eastern Europe. Little help was forthcoming from the western powers, which, in the final analysis were reluctant to quarrel with the Soviet Union over Bulgaria.

Petkov was the son of a former Minister President who had been assassinated in 1907. In 1945, he became leader of the Agrarian Party, a constituent member of the Fatherland Front, the coalition that had seized power following the Red Army occupation in 1944. His immediate predecessors, Gichev and Gemeto, had been removed from office as the result of communist intrigue. Gichev was imprisoned while Gemeto escaped from house arrest and fled to the west. He was subsequently accused of being an agent of the British and sentenced in absentia to life imprisonment.

The Fatherland Front was first put forward in 1941 as a left-wing coalition to oppose the Monarchist Government. It failed then because most factions had refused to work with the communists who, typically, had demanded complete control of the coalition, in spite of their comparative deficiency in numbers. A year later, the Fatherland Front finally emerged as a loose but secret organisation made up of communists, agrarians, liberals and social democrats. It was compelled to remain a clandestine organisation as the official opposition refused to have anything to do with it due to their anti-nazi stance and the existence of communists within their ranks. However, the Front continued to grow in strength and numbers and by 1943, it had established a central committee consisting of four people, one of whom was Petkov.

A coup in September 1944 brought a Fatherland Front Government to power. This consisted of fifteen ministers, including four Agrarians and four Communists, the latter, significantly, holding the ministries of the Interior and of Justice. Apart from the key ministerial posts held by party members, the Communists were assisted in their nefarious activities by the presence of the Red Army, and the incumbency by the Soviet Union of the Chair of the Allied Control Commission, a body that would stay in Bulgaria until a peace treaty had been formally agreed and signed. The Chair of the Commission virtually gave its occupant, Biriuzov, the powers of a Governor General and the Communists took full advantage of this as they systematically stripped Bulgaria of all the paraphernalia, trappings and accessories of the former regime. Using their control of the Ministry of the Interior, they consolidated their power over the various Government institutions by sacking 30,000 officials and replacing them with their own apparatchiks, who had been exempted from traditional educational requirements, receiving only rudimentary training in administration and finance, a bare minimum but sufficient to carry out the instructions of their new masters.

Following their success in purging the civil service, the communists then undertook a similar exercise with the Bulgarian Workers Union, winding it up completely and replacing it with the broader based General Workers Professional Union, which by 1945 had a membership of 264,000 white and blue-collar workers. Influential Workers Councils were then set up, which were to provide a valuable training ground for the officials who would eventually be charged with managing the nationalised industries after the communist takeover but there was much work to do before this became a reality.

Shortly after the September coup, the Peoples Militia and the Peoples Courts were established to facilitate the purges carried out during the next three years. The People's Militia replaced the former Police force, which had ceased to exist following the removal of the previous regime. This new force was completely run by the communists who occupied every influential position, both locally and nationally. Initially, the People's Courts had been set up to try collaborators and war criminals, but Bulgaria's refusal to participate in the eastern war or the holocaust ensured that the numbers in either category were small. This did not prevent a greater number of people per head of population from being tried, convicted, imprisoned or executed in Bulgaria than in any other emergent communist state in Eastern Europe. Officially, the Government admitted to 11,667 people having been purged within six months of the establishment of the People's Courts but the official figure, like many others given out by former communist states is at best, a conservative estimate. More realistic calculations put the numbers at anything between 30,000 and 100,000.

Similar activities taking place across the rest of Eastern Europe were justified by their perpetrators as the judicial punishment of traitors, pro-fascists or Nazi sympathisers but, as there were relatively few of these in Bulgaria, the wave of mass executions was attributed to revenge by those who had been interned or imprisoned during the war and to political expedience by the communists who were determined to eliminate their opponents, either potential or actual, as rapidly as possible. Having established a power base at grass roots level, the communists started to move against the deposed political leadership. They apprehended every single member of every cabinet since 1941 along with every member of the existing Subranie and, at the end of December 1944, they put them all on trial.

The "trials" had been completed by the end of January 1945 and on 1st February the Chief Public Prosecutor demanded the death sentence for fifty of the accused. In the eyes of the communists, to be accused is to be guilty and, as a warning to any others who sought to oppose them, instead of the original fifty deaths asked for, one hundred of the defendants were executed. Sentences were carried out the same night by firing squad, instantly rendering the Bulgarian right and centre parties leaderless and eviscerated. The Communists then turned on the Agrarian Party, and, having disposed of Gichev and Gemeto, they found themselves confronted by the more formidable figure of Nicola Petkov.

Petkov's reputation as an anti-fascist and his opposition to Bulgaria's pro-German stance meant that he was immune from being denounced and purged as a nazi sympathiser and his razor-sharp political acumen made him a difficult and astute opponent. He had quickly become a constant and forthright adversary of the communists and had called for their domination of grass roots Fatherland Front organisations to cease. Along with his Social Democratic ally, Kosta Lulchev he had opposed attempts by the communists to seize control of youth organisations and condemned the closure, harassment or takeover of journals and periodicals which were sympathetic to the non-communist cause. He had looked on with dismay as established communist icons Dimitrov and Kolarov were voted on to the executive committee of the Fatherland Front, even though both were in Moscow, having resided there since before the war without giving any sign that they ever intended to return to Bulgaria.

In May 1945, Petkov lost control of BANU, an umbrella group incorporating a number of land and peasant based political parties, to a communist collaborator, Alexandur Obbov in a vote that was allegedly rigged at the behest of Dimitrov. Petkov promptly resigned his leadership of the Agrarian Party. Although he remained a member of the Government, communist harassment now compelled Petkov to organise his own faction outside the Fatherland Front. Five months later, Petkov's Social

Democrat collaborator, Lulchev was relieved of the leadership of his party in a similar coup as the communists moved relentlessly to secure control of the Fatherland Front. Having achieved this, they now addressed the issue of the national elections, scheduled to take place on 26th August 1945 as decreed by the Yalta conference. To protect their dominant position, the communists insisted that the Fatherland Front should contest the elections with a single list of candidates, most of which would consist of communist nominees.

By now, opposition to communist domination had concentrated upon Petkov and his followers. The unbridled excesses of the purges had generated a feeling of fear and trepidation throughout the country but people knew that if they spoke out against such atrocities, they, themselves, risked being denounced, tried and executed. In these days of the Red Terror, protest was no longer an option. Peasant farmers, fearful of collectivisation, saw Petkov as their saviour, while urban dwellers under threat from communist apparatchiks, empathised with him, thus inspiring him and his supporters to counteract communist activity in the forthcoming elections. He objected to the declared intention of the Fatherland Front to contest the elections with a single list. He denounced this as undemocratic since it meant that the communists would field more candidates than the Agrarian Party even though there was five times more support in the country for the latter. He therefore insisted upon separate lists for every constituent party in the Fatherland Front and asked the western powers to intercede on his behalf with the Soviet Union to avert a single-list election and to prevent what he claimed were illegal pressures being brought to bear on the electorate by the communists. As a result, the Soviet Union agreed to the postponement of the elections until 18th November 1945.

With the assistance of the Western powers, Petkov had caused the Communists to back down and accept that Soviet influence was not irresistible but this had not been his only success. The Government declared that it was prepared to permit opposition candidates to stand as nominees of political parties rather than as individuals as had been proposed originally. As a consequence, four opposition parties declared themselves, Petkov's Agrarians, Lulchev's Independent Social Democrats, the United Radical Party and the Democrats. Government press restrictions were also relaxed to some degree, although the radio remained in sole Government control.

With the continued support of the Western powers, Petkov, having resigned from the Government, went on the offensive. Not content with the concessions he had already gained, he insisted that the parties of the Fatherland Front, like those of the opposition, should run as separate entities in the election. He also wanted an end to communist intimidation of local communities, independence of the judiciary from political interference, the resignation of the Government and the communists to relinquish control of the Ministries of Justice and the Interior. Petkov believed that the postponement of the elections had seriously damaged the communists and undermined Soviet influence in Bulgaria. Confident in this belief, he made it known that if his conditions were not met, he would advise his supporters to boycott the elections. If the opposition were to stay away from the poll, it was likely that this would invalidate the eventual outcome so that the Western powers would not recognise any Government that might emerge.

Petkov was also aware that, until Bulgaria had a universally recognised Government, not only would it be difficult to raise the foreign loans that were urgently needed to offset the escalating cost of the occupying Red Army, no peace treaty could be concluded, which meant that the Western powers would need to remain in Sofia indefinitely. The significance of the latter in Petkov's strategy was revealed when on 10th October 1945, the United States declared that they supported the reservations expressed by Petkov concerning the impartiality of the forthcoming election and they appointed an independent observer to keep a close watch on the communists during the electoral process and to advise them of his findings.

On 11th October 1945, Petkov and his supporters withdrew from the election, which inevitably went ahead without them with a predictable 88% of the seats being won by the communist-dominated Government coalition with the remaining 12% going to what remained of the opposition. The United States refused to recognise the result as their observer had submitted an adverse report. Encouraged by this, Petkov repeated his earlier demands and added to them the immediate annulment of the elections. In December 1945, a summit meeting in Moscow agreed that two opposition members should be admitted to the Bulgarian cabinet but this did not appease Petkov. A month later, the Soviet Government sent Vyshinsky, Deputy Commissar for Foreign Affairs, to Sofia but his efforts to persuade Petkov and Lulchev to join the Government and to heal the rift between the Fatherland Front and the dissenters failed abysmally. For their part, Petkov and Lulchev remained resolute in their demands for the immediate dissolution of the Subranie, free elections to take place as a matter of urgency and for the communist custody of the Ministries of Justice and the Interior to be surrendered forthwith. Having thus dug in their heels, Petkov and Lulchev had confounded their opponents and created a political stand-off that was to remain unresolved for another year.

Having failed to unravel the political impasse with Petkov and Lulchev, the communists turned their attention to gaining control of the military, removal of the monarchy and the establishment of a Marxist-Leninist constitution. On 3rd July, 1946, the Subranie passed a bill which transferred responsibility for the military from the ministry of war to the cabinet, thereby bringing it under the direct control of the communist-dominated Government. By means of trials and dismissals, a number of influential military leaders were disposed of and, after a further 2000 or so officers had been dismissed for being "reactionary," any threat the Bulgarian army might have posed to a complete communist takeover had been successfully extinguished. Two months later, a referendum on the future of the monarchy resulted in an overwhelming vote in favour of a republic, which was subsequently declared on 15th September compelling the nine-year old King Simeon to seek exile abroad.

A formal constitution was to be adopted by a Grand National Subranie and elections for this body were scheduled to take place on 27th October. The opposition could not guarantee they would receive the same level of western support they had enjoyed a year earlier, which prompted Petkov and his supporters to take part in the elections as a united front with a single list of candidates but they were soundly defeated. Out of a total number of 364 seats, the Communists gained 277, Petkov's Agrarians 69, Lulchev's Social Democrats 9, the Liberals 8, leaving the radicals with but a single seat. Petkov claimed that the opposition vote had been unfairly tampered with and he openly accused the communists of intimidation and obstruction of opposition supporters so that 60% of their number had been too frightened to turn out and vote. He also complained that opposition parties had been granted neither free access to the press nor unrestricted rights of assembly. Any meetings that had taken place were violently disrupted by communist agitators. In addition, various opposition supporters had been imprisoned, or physically barred from entering polling stations to prevent them from voting while others had had their voting papers withheld. By contrast there was evidence to suggest that pro-communists in the military had been provided with more than one ballot paper. In spite of the fact that Petkov's protests were supported by the western powers, the result of the election stood and communist hardliner Georgi Dimitrov, recently recalled from Moscow, became Minister President.

In spite of the outcome of the elections, the influence of the opposition increased as did popular support for Petkov, particularly from the Agrarians and other farming organisations but the communists were relentless and they resolved to remove all obstacles from their path. Opposition newspapers and periodicals were forced out of business as communist-controlled unions ordered their members neither to print nor distribute them. It was even proposed to "democratise" the Church, whose leaders turned to Petkov for help.

In February 1947, the Treaty of Paris was finally signed fixing Bulgaria's boundaries to their 1940 locations. A number of stipulations were also imposed, the most significant of which being that all citizens were to have equality and full civil rights, there was to be no fascist or military regime and Soviet troops were to leave Bulgaria within 90 days of the treaty's operative date. Petkov was encouraged by the last proviso and believed that the power of the communists would crumble without the backing of the Red Army but there were two drawbacks. The Allied Control Commission would also be required to withdraw along with the Red Army and Petkov had underestimated the cynical ruthlessness of the communists. In the Subranie, the opposition fought tooth and nail to prevent the imposition of a Marxist-Leninist constitution, while the communists refused to accept any alternative proposal. Exchanges became bitter and acrimonious as Petkov taunted Dimitrov with the accusation that the current expenditure on prisons and police activity was four times what it had been in 1942. Other opposition members demanded that the communist party be banned as a "fascist" organisation but the communists were merely biding their time.

In the first week in June 1947, they made their move. On 4th June, the United States Senate ratified the peace treaty and the day after, Petkov was arrested on a range of trumped up charges. The main charges were conspiracy to overthrow the Government, undermining military morale and discipline and organising terrorist activity. There were many other charges in the 9000-word indictment but none of them had any substance. Petkov was merely an obstacle to communist control of the state and he needed to be removed. When the "trial" commenced, proceedings were conducted along well-practised Stalinist lines. Petkov was denied access to a defence lawyer neither was he allowed to give evidence or address the "court" in any way as this was declared to be of "no use or importance." Prosecution witnesses, on the other hand, had been prompted, coached and thoroughly prepared so that the outcome was a foregone conclusion. On 16th August, the farcical show trial had ground to an end, the inevitable guilty verdict had been returned and Petkov was sentenced to death. Outside the Sofia courtroom, a stage-managed demonstration of peasants specially brought in for the purpose demanded "To a dog, a dog's death."

The peace treaty came into force on 20th September 1947 and Petkov was hanged three days later. Representations made by Britain and the United States against the execution were snubbed as Petkov, a devout Christian was put to death having been denied the sacrament, the last rites and, subsequently, a Christian burial. After the removal of Petkov, the communists made short work of their remaining political opponents as, one after another, all possible sources of resistance were systematically suppressed and disposed of until the whole of Eastern Europe was in their icy clutches and as Churchill so eloquently put it," from Stettin in the Baltic to Trieste in the Adriatic an iron curtain descended across the continent of Europe."

EXPLORING SOFIA AND A POTENTIAL EURO-SCAM

The next day we were into heavy duty sight seeing. By lunchtime, we had been to two museums, one of which had formerly been a mosque, a textile shop and yet another museum containing various forms of quartz. After lunch, Svetlana took us to the Alexander Nevsky Church and another chorus of "No photo!" from Giant Haystacks. We then went across the road to the Russian Church and it was open. Unfortunately, when I finally got inside this intriguing architectural curiosity, it was a bit of a let down. I am not sure what I expected to see but I didn't see it. There were icons for sure and there was heavy incense, too, but it was all pitch black and very ordinary. I might just as well have been in one of those hippy shops they used to have in the Kings Road during the seventies.

The last site we visited was the strangest of all, a last hangover from the darkest days of communism. It was closed, too, and unlikely ever to reopen even if communist rule were to be restored. The object in question was the mausoleum of the late and, I suspect, unlamented Georgi Dimitrov, who had been, as I mentioned earlier, the first Minister President of the Bulgarian Communist state.

Early in his career, Dimitrov, a Socialist member of the Bulgarian Parliament, campaigned against his country's involvement in the First World War and was promptly imprisoned for sedition. In 1919, he moved to Moscow where he became a member of the Executive Committee of

Comintern. After he returned to Bulgaria, he risked further imprisonment by leading an unsuccessful Communist uprising. He moved to Berlin in 1929 and became head of the Central European section of Comintern. After the Reichstag burned down, Dimitrov was one of several prominent Communist leaders arrested and charged with starting the fire. At his trial, he defended himself so ably that his prosecutor, Hermann Goering was made to appear ridiculous and Dimitrov was acquitted. Marinus van der Lubbe, one of his co-defendants did not fare so well. He was found guilty and executed for the crime.

Dimitrov held the post of Minister President until he died on 2 July 1949 whilst visiting Stalin in Moscow amid rumours that he had been poisoned on the orders of the Soviet leader. After his death, his body was embalmed and displayed in this featureless and undistinguished building that now stood before us until 1990, a year after the collapse of Communism in Bulgaria, when the corpse was removed and finally interred in the Central Cemetery in Sofia. In 1949, it took the Bulgarians six days to erect this monstrosity which was based roughly on Lenin's tomb in Moscow. As soon as the dead leader had been successfully preserved and installed, a tailor was charged with making a new suit at regular intervals with which to dress the body – one source said every week but even Lenin didn't get this treatment. Even so, it was a criminal waste of money.

Under Communism, Bulgaria was nothing but a third-rate banana republic, whose people were poor and half starved having been robbed blind by a self-serving Marxist-Leninist dictatorship. If he were lucky, the average Bulgarian would probably have to work for half a year before he could amass enough capital to buy one of those cheap and shapeless suits they sold off the peg in TsUM. Yet those in power decreed that a tailor should be employed to make several new suits a year with which to dress a corpse and at a cost that far exceeded what most of the population could comfortably afford.

I have always had trouble understanding communism and everything about it. I have never understood those who support it, those who manage to live under it or those who wish to inflict it on the rest of the world for what they claim to be altruistic motives. Many people in the world have had the misfortune to be born communists, one or two others like Lenin or Trotsky managed to delude themselves that they had achieved communism but by far the majority of these poor unfortunates have had communism thrust upon them, more often than not at the point of a gun.

Any form of dissent is ruthlessly stifled at the bidding of a few self-elevated despots who have allowed absolute power to corrupt them absolutely. A system of Government, which accepts repeated human rights violation as a trivial consequence of its right to govern should always be treated with apprehension. But, if the communists treated their people badly, look what they did to their leaders, people they were supposed to look up to and revere.

When President Kennedy was assassinated in 1963, he was given a state funeral and buried with full military honours in Arlington Cemetery. When Sir Winston Churchill died in 1965, he, too, was given a state funeral and was buried with great solemnity in Bladon within sight of his ancestral home of Blenheim. So, how was it that when Lenin, Stalin, Mao, Ho Chi Minh, Dimitrov and all the other venerable comrades expired, someone promptly flipped them over on to their faces, shoved a nozzle up their backsides, pumped them full of formaldehyde and deposited them unceremoniously into a glass case so that the rest of the world could come and gawp at them?

Next day, after a leisurely lunch, we boarded the coach and set off along route E80 across the Plain of Thrace towards our next destination, Plovdiv. We were crossing a highly fertile area but, apart from the occasional crop of sunflowers, all I could see was a sea of yellow rape seed plants. For the past twenty years, I had noticed more and more fields in Southern England being devoted to growing rape seed plants. The weekly train journey from Waterloo to Portsmouth had become increasingly animated by the gradual appearance of acres and acres of bright luminous yellow. In mainland Europe, too, there was no escaping its inexorable advance and now here it was on the Plain of Thrace and probably everywhere else I was likely to go as well.

As far as I know, the only products yielded by this plant are vegetable oil for lubricants, food for livestock and fertiliser. But, bearing in mind how much of England and mainland Europe had been devoted to growing these ubiquitous, cruciferous plants, I began to wonder whether this was another one of those Euro-scams we keep hearing about. For example, what happens when we have lubricated every cog in every wheel in every machine in every corner of Europe, when every beast has been fed and every field fertilised? Easy! They stockpile everything in huge warehouses so that we have a mountain of livestock feed, a gigantic pile of fertiliser that could have been the end product of every biped and quadruped that ever lived and an oceanic lake of vegetable oil in which the Titanic could have been submerged three times over, which, if nothing else would have kept it entirely free of rust. Then it starts to get clever.

Just supposing the EU in its infinite wisdom had decreed that, because there was a surplus of rapeseed products, those who were producing it should be instructed to let their fields lie fallow for a period of time. Of course, the farmers concerned would have to be compensated so that we would have the absurd situation where they were being paid for not growing rapeseed. Given our capitalist society, it would not take long before the growth potential of this state of affairs was noticed. With their subsidies for not growing rapeseed, Farmers could buy up more land and not grow rapeseed on that too, thereby increasing the size of their subsidy. I have no doubt that this would appeal to the French who have never shied from any opportunity to line their pockets at the expense of their neighbours. Can you imagine it, every square foot, square yard and square mile of rural France given over to not growing rapeseed? The French farmers would be in heaven, sitting around in bars all day getting drunk on Pernod and telling everyone how badly they were doing while they became richer and richer on the proceeds of European burocracy. As I looked out of the window at the passing scenery, I realised that the Bulgarians had a surprise coming. Their country would finally join the EU in 2007 and for all its faults it had to be an improvement on Communism.

As we continued our journey, Svetlana was giving us a running commentary on the intercom. After a while, she put her notes down and asked whether there were any questions so people started asking "How have things changed and What's it like to live here?" All in all, they weren't a bad crowd and they had a damned sight more energy than I had. Since we'd been in Sofia, they'd spent every night in the Rodina night club, got to bed between three and four in the morning and still made it in good time for breakfast. Svetlana's answers to the various questions she was asked painted a depressing picture very similar to those I'd witnessed in Poland, Hungary and Romania. Since the collapse of communism, things had not improved. She spoke of an upsurge in street offences, petty and violent theft and the growth of organised crime. The democratically elected government didn't seem to have much of a handle on things and even if they lasted to the next election, they were likely to be ousted by a coalition consisting of former communists, non-ethnic Bulgarians and "others," though she did not specify who these were.

Another thing I've noticed in former communist states is how the ex-communist politicians are gradually re-habilitating themselves by divesting their former personae and proving that what they couldn't retain by force, they were more than capable of regaining by guile. Throughout most of the 1990's, Bulgaria was to continue the political instability, labour disputes and strikes, which had prevented the economy from thriving, as it should have. The former Communists had re-named themselves the Bulgarian Socialist Party and had remained a dominant force, thereby ensuring there was little material progress with reforms. Although a measure of political stability had been achieved by 1997 and, after the election of former King Simeon II as Prime Minister in 2001, efforts were made to press ahead with the essential economic restructuring needed for EU membership, Bulgaria still found itself excluded from the list of countries set to join in 2004. This was not wholly unexpected as the level of corruption, a weak judiciary, discrimination against the Roma minority and grave doubts about the safety of the Kozloduy nuclear power plant had all conspired to convince Brussels that Bulgaria was nowhere near ready for EU membership.

Most of the cars we passed on the road were either beaten up old Lada's, big tinny Moskva's or rusty little Yugo's and Skoda's, complete with loud rasping engines and blue carcinogenic clouds pouring out of their exhausts. So, when Swetlana told us that car theft was particularly prevalent in Bulgaria, I could understand this since the act of stealing one of these malfunctioning monstrosities was probably the most cost effective way of acquiring one. What I couldn't understand was why someone would lay out vast quantities of their hard earned cash to buy one in the first place. Maybe it was an insurance scam.

Another thing Svetlana warned us against was hiring a car. Hire cars were no worse than any other cars on the road but they were just as vulnerable to theft, and, if an unsuspecting tourist were unfortunate enough to hire a car, which was subsequently stolen, then he would be held responsible and would be expected to compensate the hire company for the entire cost of the vehicle. The possibility of recovering a stolen vehicle was remote since car theft was run by organised crime, which meant that any stolen car could be re-sprayed, restored and sold on very quickly while the Police were paid to look the other way.

THROUGH PLOVDIV AND RILA TO SANDANSKI

Situated on the Maritsa River with a population of 360,000 , Plovdiv, known as Philippopolis in earlier times, is the second largest and second most important city in Bulgaria but, if there is a more beautiful one in the whole of this country, I never saw it. We stayed at the Trimontsium Hotel, a huge, soulless edifice that looked like it had been transplanted from the set of a Bela Lugosi movie to the bare expanse of Tsentralen square. That evening, we dined in its restaurant, a vast atmospheric chamber decorated in Hollywood gothic with heavy crimson curtains, brass lamps and dark stained wood. As my fellow tourists filed downstairs to the nightclub, I found my way to a candle lit bar. There were few people here. Two bored-looking hookers sat together at a table, looked me up and down and decided I did not look sufficiently prosperous to hustle and went on with their conversation. I ordered a brandy and struck up a conversation with the barman who said his name was Dmitri. It transpired that the candlelight was not a deliberate attempt to produce a sophisticated and romantic atmosphere. The electric wiring had malfunctioned and could not be fixed because the electrician had gone to visit his mother in Sofia and wouldn't be back for another two days. I finished my brandy and went back to my room hoping that the immersion heater in the bathroom didn't expire before I'd had a shower next morning.

The next day was another one of intensive sightseeing as Svetlana took us around the cobbled streets of old Plovdiv and showed us a myriad collection of historic buildings, which included mosques, churches and what she referred to as the typical Plovdivian, revival-style houses, which spread expansively, storey by storey, as they grew higher, and produced a dramatic overhang, which made for some interesting street photographs. Finally, she took us to the Antique Theatre, the remains of a Roman Amphitheatre built into the side of a hill and provided a spectacular view of

Street Scene, Old Plovdiv.

the city. Plays were staged here throughout the summer although we had arrived too early in the season to see one. The stage had been restored but while I was wondering about on it trying to take pictures, I noticed that the fabric of the building contained more ready mix concrete than Roman pillars.

There was much excitement at breakfast the following morning. Bob, a retired teacher in his seventies, was given a hero's welcome when he appeared looking tired. At the nightclub the previous evening, he had pulled one of the two hookers I'd seen in the bar and this was the first time he'd

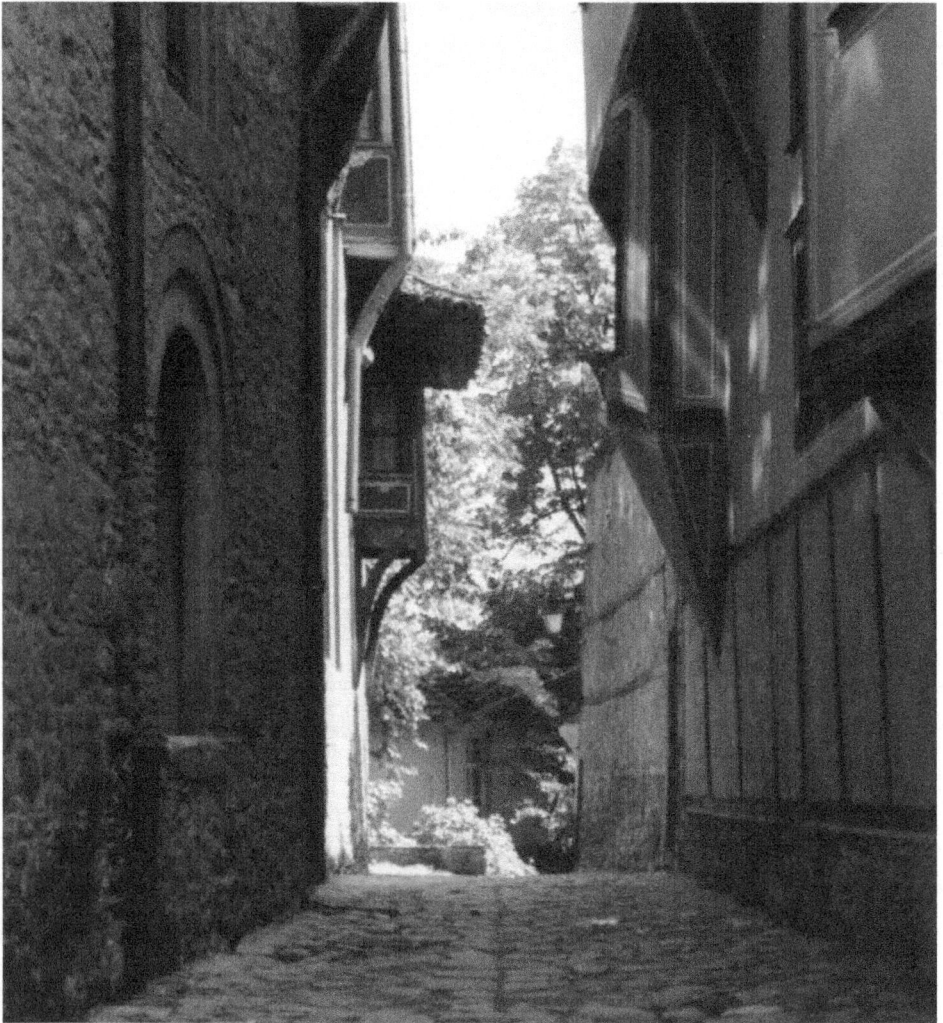

Narrow street in old Plovdiv.

been seen since. He looked as though he'd had his money's worth and I was willing to bet that it had been a long time since he'd sported a grin that wide at breakfast time. We boarded our coach after breakfast for the day-long journey to Sandanski. We would be stopping at Borovets and the Rila Monastery on the way and were expected to reach Sandanski in the early evening.

We appeared to be backtracking towards Sofia when, after about an hour, we turned south and the road started to take the inevitable upward gradient that would take us into the Rila mountains towards Borovets. For another forty minutes or so we continued our winding way onwards and upwards until we entered Borovets, formerly a small mountain village, which had now been developed as a ski resort for package tourists. There was no snow this time of year and there were no people either. The whole place was not just dead, it was downright eerie, like one of those places in a vampire movie that you are told by a half-crazed old fossil not to visit after dark. I was with a coach load of those already and right now they wanted a cup of coffee and a halfway decent toilet.

The coach stopped outside a large tourist hotel and we filed expect-antly through the open doors into a wide, wood-panelled reception and restaurant area. That, too, was deserted and Svetlana went to find some staff. This took her five minutes and when she came back, she explained we were early and they weren't expecting us for another hour. While everybody either queued to use the toilets or waited for coffee, snacks or both, I had a quick walk around and took a few photographs. The scenery was truly breathtaking. I found out later that I was looking at the slopes of Mount Musala, which was covered in pine trees and still capped with snow. However, I realised that if I stayed out here, I was likely to miss out on coffee and it might be some time before I had the opportunity to get any more.

Back on the coach, we headed north through Samokov where we began a circuitous route that eventually brought us to the town of Rila and onwards towards the Rila monastery. Actually, we had almost gone round in a wide circle since there was no accessible route that went directly through the mountains. We stopped at an open-air restaurant on the road to the monastery and they served us lunch in a clearing overlooking the fast-flowing Rilska River. I drank a bottle of ice-cold beer with my lunch and would have been happy with another one, too but unfortunately they had run out and we were a good fifty miles from the nearest supermarket.

Decorative arches at the Rila Monastery.

The Rila Monastery was one of the reasons I had come on this trip. I was disappointed that we could only stay for a couple of hours so I was determined to make the most of them. The original monastery was founded in the ninth century by John of Rila. It was looted and plundered in the eighteenth century and then the whole structure burned to the ground in 1833. The present monastery had been restored in stages, the east wing restoration having been finally completed in 1961. The centre-piece of the complex is a magnificent orthodox church with a series of arches and numerous cupolas. The red and white striped arches had an Islamic appearance and there were richly coloured frescoes on the ceilings beneath the porch. When I went inside, I was struck by the splendour of the iconostasis, which was almost ninety feet wide and lavishly decorated with gold leaf and small intricate carvings. I was not allowed to photograph this, at least, not at first, but two five dollar bills pressed surreptitiously into the palms of the door attendants soon changed all that. Maybe I should have tried that at the Alexander Nevski Church – I will if I ever go back.

We finally arrived in Sandanski at five oclock and checked into the four star Sandanski Hydro. This was not only the best hotel in town, I

Rila Monastery Front Elevation.

suspect that it was the only one in town as I never saw another all the time I was there. People visit Sandanski for the various health treatments to be taken at the Hydro and I cannot envisage any other reason for being there. According to Svetlana, the town was supposed to produce cigarettes and hot house vegetables but I never found out where. There is, of course, the black, stone Spartacus monument just off the highway but it is rather disappointing and doesn't look a bit like Kirk Douglas. As for the town, it is an eclectic collection of modern buildings, which look as if they were

Balcony overlooking church at Rila Monastery.

thrown up over night to house a crowd of people who turned up unexpectedly and then, having nowhere else to go, decided to stay.

The entire restaurant area had been taken over by a television crew who were making a programme about the Hydro so we were taken to a disused cafeteria at the rear of the building where tables and chairs had been rapidly installed for our benefit. It was makeshift and uncomfortable but it could have been worse. The food was a good deal better than our surroundings and while we felt a little short changed because we'd had to eat in little more than an outhouse after paying a premium rate for our tour, a few more beers caused us to mellow. We moved out to one of the hotel's bars and sat around a couple of tables. While we were there, I noticed a couple of attractive young women who were gesticulating in my direction from the other side of the bar. They appeared to be offering me oral sex at a price. If this was so, then it was an unfortunate state of affairs since, by then, I had consumed so much beer, they would have been hard pressed to find anything tangible with which to work.

At eleven o'clock, the bar closed and, having settled up our various bills, we went into the nightclub, a large dimly lit auditorium with concentric circles of fixed tables and chairs surrounding three sides of a dance floor and a stage behind the fourth. Ours was the only group there and it was at least another hour before anything happened but copious amounts of drinks were being served and nobody was particularly impatient. Then, an announcement was made in Bulgarian followed by another in English that was so heavily accented, it was totally incomprehensible, rather like the ones they make on Earls Court Station when a train is coming in so nobody can understand a word.

A number of musicians took their places on the stage and started to play what I assumed to be Bulgarian pop music. After a few bars, a troupe of skinny chorus girls appeared from either side of the stage and started to gyrate to the music in a manner reminiscent of Pans People in the seventies. Svetlana leaned over and told me that the girls were Russian. That seemed to ring a bell and I remembered a television programme I'd seen about a school of performing arts in Moscow. It showed how each pupil had gone through a gruelling selection process to gain admittance and how hard they had to work in order to achieve the required level of excellence. It was explained in the film that the girls would obtain employment outside of Russia but I never thought for a moment that for all their talent and hard work, they would end up in a place like this. Although more people had come in, the nightclub was still less than half full and could never have made enough to pay the wage bill, even if, as I suspected, wages were rock bottom.

After the band had left the stage, there followed half an hour of disco music when everybody got to their feet and gyrated about on the dance floor. Our group were very much to the fore, leaping around like people half their age and nobody was allowed to remain seated – including me. I don't know what they were taking but whatever it was, I was certainly in need of some long before the end.

Outer wall of the Rohzen Monsatery.

The club closed at four and after we had paid our bills, a long and argumentative process caused by the waiters having added things we'd never ordered and Svetlana threatening to report them to the manager if they didn't remove the fraudulent items, we finally called it a night. I was absolutely shattered and very drunk. There was no way I was going to be able to get up before noon tomorrow. When I told Svetlana, she was very disappointed and intimated that I would regret it. Apparently we were going to the Rozhen Monastery and if I'd liked the Rila Monastery, then I was going to love this one. I felt like I was about to pass out so in the end, we agreed that she would knock on my door in the morning to make sure I got up. I wished I'd never agreed to that.

The next morning was every bit as bad as I had feared. How I got out of bed and managed to shave and shower without injuring myself will remain a mystery. Breakfast was a non-event for me but the oldies were all up and about and tucking in as though they'd never been near a nightclub the night before. What was it with them? Didn't they get hangovers like normal people? I managed to drink half a cup of coffee but I felt sick. I felt half dead. I felt like I never wanted to see a bottle of beer again. Worst of all, I felt like I wanted to sign the pledge but I couldn't because my hand wouldn't stop shaking.

The Rohzen Monsatery.

I slept for most of the journey to Melnik and was told afterwards that I missed some beautiful scenery but I didn't care. I'd missed the Second World War, the Festival of Britain and the Coronation, too, but it wasn't going to change the way I felt, which was a pity. Melnik was a vision, an absolute warren of cobbled alleyways and courtyards. There were Tavernas, antique houses overhanging narrow, shaded streets and flowers everywhere. If only I'd been straight enough to appreciate it. In the last century, Melnik had been a thriving town but it became a casualty of the 1913 Balkan war, when it was razed to the ground. What remains has been beautifully restored but the population has dwindled to just over 500 people who earn their living either by making wine or from tourism. Normally I would have liked to have stayed and spent some time in one of the tavernas but the previous night's revelry had left me a shambling wreck and I felt I should move on.

Svetlana had much the same idea. She wanted us to press on to the Rozhen Monastery but, as I started off back to the relative comfort of the coach, she called out to me and pointed in the other direction. There was a path over the ridge and she wanted us to follow her. I could barely stand and she wanted us to walk to the monastery, all six and a half bloody kilometres of it. I knew I should have stayed in bed but it was too late for that now. At first, I just concentrated on putting one foot in front of the other while trying hard not to succumb to the overwhelming feeling of nausea, which kept threatening to engulf me.

It was a warm day and the air smelled clean and fresh. I wished I did. After about the three-kilometre mark, we stopped for a brief rest and I started to look around me. I was almost glad I came. There were sandstone rocks worn by erosion into grotesque and unworldly shapes, while a range of sandstone mountains in the distance gave the whole scene a surreal appearance. The slopes were all green and covered with a kaleidoscopic display of wild spring flowers. As we continued our walk, I noticed that my head was no longer aching and normality was beginning to return as I started to feel the first stages of hunger pangs. The Rozhen Monastery was smaller than that of Rila. It was also much plainer and its woodwork less ornate. It looked rustic – austere even, but it definitely had character.

The monastery had been founded in the twelfth century and had survived being burned and looted many times. I had a field day with the camera, especially in the Church of the Birth of the Holy Virgin but, I was just getting acclimatised, when we were told we had to go. I was about to complain that we'd only just arrived but when I looked at my watch to confirm this, I found that we had been there an hour already and we still had to walk another six and a half kilometres back. Exploring the monastery had totally distracted me from my delicate condition – so much so that I didn't have a delicate condition any more and I actually enjoyed the invigorating walk back.

We had lunch back at the hotel after which Svetlana gave us the afternoon to ourselves to explore Sandanski. After about seven and a half minutes, I had seen as much of Sandanski as I could take and I went back to the Hydro, booked myself a sauna and spent the rest of the afternoon on one of the plastic sun loungers scattered around the swimming pool. On the whole, the afternoon was a lethargic, non-event, which carried on into the evening. I found the golden oldies in the lounge getting a few drinks in before they went on to the nightclub. I stayed with them for a little while and drank cola but I couldn't stay long. This proved to be a wise move since I needed to make up for the previous night's activities, I was to have little sleep the following night in Burgas and the golden oldies were to encounter more shenanigans with the waiters in the nightclub.

Next morning when I came down to breakfast our table was full of the story. Svetlana had decided to have an early night so there was no-one to look after our merry band of revellers as they set out for their nocturnal entertainment. When the nightclub closed down at four o'clock, the waiters brought a grossly inflated bill and, when it became clear that they were not going to listen to reason, everyone got up and walked out, believing they could sort things out with reception in the morning. Having reached the lifts and thinking they were safe, they suddenly found themselves being ambushed by another group of waiters who manhandled them, physically barred their way and would not let them go until the bill had been settled. As I understood it, the bill for their drinks should have come to about £60 altogether, which sounded fair to me but the waiters decided to ask for the equivalent of £2000, which was more than the entire group could muster between them and was clearly quite outrageous. In the end, one of the women managed to sneak away, alert reception and get Svetlana out of bed. Even when she got there, she had difficulty in persuading these extortionists to see sense. They finally climbed down when she threatened to fetch the Police but it was a very unsavoury episode and clearly upset those members of our tour group who were involved and cast a shadow over the whole of the next day.

We travelled back to Sofia by way of the Rila Mountains but the usual buzz of background chatter that had been a familiar characteristic of our earlier expeditions was missing. Even when we boarded the plane from Sofia to Burgas there was no change in the mood of despondency. I suspected that they were beginning to feel that what had happened to them the previous night was by no means an isolated incident and they had to face the possibility of another week of it in Cess Pit on Sea. I did not envy them.

BURGAS, BED AND BACK TO BRITAIN

We arrived back at the hotel Balgaria at about six thirty and were told that dinner would be at seven thirty sharp. I was going to give it a miss anyway and after I'd had a quick shower and shave, I went off in search of Rosa. She wasn't in the bar when I looked, and, after checking out the ground floor reception area, I returned upstairs to find her talking to the cloak-room attendant. She hadn't forgotten that I'd promised to buy her dinner and she led me to a lift, which took us to the top floor restaurant. The only point in favour of this concrete tower block should have been the view from this restaurant but the people who designed the building managed to screw that up as well.

It wasn't their fault that Burgas was such a dump that it wasn't worth looking at, even from a great height, but it would have been nice to have had the option without having to crane my neck to the point of self stran-gulation. It was possible to see out of the windows quite easily if you stood up, but only those who were descended from giraffes could manage it while they were sitting down. I had a pleasant evening in spite of that. After dinner, Rosa was going to take me on a tour of Burgas but I pre-tended that I had to get something from my room on the way down. She followed me in and stayed for the rest of the night. On this occasion, I did not have a headache.

Because I had to leave at six-thirty, and I was the only one who was not going on to sample the rather dubious delights of Sunny Beach, the hotel prepared me a cold breakfast. At ten o'clock when they telephoned me to explain this, Rosa became agitated. But if she had been frightened when the telephone rang, she became frantic when they knocked on the door with the tray at eleven. She jumped out of bed and locked herself in the bathroom until the waiter had gone and I finally managed to convince her that it was safe for her to come out. I put the tray on a coffee table and gently led her back to bed.

She was trembling but she wouldn't tell me what it was that had frightened her. She insisted that it wasn't the Police. I couldn't figure it out at all. At first, I suspected that she might have been a hooker after all but in the morning no money changed hands, nor did she ask me for any. All she asked me for was my address and she gave me hers, too and promised that she'd write. We shared what was on the breakfast tray including a large vacuum flask of hot water and some sachets of Nescafe. Unfortunately there was only one cup so we had to take turns. It was a pity she didn't take sugar but I was hoping I'd get another cup on the plane. I left Rosa in the shower and I locked the door behind me still wondering what had reduced her to a state of abject terror. It was another year before I found out.

HUNGARY 1992

(A SLIGHT DIGRESSION)

GREAT UNCLE BULGARIA

(A SUPER SIZE PEARDROP)

Touring Bulgaria with a horde of senior citizens brought to mind an experience I'd had a year earlier. I was not on a tour myself but my peace and tranquillity were shattered when a fifty two-seater coach arrived at the hotel in which I was staying and disgorged a whole host of wrinklies while I was out for a walk. It was a blustery April afternoon in Heviz, a small spa about five miles or so from the shores of Lake Balaton, South West Hungary. I'd arrived the previous afternoon and already decided I'd made a poor choice. The town itself was picturesque with small period cottages, narrow streets and a few good taverns but it had more than its fair share of rest and retirement homes, which rather limited any social activities and ruled out completely any sort of nightlife.

The main attraction in Heviz was a spa built around the largest thermal lake in Europe, in which people immersed themselves, presumably in the hope that if their various ailments could not be cured, at least their discomfort might be eased. As I walked past, I craned my neck to look over the perimeter fence and saw upwards of a dozen sets of heads and shoulders kept buoyant by pneumatic rings above the undulating surface of the murky lagoon. Outside the main building there was a notice in several languages, one of which was English, informing would-be users of the healing qualities of the lake and warning them that the water, whilst beneficial was mildly radioactive so that prolonged immersion was not recommended. The gases in the water caused bubbles to burst on the surface at irregular intervals and, as I peered over the fence the people bobbing about down there looked like irregularly shaped dumplings in a giant cauldron of boiling oil.

While Heviz had been a disappointment, my original idea had been sound. For the last few years, I'd been spending three or four weeks at a time in Turkey, an exciting country with a history and culture I found irresistible but I felt that I needed a change so I closed my eyes and stuck a pin in a map of Europe, resolving to go wherever it struck home. I took a cheap flight to Vienna, a train and then a bus and, having finally arrived here, I installed myself in a large, not quite comfortable hotel on the edge of town, which I will call the Magyar. The hotel looked like a small mansion with wings at each end giving it an "H" configuration, a driveway and an outdoor swimming pool, which somehow managed to cheapen the appearance of the whole frontage.

Maybe it was some sort of premonition, but I had a strange experience while I was walking through one of the narrow lanes away from the lake. From an upper window of one of the houses came a haunting yet familiar melody sung in English by a man with an Irish accent. I stopped and continued to listen until I recognised it. When I was very young, my mother, a fervent Irish nationalist, used to purchase old 78 RPM gramophone records of rebel songs from Walton's, a mail order company in Dublin. One of her particular favourites was "She is far from the land," a lament for the Irish patriot Robert Emmett written by Thomas Moore and it was this I could hear now. It was the same recording that my mother used to own although I cannot remember the name of the artist who recorded it. I was thunderstruck by my discovery and my first reaction was to locate the source of the music and introduce myself to the person who was playing it but in the end, I decided against this course of action and made my way back through the paths and hedgerows to the hotel.

On arrival, I was disappointed to find a large white and red touring coach in the driveway, bearing the logo of a British-based travel group and surrounded by a crowd of ageing holiday makers waiting for their luggage to be unloaded. However, events were to turn out better than I'd envisaged and by the time we had all left here, one of these senior citizens was to throw some light on a question that had been puzzling me for decades concerning the unacceptably high level of strikes and stoppages that had occurred in the UK during the 60's and 70's and how many of them, if any, could be attributed to subversion and infiltration by agitators working on behalf of the Soviet Union.

To the best of my knowledge, the "Commies in the workplace" accusation had first been made in a House of Commons speech by former Labour Prime Minister Harold Wilson in 1966 during a strike by the National Union of Seamen but he had declined to repeat his allegation outside the House, in which he was protected by Parliamentary Privilege and shielded from any legal action that might have been taken against him by those he had accused. For this reason, his allegation was discredited by trade unionists, left wing MP's and other politicians and was never seriously addressed again until Margaret Thatcher made her "enemy within" statement during the 1984 miners strike. Harold Wilson's information had been provided by the security services who had been heavily criticised at the time by these same trade unionists, left wing MP's and other politicians for taking too close an interest in the activities of trade unions, their members, radical organisations and single-issue pressure groups like the Campaign for Nuclear Disarmament. As far as I can tell, the security services were only doing what they were paid to do and their vexatious critics would have been the first to complain if they had woken up one morning to find Soviet tanks in their city centres. On the other hand, maybe they wouldn't.

I dined in a small restaurant in the village that evening and returned to the hotel bar at about eight thirty to find it occupied by about half of today's new arrivals. I bought myself a beer and retired to the safety of a table in the farthest neutral corner to observe the newcomers from a discrete distance. There was one man – all the women had apparently retired early – who stood out from the crowd, not only because of his striking appearance but because he sounded as though he was an experienced public speaker, his booming voice being several decibels louder than anyone else's in the room. He gave the impression that he had an opinion on every conceivable subject, one that was passionately at variance with those held by virtually everyone else he had been talking to so that, by the time he came to where I was sitting, he had managed to upset every other person present, including the Hungarian bar staff who had refused to serve him.

He was a big man, not tall but well built, narrow at the shoulders, broad at the hips with the sort of belly that only comes after years of overindulgence and physical inactivity. His head was much the same shape as his torso, broad and flabby around the jowls tapering upwards to a narrowing, shiny pate. He resembled a giant pear drop and I found out later that on the outward journey, other members of the tour group, especially those who had already taken a dislike to him, had noticed the similarity, too, and had taken to calling him the pear drop man or LPD – large pear drop. He introduced himself as Eric and said he lived in Romford. I noticed his empty glass and went up to the bar to get us both another beer. He regretted that he could not return the compliment but he told me without a shred of embarrassment that he had managed to upset the bar staff by making adverse comments about the present Hungarian Government. Eric was a retired trade union official who had come here on holiday with his wife, Shirley. He told me that he had travelled extensively in Eastern Europe for many years but not so much recently. He said that he preferred things as they had been, back in the "old days." I noticed he did not say "good old days."

He told me he had spent many of his summer holidays in Bulgaria's Black Sea Coastal resorts and he clearly had much affection for them. In days to come, he would waylay anyone who was still talking to him and, because he had managed to alienate most of his fellow tourists with his other topics of conversation, he would lavishly eulogize over the virtues of Bulgaria as a holiday destination. Indeed, so extravagant was his praise for this country that he soon earned another nickname, one by which he became known to everyone with whom he came into contact, Great Uncle Bulgaria.

By the time I came down for breakfast next morning, the tour group had gone off on an excursion. I asked the reception staff to arrange for a taxi to take me the five miles or so to the town of Keszthely on the shores of Lake Balaton. I'd intended to go boating on the lake but the blustery weather had not improved and when it started to rain, I decided to cut my losses and asked the driver to take me back to Heviz. In the bar that evening Eric's wife, Shirley, a slight, grey, retiring lady told me that they had been to Tihaney, a picturesque, rocky peninsula further down the shoreline but their trip had also been marred by rain.

As part of their tour, the travel company provided excursions for the visitors every day to various locations and when Shirley told me that the vehicle had not been full on the journey over here, I excused myself for a few minutes and sought out the courier to see if I could join the following day's jaunt. The courier was a bubbly lady in her forties called Gill and, for a sum in Hungarian Florints equivalent to £20, she gave me a receipt, which, she said, would guarantee me a seat on tomorrow's trip to Pecs. Having completed that transaction, I returned to the bar to find Eric sitting alone at the table. He told me that Shirley had gone back to their room to watch satellite television. However, before she left, she'd thoughtfully gone up to the bar to purchase a glass of beer each for Eric and I.

"The buggers still aren't serving me." he said gloomily. When I asked him what he had said to cause the bar staff to behave in this manner, he sighed.

"I told 'em that the collapse of communism was the worst thing that ever happened to this country and they were all being exploited by the capitalist system. I told them I didn't think much of the present government, either – bunch of Americanised yes-men." He exclaimed.

"That would probably explain it," I replied, trying not to show any reaction at all. Eric went on to explain, as if he felt it was necessary to do so, that he had been a member of the Communist Party of Great Britain until it lapsed, apart from a brief period in the late 60's and early 70's when he "joined something else."

He seemed very intense and partially to distract him, I asked what other countries he had visited in Eastern Europe only to find that he had been to virtually all of them. Bearing in mind his apparent state of obesity, he surprised me by claiming to have skii'd on the slopes of Zakopane, Southern Poland as well as on those of Sarajevo, Mount Vitosha and Borovets. He also claimed to have trekked the Transylvanian Mountains and sunbathed on dark sandy beaches from Bulgaria's Varna and Sunny Beach, all along the Black Sea coast to Yalta. I believed the part about sunbathing although the sight of Eric doing so can hardly have been aesthetically pleasing and I immediately put the thought of it out of my mind. He hinted that many of his jaunts had either been subsidised or completely free of charge although he did not say who had picked up the bill. However, his Eastern European visits were not all in pursuit of pleasure and Shirley did not always go with him. He added that he'd also been to Moscow, Prague and East Berlin for conferences and what he called "briefings" though he never explained what these entailed.

He went on to tell me how, as a member of one of Britain's largest trade unions, he worked as a full-time organiser at some of the UK's largest manufacturing plants. This was not quite the whole truth but he would tell me that later. When I told him I was currently a UNISON steward back in London, a position I'd filled by default as nobody else wanted to do it, he assumed he'd met a kindred spirit and started talking about union politics and a lot of other things I knew very little about.

Eric was very knowledgeable about industry, politics and economics in the UK especially during the 1960's through to the end of the 1970's when he'd apparently retired. He had an encyclopaedic knowledge of Government ministers of both parties, Trade Union officials and most football teams as well. He surprised me by naming many of the existing members of the Unison National Executive Committee, which was a lot more than I could have done and I'd not only voted for some of them, I'd made a particular point of not voting for many of the others. He even gave me chapter and verse on the NALGO 1974 London Weighting Strike in which I had been involved, revealing that he knew much more about what had been going on at the time than I did. At 10 P.M., Eric decided to call it a night as we had an early start in the morning. I treated myself to one more beer before booking an early morning call at reception.

It was 6.30 when I came down to breakfast but I was still the last to arrive. The restaurant was crowded but I did not worry. I knew there would be one table where I would be guaranteed a seat. Breakfast consisted of a cold buffet of salami, sausage and a selection of other cooked meats that might easily be found in a Golders Green delicatessen. I made myself a sandwich from a crusty roll and three slices of salami, poured out a cup of thick black coffee and made my way to where Eric and Shirley were sitting. I am not at my best at that time of the morning and I was relieved to find that they were not very talkative either so that hardly a word passed between us as we finished our meal and shuffled outside to where the coach was parked.

Gill, the tour representative remembered me from the previous night as she checked everybody onto the coach and I managed to get a row of seats all to myself at the back, where I spent the journey to Pecs staring out of the window at the surrounding countryside while the remaining passengers dozed off to sleep. Pecs proved to be an architectural gem with Christian, and Ottoman buildings as well as a 19th Century Synagogue. The Jewish population of Pecs once numbered over 4000 but this had been decimated by the holocaust. The Ottomans had indulged in mass murder here, too, as they slaughtered many of the resident Christian population and pulled down their churches though some still remain. I also found the imposing Romanesque cathedral, a largely 19th Century structure that incorporated chapels and crypts from much earlier times.

ERIC THE STRIKE MONGER: THE STORY

I didn't see much of Eric and Shirley during the day as they went off on a guided tour and probably saw much more of the city than I did but later in the afternoon, I found a delightful little 18th Century tavern halfway down a narrow alleyway and, with the landlord's ginger cat curled up in my lap, I enjoyed several glasses of sparkling Hungarian ale before making my way back to the coach. I decided to have dinner in the village again that evening and when I returned to the hotel, the bar was fairly crowded but I still found Eric sitting alone nursing a glass that had clearly contained nothing but dregs for some considerable time. I went straight to the bar, bought two beers, brought them back and handed one to Eric.

"The bar staff still annoyed with you?" I asked him. He nodded. "You could always say you are sorry." I said.

"They wouldn't believe me," he replied "Besides, it wouldn't be true. They've got a bloody fascist pro-American Government," he growled.

"So have we," I told him "What does that prove?" he did not reply. Instead, he asked me whether I had ever been involved in politics. I told him I was a lapsed member of the Labour Party and that the job I had was politically restricted so I couldn't rejoin even if I had been minded to. He did not think such things were fair but it didn't bother me too much. Aside from all the politically correct claptrap about women's rights, racial equality and equal opportunities, all of which seeming to justify discrimination against white Anglo-Saxon Christian males, fairness was a concept that was totally alien to the Local Authority that employed me.

"I never had any political restrictions on what I did," he told me "It wouldn't have mattered anyway. I wouldn't have taken any notice." When I asked him what exactly he did, he said he'd generally worked as a full-time shop steward in the car industry, although he had also spent a little time as a TGWU convenor in the docks.

"What were you doing there?" I asked casually.

"Looking at disputes, solving the easy ones and seeing which of the others we could escalate into a strike." He must have noticed my raised eyebrow. "You didn't think they started all by themselves did you?"

"No," I responded recalling only too vividly the rampant strike-mongering antics of the Revolutionary Communist Party and the Socialist Workers Party at my own place of work. When I mentioned this, Eric scoffed contemptuously.

"Those people aren't interested in the working classes. They're just loud-mouthed, over-privileged college kids, who want to make a fuss and cause trouble. They haven't got a cause, not a genuine cause like we had."

"By we, I take it you mean the Communist Party." I enquired.

"Originally, yes," he confirmed, "It was them who sent me to the Ford works at Halewood. I'd been at Cowley before that and the Rootes factory in Coventry, too" He started to laugh. "Bloody Halewood, that was a laugh." He guffawed. The McMillan government persuaded Ford to open a plant there because it was a depressed area with high unemployment. Typical bloody Tories" he laughed again, "Didn't they know that the Scousers are the most militant bunch of bastards in the British Isles?" He took a gulp of his beer and continued, "We had so many walk-outs it was like doing the Okey – Cokey, in and out all the time only we didn't shake anything about." Looking at him, I could well believe that.

"Why did you do it?" I asked him. It seemed like a fair question but he seemed to have difficulty answering it.

"I thought I was helping the working classes." He replied after a while. "I started an apprenticeship as a toolmaker in 1932 at a small workshop at the back of the Elephant and Castle. It's not there now, though, didn't survive the bombing. There were a couple of chaps there who were party members and I went to a couple of meetings, met a few people and they gave me some pamphlets to read. Then I started to read Marx.."

"What did you make of it?" I asked him, deliberately refraining from mentioning that his writing lacked clarity and that I was able to make little sense of it.

"Difficult," he said to my relief "then I'd had no education so that was only to be expected but there were people in the party who helped me understand. After the war, I was married to Shirley, living just outside Coventry with two little'uns. That's when I got involved with the party again."

"Were you still in the car industry?" I asked

"Yes," he said "After I left Cowley, I was at Standard's then at Rootes. I wanted to work at the Jaguar plant but I couldn't get in. They were a real militant lot there. But the car industry was easy." He took another long pull at his beer and continued "Peter" he said, "If everything was OK in the factories I worked in, we couldn't have stirred up so much trouble but they made it easy for us. For a start, working on a production line is boring and repetitive. People get pissed off with it. They'll jump at anything for a bit of relief. All they needed was an excuse and the management were so bad, I could always find one for them. There were inter-union disputes, demarcation disputes. It could be too cold or too hot on the shop floor for the men to work. Then there were always people in another shop who were earning more than we were for the same work so we'd whack in a claim for parity and walk out until we got it."

"Then I moved to Halewood," he told me "I couldn't believe it. It was unreal. That's when I joined the Socialist Labour League. Have you heard about them?" I nodded and he continued, "Gerry Healey was running the show, a real rabble-rouser. That's when it all got to be serious," he said as he drained his glass. He passed me over some money and asked me to go to the bar to get some more beer. When I came back he told me about a colleague of his, who I will call Ron, and the mayhem he allegedly caused at Luton's Vauxhall plant around 1970.

"Ron was a natural," exclaimed Eric, "He could start a fight in a pub, set two people against each other and quietly walk away while they were beating the shit out of each other, with neither of them knowing why they were doing it. That's the sort of bloke he was, a real shit stirrer." Eric leaned back in his chair, stuck out his bulky abdomen and let forth a long, slow belch, the relief visible on his face as he did so. "Ahhh, I needed that." He sighed and continued his tale. "Vauxhall put out a leaflet to the work force containing good news and bad news. The good news was that they were going to give the workers a pay rise. The bad news was they wanted some concessions in return, you know, changes in working methods, no more restrictive practices and all that stuff. Management probably thought it was reasonable but Ron saw an opportunity and took it with both hands. He called his shop out for a meeting and when he got them there, he proposed an unofficial walkout so they could have a gate meeting, which was carried unanimously. So, off they all trooped, going the long way round so they could go through all the other shops and tell their blokes what they were doing as they went. By the time they got to the main gates, most of the workers in the factory were following them like a flock of sheep, a couple of thousand at least. Ron spoke to the crowd, a couple of other people said a few words in support, then, the next thing they knew, everyone went round to the main offices and charged in shouting anti-American slogans and smashed the place up. It made the six o'clock news that night and the morning papers the next day." He declared proudly.

"What about the Socialist Labour League?" I asked

"They were bloody serious revolutionaries," he said loudly. "They had a lot of people travelling around the country stirring up trouble. They were behind all those disputes they had in the Liverpool docks. They reckoned if they could bring the docks and the car industry to a halt, they were just about there."

"There?" I asked

"They reckoned that would be enough to enable them to take over the country." Eric said without any emotion.

"A Communist revolution on behalf of the Soviet Union?" I asked him.

"Something like that but mainly they were in it for themselves," he said "But don't misunderstand me. The "Sovs" were on the same side. The UK Communist Party was backed by the "Sovs" but Healey's lot were different – Trotskyites. I was at Halewood when the Liverpool docks stuff was going off and according to what some of the SLL people were saying, they wanted to close the docks on Merseyside, then target Ford and Vauxhall up there before hitting their factories down south. After that, they were going for the car works in Oxford and the Midlands, then the public services and the Universities. They were involved in all this student unrest, too. The Socialist Labour League people were convinced that if they could reduce the country to anarchy, they could seize power," he asserted. It wasn't the first time I'd heard something like this. I'd overheard SWP people saying the same sort of thing but it was just loose talk and I paid it no attention. I knew that if push came to shove, they couldn't organise a sexual encounter in a brothel and, while they were adept at hi-jacking protest marches with some of them even managing to wave banners, chant slogans and walk at the same time without causing themselves damage, they couldn't run a bath never mind a country.

"When did you stop?" I asked him.

"About 1975," he replied, "just before things turned really nasty."

"You mean before the winter of discontent?"

"Long before that." Said Eric, "That's what let Thatcher in. I was well out of things by then. Well, the kids were getting older and Shirley wanted a bit more security, so I took a desk job at Transport House and stayed there till I retired. But I'll tell you this," he said earnestly, "if it wasn't for the wife and kids, I'd have stayed with it and given Thatcher a bloody good run for her money!"

ERIC THE STRIKE MONGER: THE FACTS

It was ten o'clock and Eric decided to call it a night. I stayed where I was, sipped my beer and watched him leave. From the back, he looked like Alfred Hitchcock or maybe that celebrated screen villain Sydney Greenstreet. If his account of his earlier life had been true, Eric could possibly have been one of those sinister characters that Greenstreet had often portrayed. With the best will in the world, I couldn't imagine him skiing or even trekking. The thought occurred to me that all the time I had been in Portsmouth in the 60's, eking out a living as a poorly paid Local Government Officer, working Saturdays in a tailors shop to save for a deposit on a house and then scrimping and scraping to pay my mortgage, this man, if he was to be believed, had been a cog in a well-organised machine that was trying to reduce our country to a state of anarchy and me to a condition of bankruptcy and homelessness. By rights, he should have been my enemy but all I could see now as he waddled through the doorway like an oversized jelly was a rather loud, obese, old man with the best part of his life behind him – not to mention an unfeasibly large backside.

What sort of an enemy was that?

After I'd finished my beer, I went to find Gill, the tour guide to see what excursion she was running next day. When she told me they were going to Budapest, I paid her another £20 worth of Hungarian Florints and went back to the bar. I checked out of the Magyar the following morning

Fishermens Bastions, Budapest.

and used the coach trip as a cheap ride to the capital. Once more, I had an entire row of seats to myself and, as the Hungarian countryside rolled past the window, I started to think about what Eric had told me.

I recalled vividly that there had been a plethora of strikes and walk-outs during the 1960's and 70's, especially in the car industry, which had only been curtailed by the mass unemployment generated by Thatcher's government in the early 1980's. There was much anecdotal evidence of the participation of Communists in these disputes but very little proof of the scale of their involvement. I know that in the years immediately after the Second World War, the Communist Party of Great Britain attracted a great deal of sympathy and support arising from our wartime alliance with the Soviet Union. Much of this support came from within the Trade Union movement, where, during the late 1940's, the CPGB had become increasingly involved in strikes, causing much anger and irritation to Clement Attlee's Labour Government. However, in 1955 the Intelligence Services managed to obtain the secret membership records of the CPGB and from then on, the authorities became aware of every single operational party member and their activities were closely monitored.

Armed with information provided from this source, Harold Wilson was able to claim that the 1966 strike by the National Union of Seamen had been engineered by a *"tightly knit group of politically motivated men."* He did not use the word "Communist" nor did he need to. He then went on to name the people concerned and to make specific allegations against each and every one of them. He stated that, unlike the major political parties, the Communist party possessed *"an efficient and disciplined industrial apparatus controlled from Communist party headquarters and there was no major strike anywhere in the country or in any sector of industry in which this apparatus failed to concern itself."*

The seamen's strike crumbled shortly afterwards. Certain left wing commentators took the view that Wilson had deliberately smeared the strikers with unsubstantiated accusations in order to break the strike but the Prime Minister himself had been satisfied with the accuracy of the information. Indeed, by 1968, Wilson was firmly convinced that many of the strikes and stoppages that were taking place at that time had been stirred up by militant shop stewards who, if they were not actually Communist Party members, were certainly fellow travellers or far-left extremists, more interested in destroying the national economy than representing the interests of their trade union members, people like Eric in fact.

To make matters worse, in the late 1960's, two Czechoslovakian defectors identified a number of trade union leaders and Labour politicians as Soviet agents. M15 found there was some truth in the allegations and in 1970, Will Owen was prosecuted for passing material to Czechoslovakian agents in return for cash but, unbelievably, while the case was proven, he was acquitted because the intelligence he had been passing had not been classified. Tom Driberg also admitted passing secrets to the Czechs for money but no formal action was ever taken against him. As part of the same investigation, M15 interviewed John Stonehouse but he denied all allegations and the matter was not pursued. Stonehouse was later gaoled for fraud after faking his own suicide.

Wilson's critics accused him of paranoia but if that were true, he could hardly be blamed for, if rumours are to be believed, there were many plots against his Government. I found references to one of these in two separate sources citing the Daily Mirror tycoon, Cecil King and a conspiracy to supersede the Wilson Government with a cross party coalition led by Lord Louis Mountbatten. As the story goes, the celebrated scholar, Sir Solly Zuckermann, who was present at Mountbatten's Knightsbridge flat at the time King put forward his ludicrous proposition, urged Lord Louis to have nothing to do with it and his Lordship heeded the academic's advice. But the damage done to the British Establishment by traitors like Burgess, Maclean, Philby and Blunt ran deep and stories of Communist infiltration of the Trades Unions and even the Government itself would not go away and resulted in a great deal of scare mongering and hysteria. In 1971, M15 estimated that there were in excess of 450 Russian spies operating in London alone, a figure that was subsequently confirmed by a Russian defector and which prompted Sir Alec Douglas-Home, the Conservative Foreign Secretary to expel 105 Soviet Embassy staff in September of that year.

By then, the point had been reached where every major strike that occurred was being attributed to the activities of Moscow-trained agitators but I remain unconvinced. It is well documented that there was a national dock strike in 1970, which started in Liverpool over a wage claim that would have increased the dockworkers basic wage to £11 per week. The Conservative Government promptly declared a state of emergency, although the dispute ended soon afterwards when an independent Court of Inquiry offered an average pay rise of 7%. This strike ultimately cost the British economy between £50m and £100m, while the strikers lost £4m in wages, although they did receive nominal strike pay from their union. However, all reports show that the strike was a straightforward pay dispute with no evidence of any subversive activity, which is in complete contrast to Eric's claim that it had been incited by the Socialist Labour League and its revolutionary leadership.

The summer of 1972 saw another docks strike, this time against the use of containers, which signalled the end of traditional, labour intensive working practices. On 14th June, three dockers were deemed to be in contempt of court for ignoring a court order forbidding them from picketing certain haulage firms that handled containers. Warrants were issued for their arrest and as the threat of a general strike loomed, the Official Solicitor, an officer of the court, intervened on behalf of the dockers and persuaded the Appeal Court to lift the prison sentences. Unfortunately, this did not stop the secondary picketing and on 21st July, five shop stewards, subsequently known as the "Pentonville Five," were arrested and taken to Pentonville prison. A series of protest strikes immediately broke out across the country and once again there were threats of a general strike. On 26th July, the House of Lords ruled that it was the union leadership rather than the shop stewards who were responsible and the stewards were released instantly to avert a general strike.

Unlike the 1970 stoppage, which was about wages, the 1972 dock strike was a rearguard action by the dockers to prevent a fundamental change in their way of working, which would render established methods obsolete and many of their workforce redundant. They were fighting for their livelihoods but, once again, there was no evidence to suggest this was anything other than a legitimate cause rather than a fabricated dispute brought about by left-wing agitators. Any involvement by Gerry Healey or the Socialist Labour League never made the newspapers, which tends to call into question Eric's claim that this person was a viable threat to national security. It is possible that the Socialist Labour League did aspire to take over the country by undemocratic means, most far left organisations suffer from similar self-delusion, but the fact that none of them has ever succeeded speaks for itself.

Gerry Healey joined the Communist Party in 1928 at the age of fourteen but eight years later he was branded a "Trotskyist" and expelled. This accusation was absurd, as up until then, Healey had never read a word of Trotsky. A year later, all that had changed and he joined the Trotskyist movement, becoming its UK leader by the end of the 1940's. He then disappeared into the covens of the faithful, indulging in various internecine disputes over the finer points of the gospel according to Marx and Lenin before re-emerging as the leader of the Socialist Labour League and, ultimately, the Workers Revolutionary Party. The latter styled itself as the world's foremost Trotskyist Party in spite of its "Celebrity Left" reputation, due to the involvement of certain members of the Redgrave family. I often saw WRP members distributing their literature at various rallies in support of the miners in the early 90's when John Major's Tory Government was threatening substantial pit closures. They were nothing special, just as bland, boring and insignificant and having no more impact on proceedings than the Socialist Workers Party, Militant or the Revolutionary Communist Party – at least the Class War people were funny.

While Communist Party members had been active at the core of the British trade union movement particularly during the 1960's, there is no hard evidence to indicate either how many of them there were or how disruptive they had been. In any event, much of their activity would have been consigned to instant failure, since, in trying to harness the far left to undermine our country's manufacturing industry, the CPGB greatly overestimated the capability of those they chose to perform that task. In particular, they failed to appreciate the fact that the Left in the UK has always been a fragmented and disparate mass of warring factions whose hatred of each other often runs deeper than their collective hatred of capitalism, democracy or the West. Whatever mischief these people might have inflicted upon our country, their activities should not be viewed in isolation neither should any success they might have claimed.

As far as labour relations in the UK were concerned, there was far more to the industrial anarchy and disruption than could ever have been caused by a few hundred trots, commies and all-purpose loonies. Since 1945, the entire British Economy had been in severe difficulties. There had been long-term balance of trade problems, painfully slow economic growth and the pound had been de-valued several times. British industries were under-capitalised, productivity levels were so low that they were barely existent and we were losing markets abroad to foreign competitors, while those same foreign competitors were making severe inroads into our own markets at home. Inflation rose from 4% in 1966 to around 25% in 1975 in spite of various incomes policies designed to prevent this from happening. Over the same period, trades unions, especially at shop floor level, were accusing the Government of shoring up capitalism at the expense of the working classes. The unions were becoming increasingly militant so that over manning, restrictive practices, opposition to change and unrelenting wage demands became the order of the day. In short, as Labour MP Gerald Kaufman said afterwards, *the UK was a veritable adventure playground for any home grown opportunist determined to make mischief.* Any outside help they might have received was just a bonus. But, if the industrial unrest during the 60's and 70's really was the result of a concerted effort to destroy the British economy by a small band of determined foreign subversives, it did not succeed and we should be grateful for that.

I put Eric's grandiose claims on behalf of the Socialist Labour League down to the vanity of the far left, the hard left or the loony left, call it what you will, which has always exaggerated its own importance. At the time of Margaret Thatcher's removal from office, members of the Socialist Workers Party were telling anyone who would listen that it was "their" campaign against the poll tax that brought her down. Later they simplified this preposterous assertion to merely claim that it was they who had brought about her downfall. Around the same time, the Revolutionary Communist Party brought out a pamphlet called "Preparing for Power." I wonder what planet they're on now. They were virtually bankrupted in the 1990's over a libel suit against their magazine "Living Marxism" or should that be "Lying Marxism?" and I don't see them about any more, not that I've been looking very hard.

... AND IT ALL ENDS IN BEERS

The coach took us as far as Buda and drew up on Castle Hill, not far from Trinity Square and the spiky gothic features of the Matyas Church. I said goodbye to Eric and Shirley and watched them as they joined the rest of the group for an organised tour of a city that was still in the process of removing statues of newly-discredited Marxists and other visible signs of Communism from its streets. I picked up my bags and went off to find a taxi that would take me across the Danube to a low budget hotel in Pest from which I was to make nightly forays to various hostelries and imbibe large quantities of foaming Hungarian ale.

A SHORT HISTORY OF
ANTI-BRITISH EGYPT

REASONS FOR NOT GOING TO EGYPT –
NOVEMBER 1993

I decided to go back to Egypt before the end of 1993, even though my previous visit had been an unmitigated disaster, from my unscheduled stop in Bulgaria, the clumsy attempt to extort money from me by three crooked Egyptian immigration officials, nearly freezing to death while being ferried down the Nile in a floating doss-house before being driven, herded and bullied from Luxor to Hughada by a number of uncivil tour guides, who could well have been trained by the KGB. On top of all that, I'd had to share the entire unpleasant experience with a number of nerds and whingers who, in the normal course of events, I'd have crossed a busy motorway on foot to avoid.

This time, I'd planned to travel independently in November to avoid any unsuitable travelling companions being foisted upon me and, most important of all, to escape the Christmas rush, not that I had any choice in the matter. I was due to retire the following March so management decreed that I had become expendable and that my colleagues leave requirements should be given priority over those of my own. There was some justice in this, as some of my co-workers had children and were forced to plan their annual leave around school holidays while others, who had no children at all, had inevitably booked up some sort of adventure tour in an obscure part of the planet and needed to complete this self-inflicted act of human endurance before the rainy season set in. By September, I was beginning to feel particularly hard done by as, one by one, my fellow workers returned to the office suitably refreshed and invigorated having duly recovered from their annual bouts of sunstroke, malaria and dysentery, while the only break I'd managed to fit in was the 7 day, whistle-stop tour of Bulgaria in search of Spartacus the previous May – and you know what a bundle of laughs that turned out to be.

Although the idea of spending two whole weeks in Egypt might appear on the surface to be idyllic, two weeks were not nearly enough so there were two major decisions to be made. I could either take my time, stay in one place, relax and see very little or rush around as I did last time and come back feeling as though I'd just taken part in a long-distance obstacle race and still see very little. Right then, neither option was very satisfactory and I ended up calling the whole thing off, but my decision was influenced by much more serious concerns than simple logistics and time constraints. I'd planned my departure date for the second week in November and by the end of October, I'd booked (but not paid for) my flight, received my visa, and arranged my travel insurance. Then the story broke.

On 27th October, 1993, two Americans and a Frenchman were shot dead while they were dining in a luxury Cairo hotel. Four other people had been wounded in the attack, one of whom, an Italian, died later of his injuries. The attacker was originally said to be a mentally disturbed musician, although later versions of events described him as a supporter of a militant Islamist group, so he could still have been mentally disturbed. There had been six other attacks on tourists in Egypt that year and three more the year before. On 30th September, 1992, the perpetrators, Gama'a al-Islamiyya, the main Islamist movement operating in Egypt at the time, had issued a warning to tourists and other foreigners to stay away from the province of Qena, which includes the area around Luxor and the Valley of the Kings. The following day, they fired on a Nile cruiser as it passed the southern city of Assyut, injuring three Egyptian crew-members. This signalled the launch of a series of attacks on foreign tourists that was to continue for the next 5 years and culminate in the November 1997 massacre at Luxor when 58 tourists and 4 Egyptian nationals were attacked and killed by Islamic extremists near the Temple of Hatshepsut.

Although Egypt formally recognised Islam as the "State Religion" in the 1971 constitution, the country's reputation as the pinnacle of Islamic

Temple of Hatshepsut, Luxor, West Bank.

theology dates back centuries. The Al-Azhar Mosque is acknowledged to be the most influential Islamic centre in the world and its seminary is claimed to be the world's oldest university, having been established in 969 AD by the Fatimid Dynasty to teach Shia theology. The curriculum was changed from Shia to Sunni during the reign of Saladin and Sunni Muslims throughout the world continue to seek the guidance of the Al-Azhar on all spiritual matters.

Militant Islamic movements had developed in Egypt during the inter war years, although Islamofascist violence did not break out in earnest until the 1970's. Initially, this occurred in and around the city of Assyut where the university had become a stronghold for Islamic Fundamentalism. Since 1992, there had been a vicious cycle of violence concentrated in this part of Egypt and initiated by armed Islamist militants who had been carrying out shootings and bombings against both Coptic Christians and Government security forces. The latter retaliated with a series of heavy-handed crack-downs involving the arbitrary arrest, torture and extra-judicial killing of those suspected of being involved in terrorism and by holding family members hostage until the suspects gave themselves up. Many innocent people were caught in the middle of all this and if they weren't shot at, blown up, murdered or mutilated by the terrorists

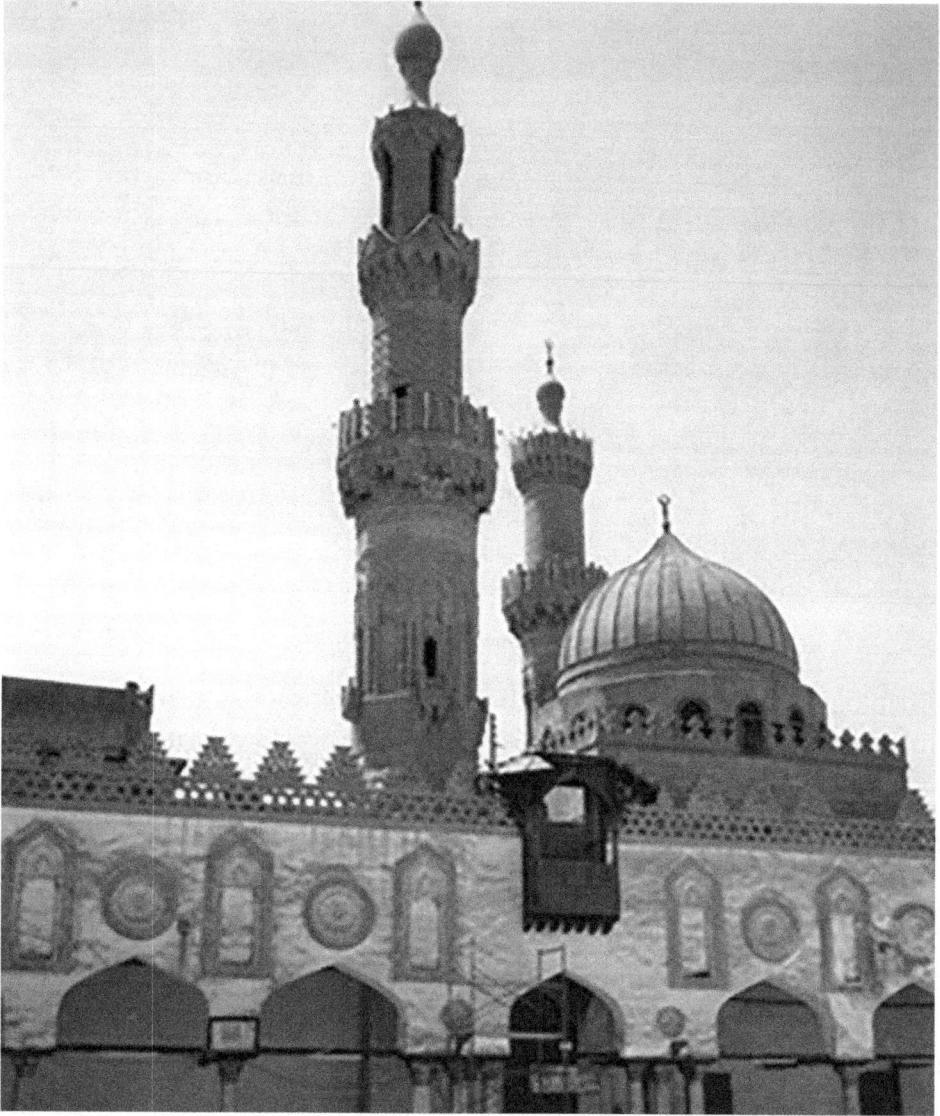

Al Azhar Mosque, Islamic Cairo.

then they were just as likely to have been rounded up, detained and tortured by those Government forces charged with their protection. Assyut and its environs never had much going for them in the first place, but since 1992, even the Egyptians have given the place a wide berth.

In the early 1990's two main Islamist groups were operating in Egypt, the previously-mentioned Al-Gama'a al-Islamiyya and Al Jihad, both of which were seeking to dislodge the Egyptian Government and supplant it with an Islamist regime. Al-Gama'a al-Islamiyya had been active since the late 1970's and was reputed to be Egypt's largest Islamist group with supporters in many countries throughout the world. Its main claim to fame was the first attack on the World Trade Centre in 1993 for which the group's spiritual leader, Sheikh Abd al-Rahman, having earlier been acquitted of any involvement in the murder of Anwar Sadat, received a life sentence in 1996 and remained incarcerated in a high-security American prison until his death in 2017. Before declaring a ceasefire in 1999, Al-Gama'a al Islamiyya gunmen had carried out regular armed attacks on those they deemed to be opponents of Islam. They also claimed responsibility for the attempt on President Hosni Mubarak's life during a state visit to Addis Ababa in June 1995. The attacks on tourists were designed to wreck Egypt's tourist industry and to de-stabilise its fragile economy. It has been estimated that, prior to the ceasefire, more than 1,100 fatalities had occurred in clashes between militants and the police.

The original Islamic Jihad was responsible for the assassination of Egyptian President Anwar Sadat in 1981. Since then, the organisation has mutated and re-emerged, carrying out armed attacks against Government personnel and car-bombings against US and Egyptian Government establishments. They claimed responsibility for the attempted murders of Interior Minister Hassan al-Alfi in August 1993 and Prime Minister Atef Sedky in November of that year. They subsequently extended their activities to include attacks on American and Israeli interests and were alleged to have received funding from the state of Iran, Al Qaeda, the usual Islamic non-governmental agencies and bogus charitable organisations as well as from the proceeds of drug trafficking and other forms of criminal activity. Subsequently Islamic Jihad merged with Al Qaeda and Ayman al Zawahri, one of its most senior members became deputy to Osama Bin Laden and succeeded him after the latter had been assassinated. He has been credited with being the architect of the Al Qaeda ideology and was one of the signatories to Bin Laden's infamous 1998 "fatwa" urging the faithful to carry out attacks on US civilians. He is wanted by the US for his alleged role in the 1998 bombings of American embassies in East Africa and the Egyptians have sentenced him to death in absentia for his part in the atrocities carried out by Islamic Jihad during the 1990's. Unfortunately the chances of justice being done in the foreseeable future are remote as he continues to hide out in the badlands on the Pakistan/Afghanistan border where no government can exercise jurisdiction.

Islamic Jihad and Gama,a al Islamiyya were by no means the first Is-lamist groups to be formed in Egypt, this dubious distinction must go to Al Ikhwan Al-Muslimun, the Muslim Brotherhood. The Muslim Brotherhood was founded in 1928 by one Hasan al-Banna and, although its influence now extends throughout the Middle East and Europe, it was banned in Egypt from the 1950's until 2011 when it was legalised. Its leader Mohammed Morsi was elected president in 2012 but was ousted by a popular military coup a year later. On 25th December 2013, the Muslim Brotherhood in Egypt was declared a terrorist organisation as it has been subsequently in Saudi Arabia and Kuwait.

Hasan Al-Banna was born in Ismailiya and exhibited a tendency towards hard core Islam from a very early age. As an adolescent, he would distribute leaflets opposing women's rights and when he was only a few years older he would preach excruciatingly long and vitriolic sermons advocating a return to traditional Islamic values. Once established, the Muslim Brotherhood swiftly became a highly politicised yet clandestine organisation, which opposed Egypt's secular society, gaining members from every social level, from artisan to professional. It soon became Egypt's strongest opposition group promoting an Islamic alternative to modern Western ideas and actively opposing the corrupt Egyptian Monarchy by which it was duly outlawed. Al-Banna was eventually assassinated in 1949, allegedly on the orders of King Farouk. During the years immediately before and after the Second World War, the Brotherhood organised terrorist cells and armed their members to wage a bloody guerrilla war to rid their country of the British, a bitter episode, which both countries have since sought to sweep under the carpet.

By the time they left in 1956, the British had been involved in Egypt for a century and a half, and, although doubt has often been cast on their motives for being there at all, especially by revisionist, far left historians, it is beyond dispute that during the period of British rule, Egypt was governed well by people who had no interest in siphoning off the proceeds for their own ends which was in stark contrast to the chaotic misrule of the Ottomans that preceded them and to the series of corrupt regimes that followed them. The irony is, when they went to Egypt, the British never meant to stay and when they landed there the first time it was to pursue a sincere, legitimate and noble cause, one they had been practising with considerable success around the world for centuries – the expulsion of an occupying French force.

A DIMINUTIVE ANGLOPHOBE FROM CORSICA

Although born in Corsica, Napoleon was educated in France, spending five years at the Military College at Brienne followed by a year at the Military Academy in Paris, from which he graduated in 1785 in 42nd place out of a class of 58. He returned to Corsica shortly afterwards and despite his elevation to the rank of Lieutenant Colonel, he became embroiled in a feud with an influential local family, which resulted in the entire Bonaparte clan being condemned to what historians later described as "perpetual execration and infamy" causing them to uproot themselves en masse and flee to France where their fortunes were to take a turn for the better.

During the French revolution, Napoleon continued to serve in the army and achieved rapid promotion. In August 1793, he was promoted to the rank of Commander of Artillery and sent to Toulon where he helped defend that city against a British blockade. He was promoted again that year to the rank of Brigadier General and continued to fight against the opponents of the revolution. In March 1796, he was sent to Italy to command the French army fighting the Austrians. Up until then, the French had been suffering from low morale, hunger and cholera as they struggled to contain their better-equipped Austrian adversaries. However, under Napoleon's leadership, they were transformed into a determined and formidable fighting force, which carried the fight to its enemy and finally turned the tide in its favour. After the French victory at Modena, the Italian population mistakenly hailed the victors as liberators but liberating the citizens of Modena was the last thing Napoleon had in mind.

Having disposed of the Austrians, the French then turned their attention to the City and its civilian population, liberating anything of value that could be carried away. This not only included money, gold and other precious metals and works of art but women and young girls, too and anyone who dared raise a hand against them was slaughtered instantly. By the time the French army returned home, it had acquired an abundance of riches and a reputation for ruthlessness, carnage, rape and pillage, which would precede it in many future campaigns.

After 1795, France had a new Government, a group of five men called The Directory. This body was determined to invade Britain and they appointed Napoleon to command an army of invasion that had been assembled along the English Channel for this purpose. They clearly chose the right man. Throughout his education in France, Napoleon had been something of a Francophobe, deeply resenting the occupation of his native Corsica by French troops. However, after his humiliating departure from the island of his birth, his attitude to France changed. Also, throughout his military education, he had learned about Agincourt, Blenheim, Oudenarde, Quebec and a whole host of other battles, from which the British had emerged victorious over the French. He knew now who his real enemies were and he wanted to destroy them and avenge his adopted country. As far as the invasion of the British Isles was concerned, however, Napoleon reached the conclusion, reluctantly, that such an invasion could not be conducted successfully until the French navy achieved maritime supremacy over the British and he turned his attention to another strategy.

If he could not invade Britain, then Bonaparte wanted to do the next best thing. He would invade British India. Napoleon had long cherished the desire to emulate Alexander the Great and lead an army overland to India and when he landed in Alexandria on 1st July 1798, he intended this to be the first stage of his grand plan. Although there was a clear route by sea around the Cape of Good Hope, the most expeditious and direct route from Britain to Bombay was via Egypt and, although this involved a short overland journey, it was far quicker than sailing around the entire African land mass. So by landing a force of 36,000 hostile troops on Egypt's Mediterranean coast, Napoleon instantly denied the British access to this short cut and directly threatened profitable British interests in India.

The French took Alexandria as soon as they landed with the loss of only 200 men. Leaving a small garrison behind them, they then headed south across the desert towards Cairo, a foolhardy expedition that could have ended in disaster. Nothing on this scale had been attempted in this part of the world by a European army since the crusades and Napoleon had neither considered the logistics nor the climate. The French army had been trained to live off the land but as they marched southwards carrying full battle equipment through seemingly endless desert, they found nothing at all to sustain them. The advance to Cairo took Napoleon's expeditionary force the best part of two weeks in searing heat with no water. Many failed to complete the march and were left in the wilderness to die.

Finally, its strength sapped after the long debilitating trek, Napoleon's army emerged from the desert at Embabeh on the left bank of the Nile within sight of the Pyramids. Here, the French army found its route to Cairo blocked by an armed force of around 40,000 Egyptians led by the fearsome Mameluke commander Murad Bey, who, it was said, could behead an ox with a single blow of his scimitar. Unfortunately for Murad Bey, he was facing an army of butchers rather than oxen and in just over two hours, his men had been soundly defeated. The relentless firepower of French muskets and artillery was far too intense for the Mameluke cavalry, which sustained severe losses before those who were still able to do so, turned tail and ran. French fatalities were comparatively light, amounting to approximately 300 while between 4000 and 6000 Egyptians were killed with many more wounded. On 22nd July, 1798, Napoleon led his victorious army into Cairo where he set up his administrative headquarters in a palace on the banks of the Nile. During the next two to three weeks, the army replenished its stocks, tended its wounded and restored its energy until the arrival of devastating news put it once more on its guard. There had been a naval engagement with the British at Abu Qir Bay and the entire French fleet had been destroyed. Napoleon's army was now stranded in Egypt with no means of getting back to France.

An intelligence report that Napoleon was due to leave Toulon with a large military force caused panic from London to Calcutta and, as there was no confirmation of where the French might be heading, a detachment of ships from the British Mediterranean Fleet under the command of Rear Admiral Horatio Nelson was ordered to keep an eye on French shipping movements off the coast of Toulon. Unfortunately, the exercise had to be abandoned after Nelson's ship was seriously damaged in a storm and his escort of frigates was scattered. However, on 14 June 1798, after undergoing repairs in Gibraltar, Nelson set sail again, his strength having been reinforced to 14 ships of the line. When he reached Toulon, he found that the French had already sailed and he surmised that there could be only two possible destinations, Egypt or around the Cape to India. Nelson headed for Egypt but when he arrived, he was astonished to find no French ships in the port of Alexandria.

Unknown to Nelson, the French fleet had first sailed to Malta where they seized control of the island and then spent a week securing possession before pressing on to Egypt so that the two convoys managed to avoid each other and the French were able to reach Egypt unobserved and unmolested. In the meantime, Nelson put in to Sicily for supplies before resuming his search for Napoleon's elusive expeditionary force. He returned to Egypt on 1 August 1798 and this time he found the French fleet at anchor in Abu Qir Bay. With only a few hours until darkness, Nelson attacked immediately, catching his opponents completely unprepared for battle.

The French had anchored in a straight line and considered they were in a strong defensive position with the shore battery on Abu Qir Island to their rear. Unfortunately, Francois-Paul Bruey, the French Admiral, had not positioned his fleet sufficiently close to shallow water to prevent five British vessels from getting between their line and the land, and, with the wind behind them, the British were able to rake individual French vessels from both sides as they sailed past them. As a result, the battle proved to be very one sided. At about 10 P.M., there was a thunderous explosion as the French flagship L'Orient, which had been on fire for the best part of an hour, disintegrated in a ball of flame sending fiery fragments of smouldering wood in all directions. The burning rudder, all 15 tons of it, was hurled half a mile from the wreck while blazing timbers rained on to the nearby British ships, Alexander and Franklin, setting them alight but the crews managed to put out the fires before serious damage was done.

By 6 A.M., the battle was effectively over and of 13 French ships of the line, two had escaped only to be detained later, two more had been sunk and the remainder had either been captured or were in the process of being subdued. However, only three of the captured vessels were subsequently deemed capable of being re-flagged and re-fitted for service in the Royal Navy, the others having been so badly damaged in combat, that by the time the sun came up, they were little more than smouldering hulks.

British casualties were reported as 213 killed and 677 wounded, although there is some doubt as to the exact number of French losses. One source gives these as 1400 killed and 600 wounded while others have estimated the number of French fatalities as being somewhere between 2000 and 5000. In all, it was a resounding victory for the British without being the catastrophe it should have been for the French, whose army was still intact, still in Egypt and still a potential threat to British India.

By the end of August, 1798, the French were in control of that part of Northern Egypt which lay between the Nile Delta and Cairo, while Upper Egypt remained in the hands of the Mamelukes. The Ottomans still considered themselves to be the rightful rulers of Egypt in spite of their ongoing dispute with the Mamelukes and on 11th August, they declared war on France. Although there had been reports that a Turkish invasion force was being assembled in Syria by Ahmed el Jazzar to liberate Egypt from the invaders, by the beginning of 1799, this had failed to materialise so Napoleon decided to take the fight to his enemy and intercept the Ottoman column before it reached Egypt. He led his army across the Sinai Desert, joining forces at El Arish with troops sent from Alexandria. Napoleon then pushed northwards into what is now Israel, where he unleashed an apocalyptic outbreak of savagery and carnage on the local population, unknown to this region since before the crusades.

The French advance was held up at Jaffa, the city being well defended by troops recruited from all over the Ottoman Empire, who provided stern resistance costing Napoleon's army 1000 dead. As an act of retribution, he slaughtered 3,800 prisoners, keeping a substantial number of others as hostages. Thus began the maelstrom of mass murder that was to become the hallmark of the French campaign in the Holy Lands. From Jaffa, Napoleon divided his forces leading the largest contingent to Acre where the French advance finally ground to a halt. Acre proved to be well fortified and defended and every assault mounted by the French was beaten back with severe losses. To make matters worse, the detached columns heading towards Carmel and Jordan to secure the route to Damascus were driven out of Nazareth and Janath respectively, causing Napoleon to detach troops from Acre to assist, thereby lifting the siege of that fortress and enabling the defenders to be reinforced from the sea by a large contingent of British Marines and armed seamen.

The French army immediately resumed its assault on Acre and continued to do so, unsuccessfully, for the next two months but each time, they were repelled incurring heavy loss of life. During one attack, the French managed to breach the outer walls but, once again, they were decisively beaten back and driven out by British seamen supported by sustained gunfire from the offshore British fleet. The following day, Turkish reinforcements landed by sea and, together with the British defenders of Acre, they comprehensively routed the French in the final battle of the campaign. On 20th May 1799, Napoleon started to pull out of Acre and head back to Egypt as the whole country rose up against him and his defeated army. The wounded and what remained of the French artillery were hastily embarked at Jaffa, only to fall into British hands soon after they set sail. As the survivors of the French army slunk back towards Gaza, they left a trail of devastation in their wake as they looted and destroyed every town they passed through, indiscriminately murdering the inhabitants as they went. What they could not carry, they burned, be it goods or crops as the retreating invaders inflicted brutal reprisals on the same population of the Holy Lands that Bonaparte had earlier sworn to liberate.

Thus Napoleon's attempted march on Syria had ended in ignominious defeat at Acre and any grandiose ideas he had of thrusting overland to India had to be abandoned. On 22nd August 1799 Napoleon left his army in Egypt and returned to Paris where, three months later, he organised the coup d'etat that resulted in France being governed by 3 consuls, he and two others, but it was Bonaparte who held the real power.

The debacle in the Holy Lands had taken a heavy toll on the French army, now under the command of General Jean-Baptiste Kleber, and it was very much a spent force but another year was to pass before a British force returned to Egypt to protect British India from the predatory French, to drive them from Egypt and to return that country to Ottoman rule.

On 8th March, 1801, the 14000 strong British invasion force landed at Abu Qir Bay and defeated the French at the Battle of Alexandria, driving them back into the city, where they remained under siege. Victory came at a price, however, with 1500 British soldiers being either killed or wounded including their commander Sir Ralph Abercromby. Alexandria eventually fell a month later, allowing the British to divert their attentions further south where Cairo surrendered to Anglo-Ottoman troops on 18th June. The French finally left Egypt at the end of 1801. During their stay there, Archaeologists in their number had assembled a vast collection of treasure, works of art and antiquities, which they were intending to take back to Paris. Unluckily for them, they were relieved of their spoils by the British, which is why the Rosetta Stone now resides in the British Museum in London rather than in the Louvre in Paris.

A small British expeditionary force returned to Egypt in March 1807 in an effort to establish a stable government and forestall any further French invasion. Unfortunately this ended in total defeat and humiliation as the British army was heavily outnumbered by Mameluke troops commanded by Mohammed Ali and the survivors were eventually evacuated from Alexandria in September of that year. The whole enterprise was ill conceived, badly planned and only succeeded in wasting the lives of many brave men.

A DISMAL BUT PROFITABLE DITCH

Following the military debacle in 1807, the British Government had little direct dealings with Egypt for decades although trade still flourished between the two countries, especially in cotton and textiles. It is questionable whether official interests in Egypt would have extended beyond the use of the overland short cut to India had it not been for the mountain of debt owed to British and other European bankers by succeeding Egyptian Governments and the construction of the Suez Canal.

The concept of an artificial waterway linking the Mediterranean with the Red Sea predated the Suez Canal by centuries and the first excavation is reputed to have been made as early as 1300 BC. Herodotus mentions a later attempt in 600 BC, which cost the lives of 120,000 men before being abandoned as unachievable. It was another century before the first canal was actually completed. This was carried out by the Persian Emperor Darius and connected the Red Sea with the Great Bitter Lake. This, in turn, was linked to an older channel excavated by Ramses II leading to the Nile. There are no accurate records as to how much this canal was used, although it was improved, adapted and extended by numerous heads of state before falling into disuse. This waterway was re-opened in the 8th Century AD during the early part of the Muslim occupation before being finally abandoned.

The notion of a north-south canal was resurrected periodically over the next millennium, the most significant venture being by Bonaparte's engineers who somehow managed to miscalculate the sea levels between the Red Sea and the Mediterranean by 30 feet, concluding that any canal that was excavated would become a raging torrent ending in a waterfall. In the 1840's, French Consul Count Ferdinand de Lessops disputed the conclusion reached by Bonaparte's engineers but when he placed his own proposal for a canal before Abbas Pasha, it was dismissed out of hand.

After the death of Abbas Pasha, de Lessops presented his scheme to his successor, Said Pasha who accepted the plan in spite of contradictory advice from various European engineers who tended to agree with Bonaparte's men and the political objections of the British Government, who feared another French threat to its possessions in India. In spite of these tribulations, excavation finally started on the Mediterranean coast in 1859 at what is now Port Said. It would proceed due south to Lake Timseh at Ismailiya and continue through the Great Bitter Lakes before joining the Red Sea at Suez, a total distance of 105 miles. An independent company was set up, 'La Companie Universelle du Canal Maritime de Suez' to finance, construct and to manage the canal for a period of 99 years, after which time, the ownership would return to the Egyptian Government. When the canal opened in 1869, its construction had cost £19m and had taken approximately 10 years to complete during which time, its workforce of around 20,000 forced labourers suffered a multitude of privations and a great number died from cholera, malaria or industrial accidents.

In the meantime, the British Government continued to express legitimate concerns about its eastern dominions. The Russians had been casting envious eyes in the direction of India for decades as they gradually edged their way through Central Asia, while there was always an ever-present threat from France. Before the canal opened, the sailing distance between London and Bombay around the Cape of Good Hope was approximately 12,400 miles. Through the Suez Canal, that distance became much shorter, only 7,270 miles. When de Lessops plans were first presented to Ismail Pasha, Said's successor, the British Prime Minister, Lord Palmerston, predicted that if the Canal ever opened, it would precipitate another war with France and now, with the canal fully operational and in French hands, Britain feared the worst.

Mohammed Ali and his successors sought to modernise Egypt and transform it into an independent Europeanised state, free from Ottoman domination. Irrigation systems were developed, canals were dug and factories were built as was a railway link between Alexandria and Cairo. The modernising process was continued by Mohammed Ali's son, Said, with the building of ships, schools and universities and by his grandson, Ismail, under whom the Egyptian economy continued to expand, albeit slowly due to its dependence on cotton, a low cost commodity subject to extreme market fluctuations. To maintain his strategy for further economic development, Ismail was compelled to borrow heavily from European bankers and the impact of an ever-increasing level of foreign debt was intensified by the cost of the Suez Canal. In short, Egypt was living way beyond its means and disaster was looming.

In 1875, its crippling debts forced the Egyptian Government to the brink of bankruptcy. Bribery, corruption and fraud all made matters worse as large amounts of public money regularly disappeared and remained unaccounted for. Between 1863 and 1875, the country's foreign debt had risen from £3m to £100m, a staggering amount considering that the income from Egypt's annual exports rarely exceeded £13m. Benjamin Disraeli, Britain's astute Prime Minister wasted no time in capitalising on this situation, and, with a loan obtained from his friends, Rothschilds the bankers, he purchased Ismail's shares in the Canal for a knock-down £4m. Although this did not come close to solving Egypt's financial difficulties, it did give the British the controlling interest in the Suez Canal.

What followed has been called colonisation by stealth or, more cynically, colonisation by debt but if it were colonisation at all, then it was colonisation by accident since, when the British invaded in 1882, they did so to protect an investment and to safeguard the repayment of monies owed. When these two objectives had been achieved, they meant to leave but events conspired against them and they were to spend the next seventy years in Egypt guarding what Joseph Conrad was to describe as a dismal but profitable ditch.

While on the surface, Egypt appeared to be a flourishing and prosperous state, this was only a façade funded by British and French capital and both the latter countries began to realise that unless drastic steps were taken and a number of urgent remedies imposed, Egypt would become insolvent and the vast amounts that had been loaned to that ailing country would be irrecoverable. In 1876, the British and French Governments forced the Egyptians to accept an international commission with powers to enforce tough financial measures designed to stave off bankruptcy but by 1877, Egypt was still spending over 60% of its revenue on foreign debt, much of this on interest payments. Even stricter measures became necessary and in 1879, fearing that Ismail was about to repudiate Egypt's entire foreign debt, the Europeans put pressure on the Ottoman Sultan to remove him from power and replace him with his son, Tewfiq. On succeeding his father, Tewfiq was immediately dragooned into accepting Anglo-French control of all the major Government departments, including the treasury, customs, railways, ports etc., which added up to a complete takeover of the Egyptian Civil Service by foreign bureaucrats, totally undermining Egyptian sovereignty.

Naturally enough, there was considerable opposition to what was happening from various quarters, including a powerful nationalist movement, the Al Hizb al Watani, the National Popular Party. Its leader, Colonel Ahmed Urabi led a coup d'etat in 1881 as a result of which Tewfiq was deposed and Urabi was appointed Minister for War with full control of the military. Following a riot in Alexandria in June 1882, during which 50 foreigners were murdered and their property looted, investors in Britain and France began to fear for the safety of their investments and put pressure on their respective Governments to act. The French, having no stomach for a confrontation with Egyptian rioters and insurgents withdrew their navy from Alexandria, leaving the British to face down the trouble alone. Urabi's troops managed to restore some sort of stability in Alexandria and he gave orders for the city's sea defences to be reinforced with new cannon acquired from Germany. The British Commander, Sir Beauchamp Seymour, envisaging his own forces as potential targets of these new weapons, ordered Urabi to remove them and when he refused, British ships proceeded to bombard the gun emplacements on the city walls. Urabi's men promptly fled from Alexandria and what vestige of law and order that had hitherto existed went with them as riots broke out and buildings were torched and looted.

After the bombardment, British marines landed in the city, quelled the riots and restored Tewfiq as Khedive. In August 1882, a British force of 20,000 men led by General Sir Garnett Wolseley landed in Ismailiya, overran Urabi's fortified stronghold at Tel-el-Kebir and put the Egyptian army to flight before marching into Cairo unopposed. Urabi was subsequently taken into British custody and exiled to Ceylon. Tewfiq remained in nominal control, although his reputation was now tarnished and his authority eroded leaving Egypt effectively under British rule, which was to last for the next 70 years. This period would prove to be extremely troublesome for the British, who were faced with a series of political assassinations of senior British personnel and a plethora of anti-British demonstrations and riots incited by various nationalist movements. The British also took control of Sudan, an Egyptian province, to a mixed reception, the Egyptians being effectively prevented from any further influence in Sudanese affairs while the Sudanese were delighted at having been effectively liberated from heavy-handed Egyptian domination. The British also attempted to put an end to the Sudanese slave trade, which had existed for centuries but, in spite of their best efforts, still persists today.

EL ALAMEIN

It was the night of the full moon on the 26th August 1942 and as they sat in their tanks and in their trenches, priming their weapons in preparation for the inevitable onslaught by Rommel's Afrika Corps, the Allied soldiers manning the thirty mile strip south of El Alamein must have wondered what in hell's name they had done to deserve their present predicament. They had been up and down the same stretch of desert for the best part of two years, only to find themselves back where they had started. Italy had entered the war in May 1940 and by December of that year, the British had overwhelmingly defeated their forces at Sidi Barrani, driven them out of Tobruk and sent them scuttling back to Beda Fomm, just south of Benghazi where they then completed the rout. The Germans, fearing that the whole of North Africa might rapidly fall under Allied control, sent a force under the Command of General Erwin Rommel to assist the Italians in their defence of Western Libya.

At this stage, the British force in Egypt found itself weakened by the transfer of a significant number of troops for the ill-fated defence of Greece and Crete against German invasion. Taking advantage of the situation, Rommel attacked the Allies at Mersa Brega and, having successfully forced them to retreat, he pressed home his advantage by pushing forward, encircling Tobruk and, making good use of captured fuel and ammunition, he drove onwards across the Egyptian border as far as Sollum, where he halted, having regained in a matter of weeks what the Italians had lost during the entire winter campaign.

In the meantime, the British continued to build up a defensive position around El Alamein while assembling a strong force with which to carry out a counter offensive later in the year. The attack, called 'Operation Crusader' was eventually mounted in November 1941 and succeeded in relieving the beleaguered defenders of Tobruk and driving Rommel back to his original starting point at Mersa Brega. However, before they could capitalise on their success, history was to repeat itself and troops were diverted to the Far East where Singapore had fallen to the Japanese who were about to invade Burma. Fortunately, this did not have such a significant effect on troop levels as did the previous year's expedition to Greece but the result was much the same. Rommel attacked once again, his objective being to recapture Tobruk and to drive the British back to the Egyptian border. In the third week of June, 1942, Tobruk finally fell and the British withdrew to the El Alamein Line, where, from the beginning of July, they had doggedly resisted everything the Germans could throw at them and finally forced a halt to their offensive but they knew this was only a temporary lull and that the enemy would soon return to the attack refreshed, re-fuelled and re-supplied, fortified by the certainty that the British were there to be overrun and once they had been disposed of, only 100 kilometres of desert separated them from the glittering prize of Alexandria.

Rommel had sought to continue his thrust forward to the Nile Delta, where he could avail himself of the vast resources that had been stockpiled by the British in the Canal Zone and, at a stroke, close down British air and sea operations in the eastern Mediterranean but his superiors had overruled him pointing out they could not support his army so far in advance of the depots at Tobruk and Benghazi and they ordered him to remain where he was until secure supply lines had been established and stabilised. However, when he learned of it, Hitler gave his support to the strategy put forward by Rommel but by then it was too late. His advance had stalled, albeit temporarily, giving him time to finalise his preparations for the final assault and invasion of British-held Egypt. The British were aware of the build-up of enemy numbers and predicted that they would attack on the 26th of August, the night of the full moon but the full moon came and went without any sign of a German advance.

Back in Alexandria all hell had been breaking loose for months as confidential documents were destroyed while civilians and other non-combatants were evacuating the city by train or any other mode of transport they could lay their hands on. Alexandria had been a hotbed of intrigue since the outbreak of hostilities – full of spies, black marketers and a host of other shady characters. Now they were clearing out and saving their own skins. They would be back after the fighting was over to salute the victors. In the meantime, they were taking themselves out of harms way and brushing up their German.

Many hard core Egyptian nationalists, from the King downwards, were working actively for an Axis victory and looking forward to celebrating their imminent deliverance from the "imperialist oppressors." Ever since they had landed in Egypt after war had been declared, it had been made abundantly clear to members of the British armed forces that the Egyptians did not want them there. They had been spat at, stoned, attacked and abused in the streets on a daily basis to the extent that many of them considered they were safer at the front. In the desert, they knew who their enemy was, whereas on the streets of Alexandria, Cairo and in a whole host of other Egyptian towns and villages, it was a different matter.

Faced with this constant hostility, the British servicemen soon began to retaliate in kind, which rapidly engendered a feeling of mutual hatred and contempt. The British referred to the Egyptians as Gyppos, Gyppies or, most frequently, Wogs, the choice of terminology often depending on whether the protagonist was an officer or an enlisted man, while the Egyptians often called the British soldiers far worse but to no avail since very few of the British understood Arabic. This antagonism was always re-kindled at public cinemas when, at the conclusion of every evening's performance, the Egyptian national anthem was played. Each British serviceman present, like the Egyptians, would stand smartly to attention while the anthem was being played and, like the Egyptians, would sing it out at the top of his voice, although the words he sang were rather different from those used by the Egyptians causing deep offence to any of the latter who might have understood English. The first line of the "British" version began "Up your pipe King Farouk," and continued with a lewd tirade against the King, the Queen, the people and finally, the country itself in terms that I cannot possibly reproduce here. I have no doubt that the Egyptians sang a similar version of "God Save the King" but unfortunately I do not speak Arabic either and would not reproduce it here if I could.

Those serving at the many ordnance depots and encampments behind the lines might not have been directly exposed to enemy fire, apart from the occasional air raid, but they, too, regularly encountered the hatred and hostility of their purported hosts. Many of them felt particularly under pressure even though none of them was likely to see a German or an Italian where they were, let alone come under fire from one. No matter where they were based, it was always considered unsafe for off-duty servicemen to venture out alone at night. One or two had done so and paid the price, their bodies having been found in the morning with their throats slit and their identification papers missing. Sooner or later the missing papers would end up in the hands of Rommel's intelligence service, which maintained many nefarious contacts in Egypt. In addition to being waylaid at night, the main difficulty faced by the men in the ordnance depots was protecting their precious supplies from the pilfering hands of the locals but the constant thieving they could understand. What they could never fathom was the sullen, smouldering hatred they experienced from the Egyptians.

From 1882, the British had never been forgiven for putting down the populist revolt led by Urabi, who is still regarded today as an Egyptian nationalist hero, or for the occupation that followed. In spite of the fact that the British had originally occupied Egypt for altruistic reasons, to save its ailing economy and to help regenerate that heavily-indebted nation, detractors could not see beyond imperialism and exploitation, neither could the Egyptians even the least hostile of whom, tended to regard the British presence with resentment. The fact that the occupiers were Christians, unbelievers, also added fuel to the flames as did their perception that Egyptians were incapable of managing their own affairs. Of course there were other concerns that bound the British to Egypt, principally the Suez Canal, which had now become a vital artery connecting Britain to its possessions in India and the Far East. Additionally, there was the very real fear that if they were to withdraw, another country such as France, Germany or Russia, might intervene to fill the political vacuum and annex Egypt for itself. Faced with this conundrum, the British had no option for the time being but to remain. Tewfiq died in 1892 and was succeeded by Abbas an anti-British, pro-German nationalist, who is alleged to have stirred up much of the anti-British agitation that was taking place at the time, but in 1914 he was deposed and Egypt was formally declared a British Protectorate.

During the First World War, Egypt became the fulcrum of the fierce campaign against the Ottomans, Germany's allies, and was used as a vast supply terminal and staging post for a multitude of British and Commonwealth troops as they left to fight in places such as Palestine, Salonika or Gallipoli. This inflamed anti-British passions even further and in 1918, at the conclusion of the conflict, Sa'ad Zaghloul, the leader of the Egyptian nationalist movement demanded complete autonomy from the British and the relinquishing of their control over Sudan, both demands being met with a refusal. He then demanded that a nationalist delegation, or Wafd, be permitted to put their case before the Versailles Peace Conference. This met with a further refusal and led to Zaghloul's arrest and deportation to Malta along with two of his colleagues. An explosion of anti-British rioting followed, as did strikes and violent clashes with British forces throughout the country, forcing the British to climb down, bring Zaghloul home and allow the Wfad'ists to travel to Paris, where they met with no success. At its height, the street fighting had become so brutal and bloody that its ferocity was later compared with that of the Indian Mutiny though, mercifully, it lasted for only two months. Even then, 1,500 Egyptians lost their lives in the unrest.

By now, Egypt was degenerating into a state of perpetual insurrection and British leaders like Field Marshall Viscount Allenby, who had been appointed High Commissioner in 1919, realised that this could not go on indefinitely and that the some sort of dialogue had to be entered into with the leadership of the Wfad. Following a series of informal meetings between Zaghloul and Lord Alfred Milner on the future of Anglo-Egyptian relationships, the Milner-Zaghloul Agreement was published in the summer of 1920, which advocated the termination of the Protectorate and the negotiation of an Anglo-Egyptian Treaty to determine the future roles and responsibilities to be carried out by the British and their reluctant hosts. When this was announced, Zaghloul was feted by his fellow countrymen, which not only alarmed the British but also some influential Egyptians such as Sultan Ahmad Fuad, who hated the Wafd'ists and saw them as a threat to his own leadership ambitions. On 23rd December 1921, in an uncanny repeat of the events of 1919, Allenby had Zaghloul arrested and deported to the Seychelles provoking further anti-British violence. By now, even hard-line colonialists had accepted that enough was enough and on 28th February, 1922, Egypt was declared independent, Sultan Ahmad Fuad became ruler, taking the name King Fuad I and a new constitution was hastily drawn up and agreed two months later. Egypt's first constitutional Parliament held its inaugural meeting on 15th March 1924 with Zaghloul as Prime Minister and the Wafd Party holding 179 of the 211 seats.

While sovereignty was nominally in the hands of the Egyptians, Britain insisted on retaining a dominant role that Nationalists found totally unacceptable, fuelling a volatile atmosphere of tension and disquiet, which frequently erupted into rioting and civil unrest. Anglophobia was all-pervading to the degree that it was even taught in schools ensuring that succeeding generations of young Egyptians were inculcated with a deep-seated hatred of Britain and all things British. Matters had not improved when Fuad died on 28th April 1936, to be succeeded by his son, Farouk, a former Sandhurst cadet, who was more interested in fast cars, faster women and collecting pornographic pictures than he was in ruling Egypt. Nevertheless, he was a co-signatory of the Anglo-Egyptian Agreement on 26th August 1936, the most significant article of which decreed that Britain should withdraw its troops from Egypt while retaining a military force of 10,000 men in the Suez Canal Zone. Unfortunately, the terms of the agreement did not include full Egyptian independence, which caused the Wafd Party to lose ground to more militant groups such as the Muslim Brotherhood and Misr al Fatah, 'Young Egypt,' an Anglophobic nationalist movement founded by one Ahmad Husayn in 1933. The Wafd party were voted out of office in 1936 in favour of a coalition led by Ali Maher Pasha, which also fell from power shortly afterwards. It was around this time that the Muslim Brotherhood began to arm and mobilise terrorist squads to mount attacks on British people and their property. These were to continue intermittently until the Canal Zone Emergency, when hostilities escalated to a level just short of open warfare

One significant clause in the Anglo-Egyptian Agreement was a mutual defence pact and the Egyptians were glad to trigger this to counteract Italian aggression in Abyssinia and Libya but while the British proved to be steadfast allies, though not necessarily for philanthropic reasons, the reliability of the Egyptians was always in doubt. In 1939, the Egyptian cabinet stubbornly refused to declare war on Germany, choosing instead to remain neutral until 1945 when they finally considered it was safe to do otherwise. Egypt did break off diplomatic relations with Germany, interned their nationals and confiscated their property. They severed relations with Italy, too, when that country entered the war but dragged their feet over the detention of its 60,000 expatriate population. Many senior Egyptians, including King Farouk, aware of the Allied setbacks in Greece and the Western Desert believed that the Axis powers would win the war and some were actively intriguing with the Germans to ensure their victory in Egypt. By early 1942, the British Government needed an ally in Egypt that it could count on and if the King could not be trusted to adhere to his part of the Anglo-Egyptian Agreement, then, if necessary, he would have to be sidelined in favour of someone who could.

In early February 1942, Sir Miles Lampson, the British Ambassador arrived at the Royal Palace with an armed force and insisted that Farouk should either sign a document appointing Mustafa al-Nahas, the leader of the Wfad Party, as Prime Minister or abdicate. Farouk signed reluctantly, claiming afterwards that a gun was held to his head to ensure his compliance. It is not known whether or not this was true but armed British soldiers were present in the room at the time the paper was signed. Although the Wfad Party was by its very nature anti-British, its leadership supported the Allies and could, therefore, be relied upon to suppress any pro-Axis activity. In any case, by that time they were well aware of the mass extermination of Jews taking place in NAZI-occupied Europe and it did not take too much imagination to realise that the same fate might easily befall Egyptian Muslims once they had outlived their usefulness to the Third Reich. Other political and religious Groups such as the Muslim Brotherhood believed that the war was not their affair and did not overtly take sides. However, the manner of the appointment of al-Nahas acted as a humiliating reminder to the Egyptians that theirs was still an occupied country and that it was the British who continued to exercise real power.

Back on the front line, the August full moon had begun to wane, but there was still no German attack. Unbeknown to the Allies, Rommel was woefully short of supplies. The fuel and ammunition captured from the British at Tobruk had been all but exhausted in July's unsuccessful attempts to break down Allied resistance. During August, a significant proportion of supplies destined for the Afrika Korps had fallen victim to Allied attacks on German and Italian shipping and to bombing raids on

German transport vehicles but Rommel had been assured by his superiors in Italy that fuel and supplies were on their way, and so, slightly before midnight on the last day of August, 1942, the armed columns of the Afrika Korps slowly rumbled forward.

The Allied Eighth Army had been expecting this advance for weeks and had been in a constant state of readiness to confront it. Divisions from Australia, New Zealand, Canada, India and South Africa as well as contingents of Free French and Greek forces joined with their British Allies to defend the borders of Egypt against a combined German-Italian army seeking to break out of Libya. In the middle of August, a new Commander had been appointed to lead the Eighth Army, General Bernard Montgomery, and from the very beginning he had informed his men that there would be no further retreat, neither was there. By 5th September, the Axis forces had been pushed back with Rommel attributing his defeat to British air supremacy and to the accuracy and firepower of Allied artillery.

Both sides took advantage of another lull in the fighting to regroup, reinforce and rearm. Rommel availed himself of the pause in hostilities to attend to his own health. For some considerable time, he had been suffering from an intestinal complaint as well as from frequent fainting fits and during the last two weeks in October, he travelled to Austria for treatment, not knowing what was to occur in his absence.

At nine-forty pm on 23rd October, 1942, every howitzer, field gun and tank the Eighth Army possessed opened up simultaneously along the whole thirty miles of the British front in a devastating display of firepower not experienced since 1918, dealing the enemy a series of grievous blows while diverting their attention from the infantry advance. Rommel was re-called instantly but by the time he had reached North Africa, the damage had already been done. On 5th November, a further British thrust was to prove decisive and force the Germans to withdraw, fighting a series of rearguard actions as they did so. Three days later, an Anglo-American force commanded by General Dwight Eisenhower landed at the Western end of the Mediterranean, effectively sealing off the German retreat and guaranteeing their surrender six months later.

As the war moved further away from Egypt, the Wafd Government came under threat after detailed allegations were published in 1943 accusing al Nahas of corruption. This caused the Wafd to lose popular support and its Government collapsed a year later to be replaced by a regime led by Ahmed Maher Pasha, brother of al Nahas' predecessor. The Wafd

Party then boycotted the 1945 General Election, which resulted in a sharp swing to the right bringing Mahmud Nuqrushi to power and with him the expectation that the British would finally withdraw from Egypt, as they'd already promised to do from India. Unfortunately for the Egyptians, the British had other ideas.

TERROR IN THE CANAL ZONE

The conclusion of World War Two saw the British Empire in decline, having heroically sacrificed itself in the defeat of one of the most terrifying embodiments of evil ever to threaten the security of the world. To fund its substantial contribution to hostilities, the British Government had mortgaged itself to the point of bankruptcy and the Americans were now holding all the IOU's, which they would continue to call in over succeeding decades. The election of a Labour Government in Britain in 1945 encouraged the Egyptians to believe that the new regime, opposed as it was to the concept of colonialism, would finally remove its troops from their country and in December of that year, Nuqrushi demanded that the 1936 Treaty be renegotiated to secure a total British withdrawal and the return of Sudan to Egyptian rule. Britain was unable to entertain the suggestion of a withdrawal at that time, since the Suez Canal had become essential to the British G.H.Q. Middle East in Cairo, which was faced with the massive logistical task of evacuating British troops from India while at the same time supporting those involved in policing the escalating state of emergency in Palestine.

Once again, Britain's refusal was met with a violent eruption of Anti-British rioting and anarchy in which attacks were made on British citizens and property in all major Egyptian cities. In Cairo, the British Army barracks at Kasr-el-Nil, in what is now Midan Tahrir, was effectively besieged by hoards of frenzied rioters, and, after allowing them to create havoc for the best part of a day, the Egyptian Police finally dispersed the demonstrators causing 140 casualties in the process. Another insurrection in Alexandria claimed the lives of two British Military Policemen, one of whom was decapitated by the insurgents, who then carried his severed head through the streets as a trophy.

After a further round of negotiations, British Prime Minister, Clement Attlee, agreed to remove his troops from all Egyptian cities by 1949 but he could not agree to demands to return Sudan to Egyptian rule. Egyptian nationalists proclaimed "The Unity of the Nile Valley" as a pretext for absorbing Sudan but the British Government had already reached an agreement with Sudanese leaders that Sudan should be an independent state in its own right and this issue was ultimately determined by the newly created United Nations Organisation who ratified Sudan's independence on 1st January 1956.

In the meantime a low-key withdrawal of British military personnel from Egyptian cities was quietly taking place and on 9th February 1947, the Mustapha Barracks in Alexandria was handed over to the Egyptian Army, while the Kasr-el-Nil Barracks in Cairo was vacated a month later. This took place at 5 A.M. amid heavy security to minimise the possibility of an untoward incident. By this time, the Muslim Brotherhood, impatient at the slow rate of progress made in negotiations declared Jihad, holy war, against the British. Even though British Headquarters had now been relocated to Moascar on the outskirts of Ismailiya in the Canal Zone, this did not satisfy the nationalists who continued to demand a complete British withdrawal from Egypt. Their desire was heightened by the establishment of the state of Israel in 1948 and the defeat of the combined Arab armies that followed it. The Egyptians, whose army had taken part in this ill-fated campaign, unfairly blamed the British for bringing about the Jewish state, adding to the anti-British fury that was slowly simmering beneath the surface. This undercurrent of discontent continued to percolate until 8th October, 1951, when the Egyptian Government, led once again by al-Nahas' Wafd Party, unilaterally revoked the 1936 Anglo-Egyptian Treaty and tacitly authorised the Muslim Brotherhood to form "Liberation Battalions" to fight a guerrilla war against the British. In addition to the irregulars assembled and armed by the Muslim Brotherhood, there were also Police Auxiliaries, an armed paramilitary force consisting of a sizeable collection of criminals, cutthroats, sadists and psychopaths whose primary objective was to terrorise and to murder British personnel, regardless of age gender or status. It was rumoured that the Egyptians had swept the gaols to recruit convicted murderers and the criminally insane to serve in the auxiliaries and the atrocities perpetrated by these evil people gave credence to this rumour, as, for the next few years, an undeclared state of war broke out in the Canal Zone.

When news of the unilateral abrogation of the 1936 treaty reached London, Churchill, who had recently been re-elected Prime Minister, was outraged and gave instructions for a plan to be drawn up to re-invade Egypt and enforce the Anglo-Egyptian Treaty. The plan, codenamed "Operation Rodeo," involved troops from the Canal Zone, supported by units from Malta, Libya and Cyprus as well as aircraft and warships. In the end, the plan was never implemented. Instead, the Canal Zone was placed under Martial Law after the Egyptians had blocked food and other supplies from reaching British troops and had forbidden all Egyptian nationals, who made up a workforce of about 70,000 people, from continuing to work in British bases. In December 1951, Egyptian anger was further provoked when Cairo Radio, a vehemently anti-British organ of disinformation, reported that British units had bulldozed fifty Egyptian mud huts to open a road to a water supply. This was only half the truth as was their version of an attack by the British Army on an Egyptian Police Barracks in Ismailiya a month later. By then Cairo Radio and a number of other Arab radio stations were working around the clock, stoking up a constant stream of Anglophobic hatred, which finally boiled over on what was to become known as "Black Saturday." The trouble started when the Police in Cairo mutinied in protest over the attack on their colleagues in Ismailiya, while a Cairene mob rampaged through the streets burning and looting many British – owned buildings and killing anyone they found inside. In all, thirty people were killed, hundreds more were injured and over £50m worth of foreign owned property was destroyed including the Turf Club and Shepheards Hotel, both of which were burned to the ground. The bulldozing of the huts and the attack on the police barracks will be dealt with fully in the following chapter.

Under pressure from the British, who suspected Government involvement in the riots, the King dismissed al-Nahas, a hasty knee-jerk reaction which led to six months of Government instability during which time four Prime Ministers came and went in quick succession until it became clear that the Egyptian ruling classes were no longer capable of fulfilling that role. There followed a coup d'etat in July 1952 by the "Free Officers," a clandestine military group led by General Mohammed Neguib. The new rulers were a mixed collection of idealists whose doctrine embraced a wide range of principles including socialism and pan-Arabism, underpinned by Islam. They sought social revolution, an end to the corrupt monarchy and its incompetent Government as well as the removal of the British presence from their country. Farouk was deposed and sent into exile, while Egypt became a republic ruled by the Revolutionary Command Council set up by senior members of the Free Officers. Amongst their numbers were Anwar Sadat and Gemal Abdul Nasser, who, like many Egyptians their age, had regularly taken to the streets in the 1930's in protest at continued British interference in Egyptian affairs, Nasser having received a minor gun shot wound for his trouble. Now, they were close to putting an end to British influence. For the first two years of military rule, Neguib shared power with his deputy, Nasser, but as time went on, policy disagreements between the two caused a serious rift and in 1954 Nasser superseded Neguib and went on to lead Egypt into a new era of international prominence.

Although, the 1936 Anglo-Egyptian treaty was due to expire in 1956, by the early 1950's, following advances in the fields of aviation and nuclear weaponry, the strategic and commercial importance of the Suez Canal had begun to recede. Also, the sustained harassment by Egyptian irregulars and, indeed, the all-pervading hatred and antagonism that had been cultivated against the British, made their continued presence in the Canal Zone untenable. So, in October 1954, Britain agreed to the gradual withdrawal of its troops but even after this agreement had been concluded, terrorists maintained their murderous attacks on British Servicemen right up until 1956 when the very last of them was preparing to depart.

Even before Al Nahas abrogated the 1936 treaty, life for a British serviceman in Egypt was extremely risky and it was a common occurrence for stones to be hurled at passing British vehicles or for the odd pot shot to be taken at a British sentry, often with fatal consequences but when the Egyptian Government gave the Muslim Brotherhood and the Auxiliaries carte blanche to attack all British personnel and installations, the gloves came off with a vengeance. The armed conflict that later became known as the Suez Canal Zone Emergency lasted from 1951 until 1954 and was at its most intense between October 1951 and June 1952. During this period, it has been estimated that British service personnel were being killed at the rate of five a week, although there is still considerable doubt as to the precise number of fatalities suffered and the exact number who actually died as the result of terrorist activity. Many are shown as having died through illness or accident, though those who were there have disputed the stated causes of many of those "accidental" deaths. The main reason for this conflicting evidence is the reluctance of successive British Governments to reveal the true facts or indeed make any admission at all of what actually occurred. They even refused to issue a campaign medal until fifty years after the event, much to the chagrin and distress of those who served and of the relatives of those who died.

What follows is an attempt to highlight the most important events during the most critical period of the Emergency, that is, from October 1951 through to February 1952. While I have tried to piece together the facts, accounts have varied from one source to another and there have been contradictions in dates, times and even locations. It is also possible, due to the huge number of incidents that took place over that period that I might have inadvertently mistaken one confrontation for another. If this proves to be the case, I trust that those who were there and who know better will forgive me.

As stated earlier, the Cairo Government started to incite trouble in the Canal Zone by blockading the area, sponsoring anti-British demonstrations and inflammatory articles in the local press while all the time Radio Cairo continued to pump out its Anglophobic bile. After a series of terrorist attacks and provocation, the British withdrew from all Egyptian cities in the Canal Zone and, for their own safety, confined the troops to their bases, most of which were situated in and around Ismailiya. The Egyptians then ramped up the violence, with increased rioting, sniping at sentries, stabbings, throat slitting, overturning and burning of military vehicles and armed attacks on military convoys, especially those travelling at night along the road between Suez and Ismailiya . The terrorists also planted bombs and landmines on highways used by the British and stretched wires across roads at head height in the hope of decapitating dispatch riders or the drivers of jeeps or Land Rovers. Most of these vehicles were driven with their windshields down to facilitate the return of fire on attackers and a piece of angling iron had to be welded to each bonnet to prevent the decapitation of the driver. Any unescorted military vehicle being driven through Ismailiya was likely to be stoned by organised mobs, fired upon by snipers or attacked with grenades, while those being driven outside of town could be ambushed or run off the road by Egyptian vehicles and its occupants abducted and murdered. There were many attempts at both as Egyptian terrorists used vehicles as ram-raid weapons on a daily basis and the Royal Army Service Corps alone lost more than 50 drivers as a result of such attacks.

A week after Al-Nahas' abrogation of the 1936 treaty, his Government initiated the first of a series of riots in Ismailiya. It started very early in the morning when a crowd of 'students' attacked British military living quarters at Arishia, four miles from the base at Moascar. People first became nervous when a large group of Egyptians disembarked from the Cairo train at the local station. This particular train was not scheduled to stop until it reached Ismailiya, confirming suspicions that the Egyptian authorities had instigated what followed and had made sure it occurred after the service men had left for their daily duties at Moascar. The crowd swept through the settlement screaming anti-British slogans, looting, burning and destroying the contents of the blocks of flats occupied by British families. Women and children were threatened and terrorised but none was harmed or physically attacked. The purpose of this stage-managed mayhem appeared to be harassment rather than injury and a warning to the British Authorities that service families were vulnerable. Egyptian Police turned up during the riot but, rather than come to the aid of the threatened families, they either stood around and watched or actively participated in the looting and burning of their personal effects. The rioters broke into every single home bawling out threats and obscenities while brandishing wooden clubs and other makeshift weapons. They stripped the apartments bare, stealing anything they deemed to be of value and burning the rest, be it furniture, clothing or other belongings on large bonfires they had built in the street. This carried on until late in the afternoon when British Troops arrived, dispersed the mob and detained about two hundred of the ringleaders.

Elsewhere in Ismailiya, the rioting was worse. Just after 8 A.M., a mob of Egyptians emerged from the main railway station and held what appeared to be an impromptu demonstration in the square outside. As a large crowd started to gather, several Cairo-based agitators whipped them up into an anti-British frenzy and they started to overturn British cars and trucks, loot their contents and set them ablaze. A number of service families had been in town shopping for groceries when the trouble started and most of them managed to return home before the situation deteriorated.

Unfortunately a group of about thirty women and children had been unable to get clear of the area but they managed to conceal themselves in the NAAFI store on the other side of the square, where they were protected by a small group of military police.

The instigators then led an assault on the NAAFI, forced their way in and started looting the contents while the women and children cowered in a recess at the rear of the building. By now a series of similarly staged riots had broken out all over Ismailiya and the Lancashire Fusiliers were sent in to restore order. By the time the troops arrived, the square in which the NAAFI building was situated had filled with rioters who were dancing around an inferno of burning buses, cars and army lorries and hurling stones and bottles at any European unwise or unfortunate enough to show their faces. As soon as they saw the army, the rioters turned their fury on them and proceeded to pelt them with stones and bottles, while the soldiers advanced towards them on foot. The NAAFI building had now been torched and was swarming with Egyptians who were stealing everything in sight. The first priority for the army was to locate and rescue the women and children. Several shots were fired in the air, which drove the crowds back and enabled a number of soldiers to gain access to the stricken building, locate the families and escort them through the hostile crowd and the constant hail of missiles to the safety of waiting vehicles.

By now, many of the rioters were drunk with the whiskey they had stolen from the NAAFI and emboldened by the alcohol, they made a renewed attack upon the soldiers with another avalanche of rocks and bottles. Considerably outnumbered and unwilling to fire on unarmed civilians, the second lieutenant in charge radioed for assistance and, with the crowd still growing in numbers, ordered several more rounds to be fired into the air to drive back the drunken horde. When they heard the shots, the remaining Egyptians still looting the NAAFI, including one or two Egyptian policemen, panicked and ran into the street where, still clutching their contraband, they merged into the baying mob and made good their escape. Reinforcements arrived soon afterwards dispersing the crowd by aiming a volley of automatic fire over their heads.

At this point, a large party of Egyptian police entered the square but these people had no interest in restoring public order. Instead, they tried to persuade the troop commanders to exercise restraint and allow the rioters to carry on with what they were doing. They did not seem to care that the mob had already destroyed a considerable number of vehicles, endangered the lives of women and children, burned the NAAFI while looting £30,000 worth of goods and at that precise moment, was trying to break into a block of British married quarters on the opposite side of the square. All over town, the army was confronting and endeavouring to pacify angry mobs and drive them back in the direction of Arab Town, the Egyptian quarter, from which most of them had originally emerged. Extremists were still trying to stir up trouble and the army set up cordons at strategic points to contain it. This situation lasted well into the night and a 7 o'clock curfew was imposed on Arab Town for the following two nights. The army remained in control of Ismailiya for another two days until they were sure that the trouble had completely died down before returning to their bases. For many months afterwards, Ismailiya was to become a riot-torn battleground on which numerous lives were lost on both sides of the conflict.

Enclaves of terrorists began to install themselves in towns and villages all over the Canal Zone and attacks on service personnel, property and vehicles intensified by the day. A large contingent of the Egyptian Army positioned itself five miles from the Canal Zone perimeter, presumably as a provocative measure but they knew they could not win an all out battle with the British and they kept their distance. Further Egyptian forces moved into the Delta and Alexandria, while another division warily observed British activities from the safety of Southern Sinai. With the situation deteriorating rapidly, the 3rd Infantry Division and the 16th Independent Parachute Brigade were flown in bringing troop numbers in the Canal Zone up to 80,000.

Early in November 1951, a meeting of the Muslim Brotherhood took place at a safe house in the Egyptian Quarter of Ismailiya at which Mohammed Farghally, the local Brotherhood leader, informed a select gathering of prominent agitators and terrorists of a change in policy by their masters in Cairo. From now on, there would be no more incidents, stage-managed riots or attacks on service families, particularly in towns. The object of such attacks had been to provoke acts of retaliation from the British forces and, as there had been none up until then, the propaganda machine in Cairo was having difficulties in explaining the activities of their "freedom brigades," since, even to the most gullible of Egyptians, stories of gratuitous intimidation of British women and children were not considered to be particularly heroic. Later that month, 1200 service families were either evacuated to safe areas or returned to England as the

Egyptian police and the so-called auxiliaries stepped up their activities. In spite of the diktat of the Brotherhood leadership in Cairo, rioting and civil disturbance were to become daily occurrences, especially in Ismailiya.

While many Egyptian workers had left the Canal Zone, there was still a sizeable civilian population living in places such as Ismailiya, Suez and Port Said and the police force remained to "keep order." This of course was complete fabrication. The role of the police was to act as an armed hostile force operating under the noses of the British while coordinating and taking part in guerrilla warfare and other terrorist activities. The role of the auxiliaries was considerably more inhuman and sadistic as British servicemen soon discovered to their cost. A British Major in charge of a small group of foreign workers disappeared while carrying out mosquito spraying for the United Nations. His body was later found in the desert, buried up to his neck in sand with his testicles sewn into his mouth. There were also deep knife and machete wounds on other sensitive parts of his torso, which, as the state of emergency continued, became the hallmark of the auxiliaries. Any servicemen unfortunate enough to be taken alive by these people usually died of torture and mutilation at their hands. Several days after the murder of the major, two British squaddies in a NAAFI truck were ambushed, abducted and tortured to death. Military Police later recovered their badly mutilated bodies from the murky waters of the Sweetwater Canal.

The Sweetwater Canal had been excavated originally to provide drinking water for labourers working on the Suez Canal. By the time of the emergency, it had been neglected to the degree that it resembled an open sewer and no British soldier would go near it for fear of contracting a disease. It also acquired a more sinister reputation as a receptacle for the mutilated remains of British servicemen who had been sadistically murdered by the auxiliaries. Sworn statements exist attesting to many such cases. On 18th November 1951, six unarmed British Servicemen were abducted by Egyptian Auxiliaries. Their bodies were later found in the Sweetwater Canal. Two had had their fingers and legs chopped off with blunt instruments, probably shovels, while the other four had had their testicles severed and sewn into their mouths. A number of similar incidents occurred around this time including the ambush and murder of a British officer, Major Rose, Deputy Commander of the Royal Engineers and eight Mauritian soldiers who had been travelling along the coast road from Port Tewfiq. A Post Mortem report stated that the bodies of the

Mauritians had been mutilated after death by being struck with blunt and sharp instruments. The Egyptian police delivered the body of Major Rose to a military hospital some time later. He had been brutally murdered but the extent of his injuries had been so horrific that, even after fifty years, no service journal or website had ever felt able to publish details. In 2004, however, the post Mortem report was published in full in a book by Canal Zone veteran Douglas Findlay entitled "White Knees, Brown Knees." It does not make pleasant reading.

The Cairo propaganda machine was hard-pressed to manufacture any political capital out of incidents such as these but it tried. For example, one Saturday evening, an ambulance brought three British soldiers suffering from multiple knife wounds to the Medical Reception Centre at Moascar. One was found to be dead on arrival, another died later of his wounds and the third man was said to have been "critical." An account of the incident in the Egyptian press stated that it had been a *savage attack by British troops who fired at three Egyptian children and kidnapped them.* The three soldiers had been unarmed and off duty at the time.

In another incident, British troops searched the village of El Hammada for weapons but, having been forewarned of the search, the Egyptian authorities dramatically increased police numbers in the village in order to oppose the British forces and create an incident. The police fired on the troops as soon as they were in range and in the resulting engagement, five Egyptians were shot dead before the rest of them surrendered. Five terrorist suspects were subsequently arrested and a cache of weapons including 155 rifles, two Sten guns, three pistols and several boxes of ammunition were confiscated. Before the search was due to begin, a Valetta aircraft equipped with a loud hailer flew over the village to explain to the inhabitants what was due to happen. As a warning, six Meteor jets followed in the wake of the Valetta but no aircraft fired on or bombed the village. This differed significantly from the version of events broadcast by Cairo Radio who reported that sixty jets flew over the village, strafing and bombing indiscriminately and "*a barrage of bombs fell on the houses and police buildings.*" The British Ambassador later sent a strongly worded note after "Al Misri," the leading Cairo newspaper had offered a £100 reward to any Egyptian who killed a British officer.

A series of unprovoked attacks by Egyptian police on military ambulances drew another such note accusing them of deliberately murdering British troops. Later, there was a raid by a mob of auxiliaries on the military hospital at El Ballah, where they opened up with automatic gunfire on areas where sick and wounded service personnel were being treated. The terrorists also shot and wounded a number of doctors and nurses as they were leaving the hospital building before being driven off by sentries. A few days later, a group of terrorists ambushed a patrol of Cameron Highlanders as they were carrying out reconnaissance on a road outside Tel El Kebir, killing an officer and a private and wounding three others. Under fire from several directions, the Highlanders withdrew to a roadblock where they were joined by a detachment from the Brigade of Guards. In the ensuing firefight, a number of terrorists were killed and wounded without further British losses.

By the time the Egyptian press had reported the story, it had been distorted beyond all recognition. One editorial carried the words, *"Thousands of soldiers armed to the teeth, hundreds of tanks and armoured cars, dozens of field guns and an incalculable number of weapons of destruction were used against the village of Tel El Kebir. The Egyptian people armed only with faith in the justice of their causes (sic) inflicted on the British heavier losses than they sustained in any battle during the last war except at Dunkirk,"*

The fiction continued by citing the number of British casualties as one hundred and twenty as opposed to the truth of two killed and three wounded. Another fabricated incident, one of many reported in Cairo newspapers, accused British authorities of executing seven of the terrorists captured at Tel El Kebir and mutilating their bodies by throwing them to the dogs.

THE EMPIRE STRIKES BACK –
CLEANING OUT THE RATS NESTS

Up until the end of November 1951, British troops had only been allowed to use minimum force when attacked by terrorists and by then their patience, restraint and self-control had been all but exhausted. They had been ambushed, shot at, knifed and stoned. They had also buried the butchered remains of comrades who had been tortured to death by the hated auxiliaries. The troops felt that retaliation was long overdue and in December 1951, the order finally came.

Since the start of the emergency, terrorists had systematically targeted the water filtration plants near Suez, which provided much of the drinking water consumed by British personnel in the southern sector of the Canal Zone. Water had to be collected from the plants in tankers and transported to the various British bases and hospitals, many of which were situated in the desert. Water convoys going to and from these filtration plants were considered soft targets and were frequently fired upon by the terrorists who had occupied some houses, mud huts and disused buildings overlooking the road so that after a few weeks, only armoured vehicles could approach the plants safely. This made it extremely difficult to ferry food and provisions to the troops who were guarding and maintaining these establishments. Local commanders had been trying to persuade the Egyptian governor of Suez and the police to provide a safe thoroughfare for British vehicles but after a further series of attacks on British transport vehicles, there was no indication that a negotiated settlement would be reached. Faced with a critical water shortage – the British Military Hospital in Suez had run out of drinking water the previous evening – and increasing armed attacks on water convoys, the decision was taken to establish a new direct route to the plants and to destroy any building close to it that might be used as cover by terrorists. The Egyptians were given fair warning of the British intentions and compensation was paid to the Egyptian Government in advance for the buildings that would have to be demolished. The only question that remained was how much armed resistance to expect and how it should be dealt with.

The main objective was to protect the engineers involved in the demolition and road building and as the completion of this work was now considered to be critical, maximum cover would be provided and any Egyptian aggression would be dealt with in kind. And so, as the sun rose on the western outskirts of the town of Suez, men from the 16th Independent Parachute Brigade were taking up positions in the narrow alleyways while on the rooftops, their comrades pointed Bren guns, machine guns and heavy trench mortars at anything that might constitute a threat. On the desert road outside of town a convoy of sand-coloured tanks and bulldozers waited impatiently for the order to move while 2000 infantrymen from the Buffs and Royal Sussex Regiments were set to follow them in. Any Egyptians who were looking for a fight today were guaranteed to get one but, with Auster spotter planes and Meteor jets buzzing overhead, the police, auxiliaries and other Egyptian irregulars quietly abandoned their erstwhile secure positions and slunk away in twos and threes so that, when the British arrived with their bulldozers, cranes and tanks, they found the whole complex of buildings deserted.

Before the demolition work could start, a thorough search was made of the empty houses, which revealed a large quantity of explosives and ammunition as well as a sizeable cache of grenades, bombs and a Browning automatic rifle. During the day, as work was progressing, a terrorist threw a bomb at one of the filtration plants, blowing a gaping hole in one of the storage tanks and flooding the installation. As darkness fell, a mob of Egyptians started to throw rocks at sentries on guard duty but they dispersed after a few rounds were fired over their heads. While the exercise was hailed as a success by the British authorities, Cairo Radio and the Egyptian press distorted the facts and milked the incident for all it was worth. No mention was made of the generous compensation paid to the Government for distribution to those who had lost their homes but that was explained later when it was learned that none of the money had actually found its way to those for whom it had been intended and it probably ended up in the pocket of a corrupt Government Minister or some similarly influential member of the burgeoning Egyptian kleptocracy. However, many of the British soldiers involved in this exercise were genuinely disappointed that they had not been able to engage the enemy. After months of being on the receiving end of ambushes, attacks, abductions and murder, they felt cheated of an opportunity to administer some retribution but their time would come – and soon.

During the remainder of December news had been filtering through that the Egyptians had reinforced their "Liberation Battalions" operating in the vicinity of Ismailiya with a number of irregulars and auxiliaries from the Delta area. At one minute past midnight on January 1st 1952, they made their presence known with a series of synchronised attacks on a number of British positions around Ismailiya. One such assault on the Royal Lincolnshire Regiment lasted over four hours during which a significant number of casualties were inflicted on the attackers. Every night from then on, there were intermittent outbreaks of automatic gunfire and explosions directed against British positions but in every case the Egyptians were beaten off. On the night of 13th January, several heavy engagements were taking place in Ismailiya and the sound of gunfire could be heard four miles away in Moascar. A group of terrorists installed themselves in the minaret of a mosque using it as a vantage point from which they rained gunfire and explosives on the troops below. Three months into the emergency, this had become a familiar strategy of Egyptian terrorists, who were always seeking to portray themselves as victims rather than aggressors. This time they were trying to provoke the British to respond with heavy weapons, inflict severe damage on the mosque and create an international incident that would reverberate throughout the Islamic world and bring down the wrath of the entire Middle East upon the heads of the British. Fortunately, nobody took the bait and the terrorists were gradually picked off by sniper fire. This did not prevent them from using the same ploy again and again but the mosque remained intact.

By the third week in January, 33 British soldiers, many of whom were unarmed and off duty, had been killed in ambush or by sniper fire. In one such incident, on 24th January 1952, two military policemen drew up in a Land Rover outside the police station in Ismailiya where they had been required to go on police business. On being invited to enter the compound, they were then shot dead in a cynical and unprovoked attack. Before that, in November 1951, before Ismailiya had been declared unsafe, two British officers had been out shopping with their families when the group was fired upon from the same police station. The men managed to scramble their families to the safety of a nearby house but both received bullet wounds while doing so. They took cover under a nearby pile of stones and, being pinned down by persistent gunfire, they had no option but to remain where they were. When the families were rescued next morning by an armed patrol, there was no sign of the officers. Their bodies were found later, some distance away. They had been badly beaten and riddled with bullets.

After more serious clashes between the army and the Egyptian police, General Sir George Erskine, the British General Officer Commanding gave the order for a pre-emptive strike on the police barracks in Ismailiya to disarm the police. This complex of office buildings and barrack blocks had been the epicentre of armed insurrection against British forces since the start of the Emergency and had served as a base for a large contingent of auxiliaries and other paramilitaries who regularly carried out armed raids against British troops and installations. The police headquarters was an extensive set of buildings sprawling across an entire city block and consisted of two main compounds, the Bureau Sanitaire, which comprised two large, two-storey buildings and five wooden barrack blocks enclosed within a boundary wall, and the Caracol, a large administration block further down the street.

On the afternoon of 24th January, 1952, Brigadier Exham, Commander of the Third Infantry Brigade informed his senior officers that "Operation Eagle," the disarming of the Ismailiya police and militia, would take place at dawn the following day. A strict security blackout was imposed and information would only be dispensed on a "need to know basis" until the operation was imminent. Many of the troops based around Ismailiya, who were not involved in the action, had no idea what was happening until it was all over. Unfortunately, the security blackout did not apply to the Egyptians who had been well aware of the attack for some weeks due to their efficient "intelligence" network operating inside most of the British camps.

In defiance of the edict from Cairo banning them from working on British bases, local labourers collected the refuse from each of these establishments, took it away and, before disposing of it, sifted through the bags for any "binned" documentation, such as Company Part 1 Orders, which might provide them with clues as to what the British were planning. From scanning these papers, Egyptian workers knew exactly who would be on guard duty at any base on any particular night. They knew when supplies were being delivered, when patrols were going out and what their routes and objectives would be. When this information started to be broadcast on Cairo Radio, orders were given that all rubbish should be burned in future but that did not put an end to Egyptian "espionage."

There were Egyptians on many bases, pushing brooms and washing laundry, while the NAAFI employed a considerable number of assorted Middle Eastern nationals. British officers were often betrayed by their own arrogance, speaking openly in front of their Arab barbers, clearly unaware that the "ignorant wogs" were fluent in English and would convey everything they had heard to Egyptian terrorists, which was why, when British troops drew up outside the police complex at dawn on 25th January, the police were waiting for them.

The Egyptian military in Cairo ordered the Ismailiya police to resist any armed assault by British forces at all costs and had drawn up a battle plan to defend the complex. On the day, the defence strategy would be orchestrated by a few senior police officers from the safety of the Ismailiya Hotel, some distance from the action. Even before the planned assault on the police barracks had been formulated, the Egyptians had reinforced the police strength with large numbers of army-trained irregulars, who had been brought into Ismailiya surreptitiously by train over a period of many months. It was calculated afterwards, that by the time the British attacked, there were 600 auxiliaries and paramilitaries barricaded in the Bureau Sanitaire and another 340, along with 60 regular police officers, occupying defensive positions inside the Caracol. While British security had been inept in its attempts to prevent the Egyptians from determining General Erskine's intentions, its success in excluding its own side from the secret was embarrassingly effective, as was demonstrated when an incident outside the police headquarters the night before the attack threatened to expose the whole operation.

On the night of 24th January, a call went out to all British patrols in the area of Ismailiya ordering them to head for the police station. Earlier that evening, as mentioned on the previous page, two military police officers had been shot dead by Egyptian Police and the vehicle containing the bodies had been left in the courtyard of the Police compound in full view from the road, a blatant act of provocation. Within an hour, a number of British armoured cars, jeeps and other vehicles had assembled in the street outside the padlocked main gates. The British ordered their men to park their vehicles away from the gates on the opposite side of the road but to keep their guns aimed at the barracks. Some time later, a car containing a loud hailer and some senior British officers arrived and asked for the officer in charge of the police compound to show himself. This was answered by a barrage of Egyptian invective, which translated loosely into something like, *"Come on if you think you're hard enough."*

Shortly afterwards, the British contingent was enlarged by the arrival of a number of tanks from the 4th Royal Tank Regiment, more armoured cars and several trucks full of infantrymen, while the senior British officers continued their efforts to persuade the Egyptians to release the bodies of the dead military policemen and their vehicle but without success. The British continued their vigil outside the Police station until first light when things started to happen and General Erskine's troops started to arrive. Many of these had been unaware of events that had occurred the previous evening and throughout the night.

At 6.20 A.M., a broadcasting van drew up outside the Bureau Sanitaire and, using a Centurion tank as cover, informed those within the compound to surrender but there was no response. This proved to be a foolhardy reaction. By the time the broadcasting van had taken its position by the gates, the entire police compound had been surrounded and cordoned off, Arab Town had been completely sealed off from the rest of Ismailiya to prevent reinforcements from reaching the police, while several more tanks and considerably more troop carriers, armoured cars and infantrymen had taken cover in the neighbouring streets, waiting for the order to move. Meanwhile, over at the Caracol, a similar force was assembling on the banks of the Sweet Water Canal, where some were observed from a spotter plane digging trenches and preparing firing positions.

A second broadcast was made outside the Bureau Sanitaire, during which, much activity could be seen through the railings as policemen and auxiliaries took up defensive positions on rooftops, behind wire entanglements and in the fortified trenches they had dug in the gardens a week or so before, when they had first been alerted to the likelihood that they would be attacked. From the cover of their vehicles, the troops could see clearly that their adversaries' positions had been heavily sandbagged and well prepared and that large quantities of ammunition were being passed out to the defenders while they waited for the British to make their move.

As there had been no reply to the second call to surrender, a Centurion tank pushed down the main gate, demolished part of the perimeter wall and came to a halt just inside the compound, effectively blocking the main entrance before a third message was broadcast. This time, several trigger-happy police defenders loosed off a few rounds from their fortified positions while the British continued to hold their fire. After another fifteen minutes, it was clear that the police were not going to respond to further broadcasts so the Centurion tank at the main gate fired a blank warning shot into the compound provoking a sustained outburst of fire from police positions, which was returned with gusto by troops from the Royal Tank Corps and the Lancashire Fusiliers. In the meantime, teams of snipers, who had taken up positions on the roof of a building behind the compound, began picking off their Egyptian counterparts on the roofs and upper floors of the administration blocks until these had been cleared. Then the Centurion tank at the gate fired two live high explosive shells at the building immediately facing it drawing volley upon volley of rifle and automatic fire in return as the infantry broke cover and took up positions all around the perimeter wall. An officer from the Lancashire Regiment tried to attach a towline to the Military Police Land Rover inside the compound but Egyptian police on the roof shot him down. After fifteen minutes of sustained gunfire, the British were ordered to cease firing and, when another broadcast was made and ignored, hostilities were resumed. After a total of five broadcasts had been made, it was obvious to all concerned that conciliation had never been an option and orders were given to enter the complex and disarm the occupants "using only as much force as was required."

At 8.35 A.M., the infantry moved in towards the main buildings under a smokescreen and continuous volleys of covering fire from their comrades. Several soldiers were killed and wounded as they broke cover. A series of actions then took place simultaneously as each of the buildings occupied by armed police came under attack but the police were securely installed and resisted stubbornly as they came under increasingly heavy fire. Tanks fired a number of rounds at fortified positions, while a nest of

Egyptian snipers on the roof of the main Bureau Sanitaire building was taken out by a grenade attack as the police started to take heavy casualties.

Fighting had also broken out at the Caracol as negotiations for a police withdrawal broke down and a company of Lancashire Fusiliers, three tanks and three armoured cars advanced towards the main building. A search party had been sent to look for Colonel Malik, the Eyptian army liaison officer with British forces. He was finally located at the home of an Egyptian general who he been trying to persuade to accompany him to the Caracol to negotiate a peaceful settlement. Unfortunately the general refused to leave his house unless someone called a halt to the shooting but this was easier said than done, as a full-scale battle was now raging at the Bureau Sanitaire and shots were being exchanged at the Caracol. Shortly afterwards, a number of Egyptian army officers arrived outside the Caracol building but none of them was inclined to persuade the police to surrender. In the end, the British ordered a tank to fire a blank round at the building as a warning but this had the same effect as the one fired earlier at the Bureau Sanitaire and shooting broke out in earnest.

At this stage, a message was received that the Egyptian general had no intention of interceding even though he was told that unless he did so, the buildings would be blasted with tank and artillery fire, there would be great loss of life but, with his help, this could still be avoided but he remained unconvinced and was clearly aware of the "No Surrender" order issued to the police from their superiors in Cairo. By now, armed Egyptian irregulars and auxiliaries were massing in Arab Town and a detachment of the East Lancashire Regiment was sent to engage them and keep them away from the police complex. Earlier, a number of auxiliaries had been detained just beyond the military cordon in a secluded patch of open space known as Stalio's Gardens and a cache of weapons had been recovered.

Meanwhile, the troops at the Bureau Sanitaire had met with some success and had cleared a number of the buildings, although the main two-storey block was still occupied by armed auxiliaries, as was the upper floor of the second building. Everywhere else in the compound, the police were beginning to surrender and were emerging from cover with their hands above their heads but this had come at a price. The Lancashire Regiment had taken casualties, one officer and three other ranks having been killed and a further ten other ranks wounded. The Commanding Officer decided to withdraw the Lancashire's at this juncture to avoid further loss of British life, and decided to dislodge the remaining incumbents with tank and artillery fire. A number of high explosive rounds were then fired at the remaining blocks to deter further opposition and the Lancashire's were sent in again, fighting their way to the upper floors, meeting and taking out isolated pockets of resistance on the way. By 11 o'clock, the battle of the Bureau Sanitaire was over and prisoners were being taken to holding facilities in nearby French Square before being transported to a camp at Lake Timsah where they were held as prisoners of war.

Back at the Caracol, troops had been withdrawn temporarily but negotiations had once more broken down and the order was given to bombard this building, too, with tank and heavy weapons until the insurgents surrendered. As the apparently shell-shocked and bemused survivors finally stumbled from the battle-scarred building, it had been intended to separate the genuine police from the auxiliaries and incarcerate the latter for the remainder of the Emergency but this did not prove to be possible as all those who surrendered were wearing police uniform. When British soldiers began searching the building for weapons afterwards, they found large quantities of Djellabahs and other discarded civilian clothing showing that the auxiliaries had hurriedly changed into police uniform before giving themselves up and that most of them were neither shell-shocked nor bemused. By the early afternoon, the entire compound had been cleared of Egyptians and a huge arsenal of arms and ammunition was removed, including a number of American-made Garrard and Thompson sub-machine guns. This should come as no surprise as the Americans had a long history of arming "freedom fighters" particularly in countries occupied by the British and French.

The British had been taken aback by the ferocity of the resistance offered by the Egyptians, who, up until then had not been considered to be the best fighting force in the world and had earned a reputation for running away in the face of anything other than feeble opposition. On the other hand, as they were surrounded, their only options were either to fight or give in and their orders from Cairo had been quite clear on that issue. The British viewed the Egyptian resistance as a brave but futile exercise that ultimately achieved an unnecessarily high number of police casualties and a golden propaganda opportunity for Cairo radio and the Egyptian press, which they seized with both hands.

As stated earlier, news of the incident provoked the series of riots in Cairo known as "Black Saturday," when a great deal of foreign owned property was destroyed and around thirty Europeans, mostly British, were murdered and mutilated by the mob. After this incident, General Erskine, telephoned Al Nahas, the Egyptian Prime Minister, and informed him that if any further rioting took place, the British army would be in Cairo within the hour. When told that the Egyptian army would oppose any such action, Erskine tersely revised his timescale to an hour and ten minutes.

Accounts vary as to the extent of Egyptian casualties incurred during this engagement. One source gave these as forty-one dead, seventy-three wounded and 886 taken prisoner but these figures are disputed by other sources, some of which have reported Egyptian deaths to have been as high as 169. Egyptian survivors of the incident were treated as heroes on their return to Cairo. They are still revered as such today and every year, the anniversaries of the "Battle of Ismailiya" and "Black Saturday" are celebrated in Egypt by the release of doves and treated as a great military victory, while successive British Governments continue to behave as though neither incident had ever occurred.

THE MURDER OF SISTER ANTHONY

"A single death is a tragedy. A million deaths is a statistic." These cynical words uttered by Josef Stalin, who was responsible for many such statistics, epitomize the pitiless murder of Sister Anthony. For if one death could encapsulate the callous brutality of the terrorist campaign being carried out in Egypt at this time, then it must surely be this sacrilegious act. Sister Anthony, christened Bridget Anne Timbers, was born in New York in 1900, the daughter of Irish-Canadian parents. She was brought up in California before being sent to complete her education in Belgium. After attending teacher-training college in England she took up her first teaching appointment at the Sisters of Charity School for Deaf Children in Tollcross, Glasgow, where she proved to be a highly valued and popular member of staff. A deeply spiritual woman, she subsequently trained for holy orders at the Convent of St. Vincent de Paul, Mill Hill, London where she received the habit in 1926 before returning to Tollcross, to teach for a further four years.

While she was at Mill Hill, she had volunteered for missionary service abroad and in 1930, she was sent to St. Vincent's Convent, Ismailiya where she taught children from the British military garrison at Moascar but her stay was cut short by ill health and she returned to Mill Hill where she remained throughout the Second World War. In 1947, she went back to St. Vincent's Convent where she stayed until her untimely death in January 1952.

On the afternoon of 19th January 1952, a bomb was thrown at a military checkpoint close to a bridge across the Sweetwater Canal. Two soldiers were killed and several others were seriously wounded. Considerable numbers of Egyptian civilians were also caught in the blast, many suffering horrific injuries. As soon as the explosion had died down and the smoke had started to clear, the staccato rattle of automatic weaponry broke out as terrorists opened fire on the checkpoint from a number of directions to hinder the treatment and evacuation of the injured, both military and civilian. Reinforcements soon arrived on the scene and proceeded to inflict heavy casualties on the terrorists, who started to withdraw to more secure positions. Seeking to continue hostilities, some of them carrying bombs and rifles broke into the nearby convent and found their way to an upper level from which they opened fire on the troops below. With a pitched battle going on in the street outside and a group of terrorists upstairs, the first priority of the nuns was to keep the children as far from harm as possible so they took them to a large room in the basement where they all sang loudly for the remainder of the afternoon to drown out the noise of the gun fire.

In the meantime, in a singularly selfless act of courage, Sister Anthony and her colleague Sister Morin went to confront the terrorists to ask them to leave what was, after all, a place of worship, whereupon a terrorist shot her at point blank range killing her instantly but leaving Sister Morin unharmed. There are conflicting accounts of the murder, some of which indicate that the terrorists had entered the convent specifically to kill Sister Anthony and there is anecdotal evidence to support this. Leaving aside the armed conflict and its attendant anti-British race hate, Egypt has a long history of persecution of Christians and Ismailiya, being the birthplace of Al-Banna, founder of the Muslim Brotherhood, was a hotbed of what was later to become Islamofascism. Discrimination and violence against Christians was commonplace in this part of the world and the life of Sister Anthony, a foreigner and an unbeliever clearly had no value to the barbarians who murdered her. The fact that Sister Anthony taught children from the British garrison in Moascar also made her a likely terrorist target but other sisters taught them, too and there is no record that any of them was murdered. Sister Anthony also helped and ministered to people of all faiths and nationalities including Egyptian Muslims but who can understand the twisted minds of terrorists?

One account of the murder refers to two gunmen, separate from the rest, who entered the convent by way of a rear door, asked the victim whether she was Sister Anthony and when she confirmed this, they shot her. This contradicts Sister Morin's account but, when interviewed afterwards, the Mother Superior reinforced the view that Sister Anthony had been singled out. "I think a terrorist has been looking for Sister Anthony because everyone knew how much she had done for the British for many years," she said. After the crime, other terrorists were heard to say things like "The job is done," "It's time we got her" and "We've got the daughter of a dog." This would clearly indicate that the act was premeditated. It is also possible that the two sets of terrorists were unconnected but this is doubtful. A more likely explanation was that the murder was an opportunistic act, committed on impulse by religious bigots, who knew that Sister Anthony had been earmarked as a potential target for assassination.

Sister Anthony was given a military funeral, attended by hundreds of people of all races and creeds including General Sir George Erskine and, as she was lowered into her grave in the British Garrison Cemetery, buglers sounded the last post. Less than a week later, the British army launched their attack on the police barracks and it would be naïve to suggest that these two events were unconnected.

PERFIDIOUS ALBION

There was no noticeable change in the nature or frequency of attacks on British troops after the assault on the Ismailiya police barracks. Vehicles were still being ambushed, bomb outrages continued to target British and Egyptians alike, bases were being raided and British personnel were still being abducted, murdered and mutilated. In spite of guards being posted on all military camps and installations, the amount of equipment and personal possessions being stolen by the Egyptians was staggering and probably fuelled an entire alternative economy amongst the Canal Zone's indigenous population. Egyptians employed in military bases proved to be shrewd and cunning thieves, pilfering just about anything they could lay hands on, concealing it about their persons and calmly walking it past the sentries at the conclusion of their shifts. All manner of things went missing like clothes, boots, knives and forks, in fact anything that could be rapidly lifted and slipped into a pocket or a fold in a djellabia. When it got dark, their paramilitary comrades would cut through the perimeter fences, sneak into the compound and make off with everything they could carry, though primarily, they were after guns, explosives and ammunition. Many camps were penetrated in this way every night with the episode invariably ending in a shoot-out claiming casualties on both sides.

One curious feature of the entire campaign is the conspiracy of silence that surrounded it, one, which has continued right up to the present day. Succeeding British Governments have been reluctant to disclose the seriousness of the situation or the danger in which British troops and their dependants had been placed. During the Emergency, security was so tight that the only way anyone would know about an incident was by being directly involved in it or by being stationed at a base where it had occurred. This was odd. "Canal Zone News" a publication produced by and for the information of servicemen stationed in the Zone ran for six months during the latter part of 1951 into 1952 but only made passing reference to attacks and no mention at all of the atrocities perpetrated by the Egyptian irregulars. For example, an edition dated 7th February 1952 gives maximum coverage to the death of King George VI yet makes no allusion at all to the 26 servicemen who were killed during the preceding month. As a matter of policy, "Canal Zone News" minimised the extent of terrorist activity and deleted all reference to anything other than minor British casualties.

The facts surrounding the entire episode have been buried so deeply that the truth might never have been uncovered had it not been for the concerted efforts of a number veterans of the campaign who were determined that the world should know the full gravity of the Emergency and the price they and their comrades had to pay in the service of a country that was kept in ignorance of their heroism by self-serving, politicians. Even now, the Ministry of Defence is either unable or unwilling to provide accurate details of military personnel who lost their lives or of the precise causes of their deaths. For years, the official number of British service casualties was listed as 40 killed with 75 wounded, a figure confirmed in March 2000 by Dr. Lewis Moonie, Minster for Veteran Affairs. A few months afterwards Defence Secretary Geoff Hoon conceded that the number of deaths was slightly higher at 54, while in July 2001, Defence Services Secretary Robert Coney produced another set of statistics giving the number of deaths as 613, but this figure also included civilians and Commonwealth servicemen.

The Award Alliance Group, a society representing Canal Zone Veterans had been pressing for the award of a campaign medal or as it is more correctly known, a General Service Medal, which had been denied them for half a century by successive British Governments. As the result of the Group's dogged persistence and that of its supporters, the Government finally agreed to award a General Service Medal on 11th June 2003. Although the Sub-Committee tasked with hearing evidence from witnesses acknowledged that the casualty figures were in dispute, they only conceded that around 50 people had been killed by deliberate dissident action. Those who served in the Canal Zone at the time have challenged this finding and continue to do so.

Statistics obtained from the War Graves Commission reveal that a total of 520 bodies were interred in British Military Cemeteries in Cairo, Moascar and Fayid during the time of the Emergency. This includes the bodies of Commonwealth servicemen as well as those of 57 civilians and 63 women and children who were service dependants but it excludes wounded soldiers who were evacuated and died elsewhere, those whose bodies were flown home for burial and those whose bodies were never recovered.

The number and extent of the incidents themselves have also been under reported. Figures provided by the Civil Affairs Branch of HQ British Troops in Egypt indicate a total of 391 incidents between the abrogation of the 1936 Treaty in October 1951 and the end of December that year. This includes 154 cases of sniping, 41 bomb attacks, 18 murders and 12 woundings. The Veterans themselves estimate conservatively that there were over 30 incidents a month adding up to more than 1000 incidents throughout the life of the Emergency, most of which were hushed up and concealed from the people back in England. Also, of the deaths to which the Government was prepared to admit, many have been attributed to causes other than terrorist activity. Road accidents, accidental gunshot wounds, suicide, electrocution or drowning were some of the explanations put forward but there is nothing as unconvincing as the British ruling class when it is engaged in a cover up.

It is difficult to understand why the ferocity and the human cost of this campaign were suppressed so comprehensively and for so long. While they were stationed in the Canal Zone, British Servicemen were on official duty protecting an Anglo-French owned asset that might otherwise fall into unfriendly hands. Keeping details of incidents from the men themselves was understandable to a degree. For example, a young Durham Light Infantryman was stabbed at a base outside Ismailiya, while he was searching a line of Egyptian labourers for stolen goods. The Egyptians ran off while help was being summoned and the soldier died later in hospital. That night, every man who was not on duty left camp wielding a pick-axe handle. They formed up in columns of three and marched through Ismailiya cracking the heads of every adult male Egyptian they met. A riot was only narrowly averted and the whole episode was hushed up. Later in the campaign a servicewoman was abducted, tortured, raped and dismembered. Rumours of the atrocity only leaked out towards the end of 1954 after many British soldiers had already left for home. Had this become common knowledge, it might have resulted in a very serious incident indeed.

The only reason I can put forward as to why details of the Emergency were kept from the British public was to avert a feeling of national outrage that could easily have led to demands for war. This had to be avoided at all costs. Firstly, because Britain was virtually bankrupt and could not afford to become embroiled in a North African war and even if we could, our creditors in Washington would not have permitted it. Secondly, the Soviet Union would have used any act of British aggression as a pretext to come to Egypt's aid and, in so doing, ignite World War III. Apart from that, not everyone at home supported Britain's role in the Canal Zone.

In the eyes of some of our politicians, it was British servicemen, rather than the Egyptians who had been the aggressors. Before the rise of the Looney Left in the 1980's that virtually paralysed UK local government with nonsensical politically correct policies, there was always a Looney Left, like the Communist element in the Trade Union movement or the so-called Campaign for Nuclear Disarmament which only seemed to be interested in disarming the West. Additionally, there was no shortage of anti-British sentiment being expressed in Parliament during the immediate post war period with the likes of hard-line leftist Aneurin Bevan being particularly critical of British activities in Suez. One or two of these misguided people managed to find their way to Egypt, allegedly on fact finding missions and one in particular, Dr.Edith Summerskill, a minister in Clement Attlee's Labour Government, proved to be a major source of embarrassment. I became aware of Dr. Summerskill's irrational activities some years later when I was an amateur boxer and she was agitating to have boxing banned but, by then she had been exposed as an eccentric old fossil who was off with the fairies and nobody took any notice of her. In Egypt she seemed to want to ban the British army and this time people were listening.

Having been exposed to Egyptian media, Dr Summerskill accepted their lies and fabrications as gospel and proceeded to accuse British servicemen of provoking the meek and passive Egyptian population by their "insensitive and ill-disciplined" behaviour. To make matters worse, she repeated these groundless accusations to the Egyptian press and again on Radio Cairo, which, given her status, proved to be a resounding coup for Egyptian Government propaganda and an inexcusable shot in the foot for the British.

We received no support from our so-called allies, the Americans, either. Since 1947, they had been trying to entice the Middle Eastern countries into an American-led alliance and they saw the British presence in Egypt as a hindrance to their activities, which was why they tried to undermine it at every turn. Even earlier, Britain's precarious post-war position in Egypt was destabilised when an American delegate to the United Nations Security Council declared in full session that a vital stretch of water like the Suez Canal should be an international asset rather than one that was under the sole control of the British. In the circumstances, this was an extremely unhelpful remark although it was consistent. The Americans had long expressed the view that the British should withdraw from Egypt altogether and leave the Canal Zone base intact so that it could be reactivated in the event of an international emergency. While this might have suited the purpose of the Americans, the idea of walking away and leaving facilities and equipment valued at £270m at 1950 prices to the tender mercies of the Egyptians would have been an act of folly that would have had serious repercussions elsewhere.

As the British Empire started to unravel, the 40 year confrontation between Communism and the free world was gathering momentum and on 25th June 1950, this erupted into open warfare in Korea when the forces of North Korea invaded the South and sparked a three year conflict that would involve a US led coalition of UN troops against the Communist forces of North Korea and China, aided and abetted by the Soviet Union. In addition, the British were facing emergencies in Malaya and Kenya from Communist insurrectionists and African nationalists respectively making it essential that the Canal remained open and in their control. To make matters worse, The Soviet Union and its satellites were casting envious eyes in the direction of the Middle East and North Africa. Stalin had assembled several divisions along the Soviet border with Turkey with the oil in Persia as their ultimate objective while Marshall Tito was resisting Russian plans to enter Yugoslavia in order to gain access to the Mediterranean.

In an interesting aside, I have read several articles written by Canal Zone veterans who have called into question the assertion that Britain's primary purpose in retaining control of the Canal post 1948 was colonialism. In the war that followed the declaration of the state of Israel, the Egyptians suffered a humiliating defeat and were desperate for revenge but the British army, which blocked their way to Israel, had no intention of letting them pass. After the unsuccessful attempt by Anglo-French forces to re-take the Canal Zone in 1956, the UN peacekeeping force sent in to restore order found itself in a similar position and although its troops were initially welcomed by the Egyptians as liberators, the relationship soon soured as they, too, refused to allow the Egyptian army access to the Sinai. As a result, the "Liberation Battalions" were reactivated and the UN peacekeepers, mostly Canadians, started to take casualties, ten of whom are buried alongside their British counterparts who died in the earlier Emergency. Once again, the authorities have been reluctant to admit the true causes of death citing these as traffic accidents, drowning or sickness, a familiar story, which should be taken with a liberal helping of salt.

In his book "The Rise and Fall of the British Empire," the British historian Lawrence James repeats a story that was told to him about the final days of the British withdrawal from Egypt. It is said that, as one of the last launches moved away from the quay at Port Said, an Egyptian youth lifted his robe and urinated on the soldiers below, whereupon a soldier picked up his rifle and fired a shot at him. It is not known whether or not this story was true but, according to James, it did symbolise the final thirty years of the British occupation of Egypt. If only the Canal Zone Emergency could be dismissed so flippantly.

For the most part, the British servicemen based in the Canal Zone during the Emergency were national servicemen, young men between the ages of eighteen and twenty who had been compulsorily conscripted. They had no choice in the matter and were nothing less than innocent victims of a conflict that had been created by others. They had endured conditions of extreme privation, been exposed to serious, life-threatening sickness and despite their youth and inexperience, they had been pitted against an evil and fanatical pack of terrorists and expected to stand their ground without flinching. Yet, on returning home, they received no recognition, no medal and no thanks. For years afterwards, whenever Canal Zone veterans tried to tell people what they had endured in Egypt, nobody believed them since all but the most perfunctory of references to incidents and casualties had been suppressed. Without doubt, these young men had been comprehensively betrayed by a band of ruthless and cynical politicians who, not content with stealing their adolescence and exploiting their innocence, had heaped insult upon injury by consigning their finest hour to an oubliette in history.

BULGARIA 1994

ASSIGNATION IN BURGAS

Throughout 1993, I was making preparations for early retirement after a love-hate relationship with my work that had lasted for the best part of twenty years. I had been employed as a Committee Administrator for a London Borough, which I will call the London Borough of Wavering. A colleague suggested the name to me, when he heard I was writing a book and, if nothing else, it was an accurate description of what passed in those days for its decision-making process. However, somewhere in the dim and distant past, someone must have thought that Committee staff didn't have enough to do so they decided that, in addition to our Committee duties, we should deal with complaints from members of the public and investigate others, which had been made directly to the Local Ombudsman. In view of the fact that Wavering had a long and convoluted motto in Latin that failed scholars or disgruntled residents might loosely translate as *Maladministration? What Maladministration?* or *Cock-ups R Us*, my workload was considerable, all embracing and caused me to work excessive, unpaid overtime. If this was not bad enough, my efforts to appease the aggrieved residents of Wavering were often obstructed by my colleagues in other departments on whom I relied heavily for assistance. Unfortunately, instead of providing me with much-needed support, many of them chose instead to spend their working hours locked in interminable, unstructured and largely unnecessary meetings ensuring that their productivity output was zero and I was left to placate numerous angry residents who by now were holding me personally responsible for every ill that had ever befallen them.

A pernicious meeting culture had been allowed to develop right across the Council and became the cause of endless frustration to those of us who were trying to get things done, whilst to those who found themselves excluded from such rituals, they became the source of innuendo and rumour, the most popular being that the Social Services department was run by vampires, since they spent every daylight hour incarcerated in conference rooms and only emerged after the sun had gone down. In this, they took their lead from the elected Councillors who persistently clamoured for meetings every night of the week, primarily because they received a financial inducement in the form of an attendance allowance and, once a meeting had been called, they would sit, gabble, babble and bleat for half the night, as they had no discernible life outside the Council and, consequently, no reason either to go home or anywhere else. In the bad old days, the Planning Policy Committee would often drone on until 4 A.M., giving rise to the suggestion that they, too, might be vampires.

Every now and then, I'd get fed up with the constant stress, pressure and long hours and apply for another job but inevitably, halfway through the interview, I'd always withdraw my application on the grounds that the new post, though more lucrative, appeared to be bland and one-dimensional when compared with what I was doing already. By the time I'd made similar tactical withdrawals from a number of job applications, I'd begun to achieve a degree of notoriety and, understandably, people no longer invited me for interview, so when Wavering started to offer voluntary early retirement to reduce staff numbers, I jumped at it.

I wanted to rid my life of something that had plagued my peace and tranquillity ever since I'd first left school – work. There were all sorts of things I wanted to do, all sorts of places I wanted to go but work always got in the way. No end of times I would go off to Greece, Turkey or Morocco for a two week break, willing myself never to return but I always did. I needed the money. Now, having finally retired from work, I had a pension, albeit a reduced one and, providing I was careful, I could spend as many of the years that remained to me travelling to places I'd never seen before. My plan was to travel through Russia, China, Nepal, Pakistan and India but first, I felt I had unfinished business in Egypt and, of course, in Bulgaria.

Rosa would write to me every six weeks or so in Bulgarian Cyrillic and I used to go to the Embassy in Queens Gate where a member of the staff was kind enough to translate for me. I'd been trying to book a flight to Burgas from early October 1993 but there were no direct flights out of season, which was why I'd started to plan my aborted trip to Egypt. It was hard enough to get a flight to Sofia during the winter months, but there were only two internal flights a week from there to Burgas and neither of them was a direct connection so I would have to stay in Sofia for at least one night in either direction. I soon realised that if I wanted to visit Burgas for a week, I would have to allow the best part of another week to get there and back. In the end, I decided to wait until May, when charter flights to the Black Sea coast would be resumed.

Having let my flat through a housing association to a very young single parent with a delinquent boyfriend, something over which I would agonise for the remainder of the year, I managed to get a flight on a Balkan Airways charter, carrying people who were doing the same Spartacus Tour as I'd done the previous year, or else, they were spending two fun-filled weeks in Slurry Pit on Sea. I phoned Rosa a week before I was due to leave and when I finally made it through the formalities into the arrivals area, there she was, looking extremely tanned and blonde in a turquoise, button through blouse with a pair of faded blue denims cut off at mid thigh and a pair of stiletto heels designed to give short people vertigo. I was not sure where we would be staying, although I was hoping that it would not be with her parents. I have always found parents to be a bit off hand with me, especially when I was having my evil way with their daughters and, if my previous visits to Bulgaria were anything to go by, I was going to have enough complications without a couple of over protective parents to contend with. However, accommodation did not prove to be a problem as Rosa directed our taxi to a Balkantourist office near the beach, just a few minutes walk from the Hotel Balgaria. They were renting out private rooms in peoples houses and we took a double for the equivalent of five US Dollars a night.

Our room was in a rundown apartment block with a crumbling stucco frontage on what used to be the Bulevard Karl Marx but had now been re named Bulevard Democrazie. I wasn't sure whether there was meant to be any connection but if there was, it was lost on me. A large, elderly lady with a benevolent demeanour greeted us at the door, took the voucher Balkantourist had given me and showed us to our room. There were four other rooms leading off the entrance hall as well as a small communal kitchen, bathroom and toilet. Our room was vast, not so much a bedroom as a repository for second hand furniture. Apart from four beds, there were three mahogany double wardrobes and a full-length dining table with eight chairs. The windows were covered with mosquito netting and would have opened inwards had they not been nailed shut to keep out burglars. Although we had a choice of beds, this did not prove to be an advantage as unwholesome bedding and sheets that were heavily stained with semen limited our selection.

I had a quick shower but when I came back dripping wet and wrapped in a towel, the room was in darkness, the blind covering the window having been pulled down tightly. As my eyes became used to the gloom, I saw Rosa, stretched out seductively on the bed against the far wall wearing nothing but a pair of my silk boxer shorts that she'd obviously found while unpacking my bag.

"I waited for you," she said, softly.

"At least you didn't catch cold," I replied quickly without realising how silly it must have sounded.

"No," she persisted "I wait for you since last year. No other man."

Whether I believed her or not didn't really matter, only that we had a lot of catching up to do and I watched her wriggle out of her new boxer shorts while I carelessly let my towel drop to the floor.

After another two hours, by which time we'd both showered and changed, Rosa suggested that I left my currency with her for safekeeping. She explained how law and order had virtually broken down here and there was a good chance that we would be burgled. She wasn't interested in looking after my travellers cheques and, when I queried this, she explained that the sort of people who carried out burglaries in Burgas would not be sufficiently well connected to dispose of travellers cheques or any similar means of exchange, at least not yet but I was sure that, even as we spoke, someone was out there working on it.

That evening we had dinner in the spacious high-ceilinged restaurant of the Hotel Balgaria. It was a busy night with many customers, most of whom looked as if they might have been package tourists. A large stage rose majestically at one end of the room where a twenty-piece orchestra accompanied a number of local singers who serenaded diners with local versions of European and American pop music that had clearly been learned phonetically. Rosa told me that she used to sing here before she went to Germany, which was why she knew so many of the waitresses and cloakroom attendants. Afterwards, I suggested taking a detour along the seafront but Rosa was horrified. Apparently it was not safe to do this after dark because of what she called "bandidos", so we stuck to the comparatively well-lit roads.

The following morning, we were up and about at eight to make the short bus journey down the coast to the historic town of Nesebar. Most of the guidebooks I'd read tended to deride Nesebar or refer to it as *"once beautiful"* but this is unfair. The Greeks founded it in 510 BC as a trading post, although the name Nesebar was not used for another thousand years or so. In the meantime, it was fought over, won, lost and regained by Greeks, Romans, Bulgars and Ottomans before falling into gradual decline. Now it is a small fishing port, rich in archaeological remains, especially those of Byzantine churches of which there are a plentiful number in various states ranging from exquisitely preserved to piles of rubble with a large number some way between the two. The bus put us down close to a splendid old windmill and we sauntered across a small causeway barely wider than the road it carried until we came to a cross roads and some old Greek ramparts. We followed the road to the right, which took us to the harbour and an assorted collection of small boats.

We met many tourists who had taken the three-kilometre bus ride from Sunny Beach and we decided to go there after lunch. Rosa wasn't too enthusiastic but I put that down to the fact she'd been there many times before. Nesebar was probably what I had expected, a minor tourist attraction, littered with bijou souvenir shops selling the usual local handicrafts for as much as they could persuade the tourists to pay. Considering how small the town was, it contained a surprising number of restaurants, tavernas and bars. A short distance from the shore, we found a tiny, Greek taverna with a long, sheltered patio, which appealed to Rosa's ancestral heritage and I sat back while she ordered lunch. When they brought the inevitable Greek salad, I insisted that Rosa took my helping of Feta cheese as well as her own. Over the previous ten years or so, I had been a frequent visitor to Greece and while I love the culture and the food, I had reservations about the wine and I never wanted to see another piece of Feta cheese again – ever.

After lunch, we went back to the bus stop where the bus to Sunny Beach was waiting. It ran every fifteen minutes and normally did a brisk trade, although this time of day it tended to make the return trip half empty. On arriving at the bus terminus in Sunny Beach, I could see why all the tourists were in Nessebar. The beach itself was beautiful with golden sand as far as the eye could see, even better because it was completely deserted. Unfortunately, the surroundings were dismal. All we could see were hotel buildings, five or six storeys high but some of them were as long as a street and all of them looked pretty inhospitable. They resembled sixties office blocks, square, grey and concrete – a sort of Siberia-on-Sea. Hoteliers in the Costa Del Sol could sleep soundly in their beds at night. They would lose no trade to this bleak, soulless place.

Ten years on, a great deal of money was to transform Sunny Beach into a thriving modern resort with a variety of clubs, bars and new hotels, while many of the older establishments were to have dramatic makeovers which would cause them to metamorphose miraculously from the dismal blockhouses we were looking at now into something truly spectacular.

Rosa was a little uncomfortable and suggested we get out of the sun for a while. We went into the austere reception area of the nearest hotel and I ordered coffee for Rosa while I had a beer. When I asked what was wrong Rosa told me she had a headache. We hadn't spent much time together but I knew enough about her to know she wasn't the type to make a fuss needlessly. We left our drinks and made our way back to the bus stop where the bus to Nesebar was just preparing to leave. Once we had arrived in Nesebar, I couldn't find a taxi so we had to wait another twenty minutes by the windmill before the Burgas bus arrived and, by then, Rosa was suffering badly. I guessed she had sunstroke and she was in need of medical treatment but she insisted, doggedly, that she only had a headache. By the time we reached Burgas, Rosa's condition had deteriorated and she was slumped across her seat with her head in my lap. I had to help her off the bus, and, when she was unable to walk, the hundred yards or so back to the apartment, I sat her on a park bench in the shade while I went to find a taxi. Fortunately, this did not prove to be difficult and within a few minutes we were back in our room but Rosa was still suffering. She continued to insist that she did not want a doctor until she started to tremble uncontrollably and proceeded to throw up in a wastebasket.

I went to find our landlady, who agreed with me that Rosa had sunstroke and immediately telephoned for a doctor, who took another forty-five minutes to arrive. She turned out to be a brusque woman of a certain age who viewed me with no small degree of suspicion. She motioned me to leave and I waited in the corridor until she had examined Rosa and, presumably, treated her. Rosa told me after the doctor had left that she'd been given an injection and our landlady had been sent out with a prescription. Part of the prescribed treatment was a herbal massage and, once our elderly hostess had returned from the chemists, I was once more relegated to the hall, while the strong smell of chlorophil accompanied by much slapping and pummelling announced that the prescribed treatment was being administered. After about ten minutes, our hostess left us briefly after completing her task, only to return with a long, pale cotton nightdress, which she asked Rosa to put on in case the heavily scented solution came off on the sheets. It was a nice gesture but considering everything else that had been spilled on them, a few splashes of herbal oil would only have improved their condition. I turned the lights down and sat next to the bed while Rosa slept and at about ten thirty, I crawled under the sheet next to her taking care not to disturb her.

The following morning, Rosa was up and about before I was and appeared to have fully recovered from her previous day's incapacity. After we had showered, we set off in the direction of her home so that she could wash the nightdress our landlady had loaned her. On our way, we passed the Turkish Consulate, where a queue of sad-looking people cast early-morning shadows across the street as they waited patiently for visas. We continued our leisurely stroll along the Bulevard Lenin – they hadn't changed that one yet – past the uninspiring façade of the Balgaria Hotel and crossed the street into the Bulevard Deveti Septemvri – they hadn't changed that one either – to a large, busy square bordered by a uniform collection of shop fronts and restaurants. Rosa left me in a small bistro and, after ordering a pizza for my breakfast, she set off alone to her parents flat.

After about an hour, I'd managed to munch my way through an outsize vegetarian pizza, consumed two pots of black coffee and was beginning to feel quite human when Rosa reappeared wearing a wide brimmed straw hat as recommended by the doctor the previous evening. The doctor had also told her to stay away from the beach so we spent the day walking around Burgas, which I found interesting although I wouldn't like to have lived there. My guidebook informed me that Burgas had a population of 185,000 people – approximately the same size as Portsmouth. Like Portsmouth, it had a deep-water harbour, but there the similarity ended. I saw no warships at all only a fleet of oil tankers and container ships most of which flew Russian flags or those of other former Eastern bloc countries. There was supposed to be a large ocean-going fishing fleet, too, but there was no sign of it and I assumed it had already gone fishing and was busy emptying the North Sea of its maritime wildlife.

Outside of town there were supposed to be three large lakes, although we only saw one of them on the way from the airport. There were also a number of chemical plants and an oil refinery which I didn't see either but at least they explained the presence of so many oil tankers in the harbour. A number of the main streets in the city centre had been pedestrianised, which cut down on pollution levels and gave people an opportunity to walk safely – a necessary facility in these parts. From what I had observed, Bulgarian drivers subscribed to the Italian school of motoring,–*If you can't drive carefully, drive fast and don't forget to bribe the Police in dollars when they stop you.*

Burgas did not seem to be an ancient city and most of the buildings appeared to be relatively modern and downright ugly. The oldest building in town was the Church of Saints Cyril and Methodius which dated from the turn of the twentieth century and only looked interesting because of the mediocrity of its surroundings. From here we walked for fifteen minutes or so until we reached the sea front. Unlike most sea fronts I'd visited, this was not only run down and neglected it looked as if it had never been any other way. Between the main road and the beach, there was an extensive area of gardens, which could have been pleasant had they been properly maintained and might even have provided an oasis of greenery in an otherwise concrete and utilitarian town. Unfortunately, even in late spring, what grass there was had turned brown and lifeless and the hedgerows were spiky, jagged and devoid of vegetation. The beach area looked as though at sometime, someone had started to develop it for tourism and then lost interest in it and stopped. Close to the promenade, I could make out the remains of concrete structures, which might once have been restaurants and snack bars. The beach itself, like the one we'd seen yesterday at Sunny Beach was impressive in that it was a long stretch of relatively unspoiled sand – at least it was until I reached the area around the waters edge. The yard or two between the edge of the water and the dry sand was black and oily, the result of years of unrestrained oil spillage and the real reason why Burgas could never have become a tourist resort. We walked back down the recently re-named Bulevard Democrazie past the now-deserted Turkish consulate to our apartment to get ready for our evening out.

MEET THE LOCAL MAFIA – ATILLA THE PIMP

We decided to go back to the Balgaria for dinner and walked along the main sea front road that used to be the Bulevard Dimitar Dimov – what they called it now was anybody's guess. It was a clear, pleasant evening and many of the local people were out on the street taking the air. As we walked, we must have made an odd-looking couple. I was an ageing and rather reluctant local government officer, walking hand-in-hand with Rosa, a glamorous cabaret artiste resting between engagements. I could see that we were attracting the attention of many passers by, which should not have been a problem because I was looking at them, too. For the most part, the women were attractive in their brightly coloured blouses and short summer skirts, even though they'd overdone the makeup but, by contrast, the men were dark swarthy and unkempt with faces like Brillo pads. They also seemed to exude an air of menace, which for some reason made me feel uneasy. My feeling of unease was not helped when, occasionally, a group of these people would stop and grab my sleeve to attract my attention. Rosa would shout at them, everyone would turn and look and they would beat a hasty retreat. Rosa explained that they were pickpockets, one of whom would try to distract me while another would rifle through my pockets or steal my wristwatch. She told me that a great deal of this went on and the Police did very little to contain it.

We had dinner in the main restaurant and watched the all-singing, all-dancing cabaret. As we were leaving, I noticed a group of middle-aged men in black, shapeless leather jackets who were glaring at us malevolently. I'd seen them there on our previous visit. One of them, younger than the rest, wore a full-length, nazi-type leather coat and bore a resemblance to Alain Delon, the French film actor. He must have followed us out because suddenly, there he was in front of us making threatening noises. He grabbed Rosa by the throat and, although I didn't speak a word of Bulgarian, I guessed he was telling her he didn't want to see either of us in the hotel again. When I realised what was happening, I jumped on him and after grabbing a handful of his greasy hair, I jerked his head back and, in so doing, succeeded in breaking his grip. Then, as I managed to get between him and Rosa, he lunged recklessly at my knee with his groin. Unfortunately, the folds of his coat rendered the manoeuvre ineffective. Instantly retaliating, I tried to head butt his oncoming fist, but again, in the heat of battle, it swept harmlessly above my head as he struck the top of my exposed cranium with his oncoming belly. This unwelcome contact caused Delon to grunt angrily and, having become bored with proceedings, he pushed us both away, uttered what I assumed to be another warning and slunk back to the hotel. Rosa was angry. She was spitting nails and quite rightly too.

"He told me to keep out of the hotel." she said. "They are mafia. They are pimps. They think we take their business. We go back." She stormed off back the way we had come and I noticed something curious. As we left the hotel earlier, we had to pass a rather large doorman, who resembled a stereotypical Russian field athlete weaned on a diet of performance enhancing substances. While I was struggling with the leather boy, I noticed him out of the corner of my eye moving in our direction as if he was thinking of helping us. Now, as our would-be assailant reached the hotel entrance, the doorman approached him, smiled and put an arm round his shoulder as though he was greeting a friend. It wasn't us he was thinking of helping.

Rosa swept in past him so quickly that I had trouble keeping up with her. She went straight up to the reception counter and began a heated exchange with the entire complement of staff. While this was going on, I could see that Delon had resumed his place at the table with his shifty cohorts. He glowered at me so I gave him the middle finger at which he started to get up out of his chair but one of the others motioned him to sit down again and he did so. Rosa finished her altercation with reception and led me up the winding staircase to the dimly-lit cocktail bar. She exchanged a few words with the bar staff, and I followed her back into the restaurant. This was a different section from where we had been earlier but it was all part of the same dining hall and Rosa appeared to be looking for somebody. She strode angrily up to a table where a fat unshaven Bulgarian was sitting by himself and said a few terse words to him. It was not even a sentence but its effect was explosive. He leapt to his feet and roared at Rosa who turned tail and ran, grabbing at my hand as she went past so that I was nearly jerked off my feet in pursuit. The Bulgarian, I learned afterwards his name was Atilla, started to chase us through the restaurant while the well – dressed diners looked on in horror. We ran past a couple more of those large hotel security men but they did not intervene. As we reached the top of a flight of stairs, which led out into the street, I could feel that Atilla was nearly upon us when it suddenly occurred to me that I had no reason to flee from this excremental barrel of lard so I turned and confronted him as he huffed and puffed his way towards me.

"What do you want?" I asked him. It sounded a bit lame because he clearly wanted to tear us limb from limb but it distracted him long enough for me to catch him off balance.

"You English?" He asked as his expression changed from anger to confusion.

I responded with a straight right hand, which caught him full in the face and dumped him onto his well-upholstered backside. He tried to rise but his legs wouldn't support him and he staggered backwards until he was held securely by several of the restaurant waiters, who didn't appear to like him very much either. I saw that Atilla's left eye was puffed up and nearly closed. At that moment I noticed two of the security staff closing in and I quickly followed Rosa down the stairs. I caught up with her in the street and we made for a smart looking bar a couple of blocks away where she explained what the altercation had been about.

Atilla had been a former communist official who had been pushed out of his job after liberation. This was not an isolated incident. Rosa told me that there were many ex-communists in Bulgaria who were now making a good living from organised crime. Atilla was a petty racketeer whose main source of income was pimping and he used the hotel to market his prostitutes. Because Rosa was with me, he assumed that either she was freelancing and I was a client or we were working as a team and I was a pimp. Either way, we were on his patch and he told his evil smelling bunch of heavies to warn us off. It had been these people she had been so frightened of when she had stayed in my hotel room the previous year.

"What did you say to him to make him so angry?" I asked.

Rosa laughed, "I tell him that he is only a pimp because he can't satisfy a woman."

She told me that he preyed on young women with no family and forced them into prostitution. Generally, they came from villages inland and none of them came willingly but Atilla's boss paid off whoever needed to be paid off and nobody bothered him. The next day, Rosa asked me to go back to the hotel to make an appointment to see the manager and make a formal complaint.

I turned up at reception at nine o'clock that morning and made an appointment to see the manager at two thirty which left us ample time to relax on the beach, where Rosa continued to turn heads as she prostrated herself on her towel wearing nothing but a skimpy pair of cotton briefs to cover the only part of her shapely body that was not deeply bronzed. At two fifteen I presented myself at reception and, after the customary ten-minute wait I left Rosa talking to one of her friends behind the bar, while I followed one of the dark-haired women from reception into the elevator. We stopped about halfway up the tower block and I was shown into a small anti – room containing two low chairs and a coffee table and, as I waited for another ten minutes, I flicked through a German language guidebook, which claimed to contain a selection of interesting places to visit in Burgas. It was a very thin book. I could hear voices from inside the office, anxious female voices, but I could not understand a word they were saying. Suddenly, the wood-panelled door opened and a deferential young lady dressed as a hotel waitress came out and invited me to come in.

The manager was sitting at the end of an extended table in a long narrow room with windows along one wall and pictures of distinguished looking people on the wall facing them. She was short, stocky and aged somewhere between forty and fifty, old enough to have been in post while the communists were in power. She spoke no English but she introduced the waitress who would be acting as an interpreter. I told her what had happened to us when we had left the hotel and again in the restaurant when we had encountered Atilla. I missed out the bit about whacking him but I guessed she'd been told about that already. She listened intently to the whispered words of the interpreter but remained impassive. Either she was not very impressed by my story or she was not very surprised. She claimed to have no knowledge of the identities of the persons involved and if there was a vice ring operating in the hotel then it was the first time she had heard of it. When I complained that we had received no assistance from the various security people in the hotel when it must have been obvious that we were in difficulties, she picked up the phone.

In a few moments, the door opened and a red-faced man the size of an abnormal load manoeuvred his way awkwardly into the office. They told me he was the head of security and the manager repeated, what I assumed was my complaint. This man was not fat, nor had he ever been. From his appearance, I suspected that he had spent a good deal of his life pumping iron with the result that he was built like a concrete out-house. In spite of his smart navy blue blazer with a crest on the breast pocket, his military tie and his starched white shirt, he smelled like one, too.

After the manager had said her piece, the head of security made his report in a mechanical monotone, pausing every so often to glance vindictively in my direction. I didn't have to speak the language to know what was going on. It was just like Local Government back home. Everybody in the room was going to deny responsibility for anything. There had been an enquiry. I had been given a fair hearing and that would be the end of the matter, which was exactly what happened. Everybody was very polite. Everybody was very correct and I had a strong suspicion that everybody was being paid off by the same person who employed Atilla. I decided that I was going to get nothing more here so I thanked them for their time, the manager wished me a happy stay for the remainder of my time in Burgas and I went downstairs to look for Rosa.

I found her in the bar being tended to by the bar staff. While I had been away, she had been attacked by one of Atilla's thugs. She had not been harmed but I felt it was best to get her out of there quickly. We went back to the trendy-looking bar we had been in the previous night and compared notes. About five minutes before I came back, one of Atilla's foul-smelling henchmen came into the bar, grabbed Rosa by the throat, threatened her and left. She had seen Atilla, too, sporting a badly swollen eye. When I told her about my meeting with the manager, she became extremely angry.

"They lied to you. They all lied." she hissed.

"I know that," I said "But they would, wouldn't they? You can't expect them to admit to being involved in a vice ring, especially to a foreigner. For all they know, I might be an undercover reporter with the News of The World." Rosa would not be placated and in her place I would have felt the same. She was being ordered out of a public area by a group of people who had no authority to do so.

"We go to the Police." she said. My previous dealings with the Bulgarian Police did not inspire me with confidence in this less than august body but if that was what Rosa wanted then I was prepared to go along with it. She explained that if she made a complaint, it would be ignored since the Police knew better than to cross organised criminals, especially as many of them used to be high-ranking communists before liberation. However if a foreigner were to make the same complaint then it would be taken seriously and investigated. At least, that was the popular perception.

When we arrived at the Police station, it was closed. Crime in Burgas could continue unabated, twenty-four hours a day, seven days a week but those who were employed to fight against it only worked part-time leaving the scales of justice permanently weighted in favour of the growing criminal fraternity. It was to take ten more years of political correctness before the police in the west would catch up with their enlightened Eastern European counterparts and respond to emergency calls with recorded messages, while redressing the imbalance in the crime statistics by persecuting motorists who parked their cars in the wrong place or pedestrians who inadvertently dropped litter. At least we could be certain that the Police Station in Burgas had not been closed for Diversity Training or a Service Planning Away-Day. Having swallowed our frustration, we decided to return the following morning and spent the rest of the day on the beach, where during what remained of a sweltering afternoon, Rosa's already dusky charms became several shades darker. At about five o'clock, we went to Rosa's parent's flat to retrieve our landlady's nightdress and this time, she took me in with her.

She lived on the sixth floor of a crumbling concrete tower block that looked as though it would collapse in a strong wind. The lift smelled strongly of urine, as did the corridors and other communal areas. However, once we were inside the family's apartment, I was amazed at how bright and spacious it was. There must have been four bedrooms along with a modern, fitted kitchen, a bathroom and separate toilet. There was also a large airy lounge and an equally sizeable dining room. I was introduced to Rosa's wizened old grandfather, a wiry man with a face like a pickled walnut crowned with a few wisps of white hair, who sat in front of the television wearing a threadbare grey cardigan, worn corduroy trousers and carpet slippers with a hole in the left one allowing his big toe to peep through. I also met her mother, from whom Rosa had clearly inherited her good looks. The rest of her family were apparently still out at work though Rosa did not tell me what they did. Instead, she made tea for us all while she recounted her tale of woe and when she told them I was going to the Police both relatives stood up and shook my hand vigorously as if I were some kind of hero.

The next morning, as the rest of Burgas went about its business under a cloudless, David Hockney sky, Rosa took me to the Police station, and, as instructed by the bored looking constable on the desk, I wrote out a statement in English adding my signature to the last page. I got the impression that even if I'd written out the lyrics to every song on the Sergeant Pepper album and signed myself Nikita Khruschev (deceased), my statement would still have been treated with the same level of indifference. This must have occurred to Rosa, too, and she took me to the office of the local newspaper. Apparently, the editor had got himself into difficulties by speaking out about Police corruption and the activities of organised criminals but he had refused to be intimidated and was sticking doggedly to his task, quite an act of courage in the circumstances. The office was at the back of a building, which faced the Balgaria and we reached it by way of a narrow urine-soaked, alleyway. The editor was a small man in a shabby off the peg jacket that might well have been purchased from TsUM. He had young features on a deeply lined face, which led me to believe that his brand of crusading journalism had caused him to run foul of the communists, too.

He spoke fluent English and took shorthand notes as I slowly told my story for the third time. If nothing else, I had become word perfect by now but to my knowledge, nothing was ever done. I received a letter from Rosa two months later while I was in Portsmouth. She enclosed a newspaper cutting but I could make neither head nor tail of it. In the end, I telephoned the embassy to make an appointment with a lady who said she was the second secretary and I drove to London so that she could translate for me.

In her letter, Rosa said she didn't dare go back to the hotel Balgaria in case Atilla's henchmen harmed her. The press cutting was a brief article from a national newspaper revealing that many former field athletes, wrestlers and body builders who had previously pursued these laudable activities as members of the Bulgarian armed forces were now being employed in hotels, nightclubs and casinos to act as security guards and bouncers. The article went on to infer that these people were really being paid by organised crime to protect pimps, thieves and extortionists from being obstructed in their dubious line of duty.

None of these revelations surprised me at all but they did surprise the lady from the embassy. She went to get the ambassador and, although they had all sorts of other engagements that morning, they put them on hold for an hour or so while I told them the whole story. After I had finished, they promised they would make a report to their foreign minister and what I had told them would be investigated but I never heard from them again. Rosa went back to Germany shortly afterwards and I have not felt the need to visit Bulgaria since. It would be nice to think that our experience finally led to an investigation, which brought about a crackdown on organised crime if not in the whole of Bulgaria then at least in Burgas but I won't hold my breath.

EGYPT 1994

CAIRO: THE HOTEL SCAM

I only remained in England for another two weeks after returning from Bulgaria but I accomplished a great deal. First of all, I made a provisional booking to start my major Odyssey through Eastern Europe and Asia on September 1st. Then, having previously let my flat, I decamped to Portsmouth to stay with my sister, driving back and forth to London in order to obtain an Egyptian visa and an open ticket to Cairo. I had been agonising over whether or not to go back to Egypt since I'd called off my trip the previous October. My anxieties had not been eased by a further terrorist incident in December when extremists fired on a tourist bus in Cairo prior to bombing it and wounding eight people. To make matters worse, there had been seven further attacks in February and March 1994, which specifically targetted tourists and involved shots being fired at either Nile cruisers or the Cairo-Aswan train. However, there had been no more outbreaks of violence since 13th March and, as it was now almost June and low season, I suspected that the terrorists had suspended their activities for the remainder of the summer so I decided to take a chance and return to Egypt.

On departure day, I drove to London very early, left my car with my friends in Putney and stayed for breakfast to go over some last minute arrangements since they would be looking after my affairs in my absence. When travelling for an unspecified period of time, it is imperative to sort out in advance how you propose to live while you are moving around. In 1994, with neither internet nor international ATMs, the only readily available means of communication, apart from letters and postcards were faxes, telephones and telexes. I knew that in some countries travellers could work temporarily to raise funds while others made and still make complicated arrangements via international banking networks to ensure they have access to their money regularly. While I was in Goa, I met a beach bum from Liverpool who was getting his dole money sent to him by a friend who signed on for him and sent out international money orders every fortnight. £45 a week bought much more in Goa than it ever could in Liverpool. Ordinarily, like anyone else, I would have frowned on this type of benefit fraud but we were still in the mid-nineties and our fifteenth consecutive year of Conservative government. Entire communities had been left without money and had been forced to resort to localised bartering systems to survive. As far as jobs were concerned, either in Liverpool, or anywhere else in the UK, if you didn't have one already, you could forget it.

To fund my travels, I needed an arrangement that would hold good in any country I cared to visit, get me my money on demand and with a minimum of bureaucracy and cost. There was only one organisation in the world I knew could deliver this, American Express. About two years before I gave up work, I received a circular from Amex telling me that I met their financial criteria for a Green Card and when I applied, they told me that with my salary, I could have a Gold Card, too, so I ended up with both. There were not many countries where American Express did not have some form of local representation and I could go into any of their offices, write out a personal cheque from my National Westminster Bank current account, and, using my American Express Gold Card as a guarantee, I could obtain either US Dollars or travellers cheques, depending on local currency regulations. Since I started this arrangement, no matter where in the world I have been, I have never failed to be impressed by the high calibre of staff I found in American Express offices, apart from in Luxor where I was to find myself in serious difficulty.

I'd booked an open ticket on Air France, not my first choice of airline by any means but it was a first division organisation and as such was highly efficient. The only drawback was that I had to change at Charles DeGaulle airport, which did not exactly fill me with glee, not only because it had been named after a man who, while he had been alive, had probably been the world's most vehement Anglophobe, it was also one of the ugliest airports I'd ever set eyes on. It's bare, untreated concrete facades and interiors give it an appearance of not just being unfinished, but that the work force had downed tools half way through the job and no amount of inducement or incentive had succeeded in persuading them to carry on. I flew out again at 5.30 P.M. and by the time I'd completed formalities at Cairo airport, it was nearly midnight. On the flight, I'd befriended an expatriate Egyptian called Alex but we'd been separated while coming through customs and I lost him completely in the mass of people milling about in the arrivals hall. This left me in a bit of a fix. We had arranged to share a taxi into town and he was going to book me into a reasonably priced hotel as opposed to the sort of accommodation that was euphemistically described as a guest house but was in reality a back packers' sleaze pit. He would have been a useful contact to have in a strange city but it could not be helped and now I was here at the mercy of the touts. In the end, it was just a case of picking one in the hope that I'd get lucky. I didn't.

I was approached by an ageing Egyptian wearing a fez. I use the word ageing with some degree of caution since most people who had aged as much as he had were dead already. He offered me a room at the Ismailia House Hotel, which turned out to be a backpackers' haunt on the upper floors of a tall building overlooking the Midan Tahrir. He charged me forty Egyptian pounds for the first night and twenty for transport to get there. He also asked me for bakshish. When I gave him ten pounds he said it was not enough so I gave him ten more. When he continued to ask for more, I told him that was all there was and I could spare no more. He then went into a long litany of doom and gloom to the effect that he needed the money for his children. I asked how old his children were and he told me he had a son of twenty-five, another of twenty-three and a daughter of twenty-one. At this stage of proceedings I lost patience with him and told him bluntly either to stop taking the piss or hand back the money I'd already given him.

This approach proved to be successful as he continued to drive in sullen silence until we reached the downtown area of Cairo, although when we finally drew to a halt, I had no idea where we were. We had pulled up in a murky alleyway behind a tall concrete block, whereupon he told me we had arrived at our destination and we would be getting out here. I was more than a little alarmed as there was nothing in this alley that looked remotely like a hotel, guest house or even a hostel and I started to recall grisly stories of travellers being waylaid, robbed and left for dead in surroundings such as these. With a great deal of trepidation, I followed him, bags in hand, as he led me through a small rear entrance towards a very old and rickety lift, which creaked and juddered its way painfully to the seventh floor. This proved to be a grubby, open plan reception area, complete with desk, clerk and a large sign bearing the legend *Ismalia House Hotel*, a low budget travellers' flop house complete with a dozen or so low budget travellers, flopped out on threadbare sofas, watching football on a Japanese television set. We went up to the desk where my guide presented the receptionist with a docket and I was formally checked in. I noticed a list of rates pasted to the wall, which showed that room rent was only thirty pounds a night. The receptionist, an elderly Egyptian who should not have been working at this hour of the night, asked me whether I wished to book further nights at the rate I'd been charged at the airport so I told him I'd decide in the morning. My guide's face fell as he kissed goodbye the opportunity of further commission. He looked at me as though he was expecting another tip but I told him he'd made enough out of me already and with that I retired for the night.

I slept in late next morning and by the time I'd taken my turn in the communal bathroom – it was that kind of place – shaved, showered and dressed it was 10 A.M. but they were still serving breakfast in the small dining area adjacent to reception. I was going to ask for tea and toast but then I remembered that they rarely boiled the water over here so I changed the order to coffee and toast, which, to my surprise was served promptly. Half an hour later, I'd booked another four nights at the normal rate, and checked my travellers cheques and passport to be kept under lock and key at reception. I'd already loaded both cameras and was looking for the quickest way to the pyramids.

When I asked reception for directions, they introduced me to a short mature-looking Egyptian who answered to the name of 'Jim' and said he was a taxi driver. We negotiated a rate of fifty Egyptian pounds for the day, which involved one trip to and from the pyramids and I could stay for as long as I liked. It was a good deal, or so I thought, but Jim had other ideas. He asked me if I wanted to ride a camel while I was visiting the pyramids and that sounded like a good deal, too. That was one of the things I didn't do last time I was in Cairo and it seemed like a fun thing to do. Instead of taking me to the main entrance to the pyramids complex, Jim took a detour south to a small village – except that the number of tourist shops around signified that it had long since ceased to be a bona fide village and was now more of a taxi drop for tourists who were about to be separated from their money.

After we'd left the taxi, Jim introduced me to Mustapha, a large Egyptian, disguised as a sack of potatoes, wearing an old djellabia and a grubby Arab headdress that might once have been white. He led me to his stables and selected a tall female camel for me that might also once have been white. We agreed a fee of sixty Egyptian pounds and he made a long hissing sound at which the camel sank to its knees so that I was able to clamber onto its saddle. The man then made another hissing sound and the beast started to rise. I'd ridden my first camel many years ago in Tunisia and had ridden them again in Morocco, Turkey, Syria and Jordan so the experience was not exactly new to me. Upon rising from a kneeling position, a camel will invariably straighten its back legs first making it necessary for its rider to lean backwards sharply to avoid falling off. I have heard many stories of injuries being caused to unwary tourists who had neglected to do this and been pitched forward onto their faces for their trouble. I didn't want to be one of them, especially on my first day back in Cairo. Having stood the camel up, Mustapha handed the lead to a young boy and disappeared, only to reappear moments later riding a pony, which, considering the size of the load it was carrying, did not look as though it was going to last the course.

Curiously, we approached the pyramids from the south, skirting the Muslim Cemetery and for the next hour, Mustapha led me around the outside of the complex and if his overloaded pony was in any distress at all, the poor beast had the good sense to keep quiet about it. Mustapha also borrowed one of my cameras so that he could take photographs of me on the camel with the pyramids in the background. The only thing I hadn't done was to take a picture of the sphynx but when I put this to Mustapha he demurred.

"We cannot take our animals into the compound." he said," I need a special permit for that" and at that moment, the penny dropped. This tour was completely unofficial. I could see the compound and there were camels and horses being ridden around in there. I could have been annoyed that I had been misled but this was a leisurely way to see the sights, it was hot and I was in no mood for a slanging match. That did not mean that I did not know what was coming and I was not wrong. As we went around the outside of the cemetery, Mustapha brought his pony up level with me and asked.

"You have good time?"

"Of course," I responded having already decided what I would give him when he asked.

"Then you give me bakshish ?" he asked and when I nodded "and him too ?" he continued, indicating the boy who had been silently leading my camel the whole time.

I reached down and handed the boy ten pounds with which he seemed very happy and I gave Mustapha twenty.

"It is not enough." he said solemnly, lying through his teeth.

"I'm sorry, its all I have left," I said, lying through my teeth, too. I paused as though I was thinking and then pretended that I'd come up with an idea.

"I know," I said, "Why don't we ask the Tourist Police back in the village how much they think I should give you and I'll change some more currency at the bureau when we get there."

There was a silence although he might have muttered something under his breath in Arabic but there were no further demands for money. It used to work that way in Morocco, too. Back at the village, he had switched back to his jovial host persona, we shook hands and I went to find Jim.

"Would you like to drink some Jasmin tea?" Jim asked me when I found him and this, too, seemed like a good idea. He took me into a shop where I was brought tea. I was rather hoping that it would be a restaurant but it turned out to be a perfume shop and the owner, a gushing man skilled in the art of oriental salemanship insisted on showing me his wares. After ten minutes of being sprayed with a selection of his most exotic fragrances, I was beginning to smell like something between a Turkish harem and an Egyptian knocking shop and I called a halt to proceedings. I told him that I wasn't a tourist, I was a budget traveller, the difference being that I did not have the funds to buy up loads of expensive souvenirs nor did I have the means to carry them home. To his credit, he kept his painted smile in place and we both retained our air of politeness but his haste to get me out of his shop was only exceeded by my own haste to leave.

It didn't take any powers of detection for me to realise that I was likely to be taken on the sort of tour that can happen in any tourist destination in the world. Somewhere along the way, there was likely to be an unscheduled stop. Maybe we would go and see Jim's father, brother, cousin, or great uncle twice removed – once by the Police, but I was willing to bet that this person would have some sort of souvenir or carpet shop where I would be on the wrong end of a very hard sell. There was no point in telling Jim that I didn't want to go to any more shops because he did not want to hear that and therefore he would not listen. This was a working day for him and he was out to get as many kick backs as he could. I would have felt sorry for him had it not been my money he was after. When I got back to the car where he was waiting for me, someone must have told him that I did not buy any perfume, and, therefore he would not be getting any commission so he did not look pleased but this was about to change.

It was still fairly early in the day so I suggested to him that we went to Saqqara to see the pyramids there. We agreed an additional charge of thirty pounds and set off at once. I was hoping that this would provide a diversion and keep us away from any more souvenir shops and it did for a while. Saqqara was where Egyptian nobility was buried when Memphis was the capital of ancient Egypt. I can remember being told, incorrectly, by one of my primary school teachers that all the Egyptian pyramids were in Memphis but what did she know? She used to blush every time she discovered *Spotted Dick* on the menu for school dinners. I'd like to have been there when they told her it wasn't a sexually transmitted disease. We headed straight for the pyramid of Zoser, also known as the "Step Pyramid" which predated any of the pyramids we had just seen in Giza. It was about half the size of the Great Pyramid of Cheops and had been badly affected by age and erosion. Jim came with me into the surrounding funerary complex and took several photographs of me examining the tiles and reliefs.

We returned to Cairo on a dirt road, which ran alongside an irrigation canal where farmers were working in the fields and heavily laden camels trundled by in single file, kicking up clouds of dust as they went. After a few miles, Jim pulled up at a restaurant for lunch. The establishment he chose was clearly not one that was frequented by tourists. Even though it was quite crowded, I was the only non-Egyptian there. As we sat and munched our chicken kebabs on skewers, it occurred to me that, this time yesterday, I'd been in a taxi on the M4, somewhere between Hammersmith and Heathrow, far from dirt roads, canals and camels. While we were eating, I bought a couple of bottles of mineral water as I'd come out without any that morning and in June, it was necessary to drink at least two litres of water a day to avoid dehydration. After about an hour, we moved off again and when we made our predictable unscheduled stop, it was not at some sleazy tourist shop purportedly run by a fictitious relative of Jim's, it was at a craft school where, supposedly, children were being taught to make carpets.

This was not so much a school as a medium sized factory where about forty young children between the ages of four and twelve were working on looms, turning out traditional Egyptian hand-made carpets. Jim left me while I was given a conducted tour of the premises by the proprietor. He was not impressed by my complete disinterest in the merchandise, he was evasive when I asked about the children's welfare and he refused point blank to answer any of my questions about bonded labour. I never managed to establish whether or not the children received any formal education but in a place like Egypt, he told me, having a skilled trade was better than having no trade at all and they would always be able to earn a living, but he did not say for whom. I have never felt easy about child labour and I recalled part of the charter drawn up by UNICEF, where it said something about a child's right to education and a child's right to play. I hoped that these were being observed as I politely thanked my host for his time and left without buying anything. I was to encounter far more serious examples of child labour later in the year when I visited Pakistan.

Once more, Jim was visibly disappointed as I left the school empty handed and we made our way back to Cairo in silence. We agreed to meet up again the next day and I went back to the Ismailia House for a shower. All in all, my day could have been a lot worse and although I was taken to two establishments where I was expected to buy merchandise so that Jim could earn a percentage, I'd been well treated and left both places on good terms with their respective proprietors. However, I thought that I could save him further disappointment and myself potential grief if I made things clear to him the next morning that I had not come to Egypt on a shopping spree.

At about seven that evening, back at the hotel I was sitting in front of the television clutching a bottle of beer and watching a trailer for the world cup which was due to start next day. I was chatting to Joseph and

Bill, a couple of Nigerian students in their early twenties who had been staying at the Ismalia House for some time and said they were waiting for money to come through so they could buy plane tickets home. They seemed to have enough to get by on but I bought them both a beer and proceeded to pick their brains about decent places to eat. Ominously, they were unable to recommend anywhere so I finished my beer and headed for the lift.

I have never felt very confident about lifts in general but the one in this building was special. There were about ten or eleven floors to the building but it was difficult to estimate just how old the block was. The exterior was rendered in dirty, grey concrete but in Cairo, concrete could get that dirty within twenty four hours, while the lift looked more like a relic from the thirties, supported by a chain that could have been stolen from a 1950's high-flush cistern. I remember long ago as a young newlywed, my wife and I went up the tower of Westminster Cathedral in a similar lift. The attendant was a ghostly spectre of a man who bore a strong resemblance to the comedian Max Wall and when he saw I was nervous he sought to reassure me with the words:

"Don't worry, young sir. This is a Christian lift. It takes you up but it NEVER lets you down."

I have a clear recollection that I trembled visibly for the whole of the ascent but laughed it off as the inevitable consequence of the icy mid-February weather. I felt the same way on this particular evening but was unable to use the same excuse. The attendant smiled at me reassuringly, like one of those spooky guys in "The Curse of the Mummy's Tomb" just before an apparition appeared wrapped in bandages and crushed the victim's skull. I was relieved to be out on the street and I crossed the Midan Tahrir past the bus stands to the rear entrance to the Nile Hilton. There was a security check here and everybody had to pass through an electronic metal detector. Of course it bleeped when I walked through and I turned out my pockets to reveal the spare set of front door keys to my flat in Hayes, a few English coins and my Swiss Army Knife complete with bottle opener and that ingenious little spike designed to whittle stones out of horse's hoofs. There's not much call for those in Hayes.

When I reached the central reception area, a palatial gallery with an open plan staircase, which rose regally towards somewhere exotic that I never got to see, I was confronted by a crowd of Egyptians, much merriment and the banging of drums. Women were parading themselves wearing extremely expensive and brightly coloured traditional costumes, while the men wore Armani, Dior and Cardin dress shirts with immaculate bow ties but no jackets due to the heat. I'd somehow blundered into the middle of a fashionable wedding reception involving two prominent Cairene families and two things immediately became clear to me. Firstly, that festivities would continue long into the night and secondly, that there was likely to be little or no service elsewhere in the hotel because most of the staff were fully employed here and were likely to remain so. I went back the way I came being spared the metal detector on the way out which surprised me. For all they knew, I could have stolen the silverware.

I walked back across the Midan Tahrir – Liberation Square – which resembled a poor man's Piccadilly Circus with all the traffic problems but no Eros. Every so often, I'd be accosted by an Egyptian who wanted to be my guide, or to take me to his brother's souvenir emporium but I politely declined and they left me alone. It's funny how none of them wanted to take me to their brother's restaurant, their brother's cocktail bar, their brother's pub or even their brother's knocking shop. Maybe I was in the wrong part of town but I doubted that. It was getting on for nine o'clock but still oppressively hot when I found it.

I'd been looking for something relatively harmless to eat, preferably vegetarian. While I knew I'd get some form of stomach upset sometime – it was one of the joys of travelling after all – I did not want to catch anything just yet so I needed to eat something bland and filling. It didn't necessarily have to be nutritious but that would be a bonus. I turned into a narrow side street just behind the Ismalia House and found just what I'd been looking for, Pizza Hut. It must have been a Muslim franchise because they only sold soft drinks but in this heat, Coca Cola was better than nothing and I managed to consume an entire two litre bottle in one sitting.

I went back to the hotel where a group of travellers were sitting round the television watching a film. I ordered up a beer and joined them. They'd been in Cairo for a number of days. Some had come from the south, mainly Luxor and Aswan while the rest had come in from Israel where they'd been working on a Kibbutz. I didn't know why everybody got so excited about working on a Kibbutz, in fact I was willing to wager that the whole concept had been dreamed up by Josef Stalin or one of his cohorts. Who else could dragoon a large number of complete strangers into working ten hours a day, seven days a week for peanuts with nothing else to look forward to but a few glasses of local plonk and the vague prospect of getting your leg over a beautiful Israeli girl? Maybe I was cynical because I'd already spent a number of years working long hours for low pay at the London Borough of Wavering. The local plonk was Young's Special and my only workplace carnal adventure had involved the Director of Housing's secretary, who was neither Israeli nor beautiful.

Jim turned up bright and early and I invited him to join me for breakfast, which was a meaningless gesture because I was never asked to pay. I explained to him that I was not interested in shopping but I was not sure whether he had been listening. I'd already decided on an itinerary so it was just a case of agreeing a price. First of all we would go to the Citadel to visit the Mohammed Ali Mosque and then I wanted to spend a few hours wandering aimlessly around the El Khalili Market. After that we could improvise. On the way to the Citadel, we made an unscheduled stop, thankfully not at a shop, but at a macabre scene that Jim thought I might find interesting, one of two so-called Cities of the Dead, immense Islamic cemeteries, which seemed to stretch for miles.

It has been estimated that several hundred thousand people lived here amid the tombs and relics, which to me looked like a novel way to solve a housing crisis. Something similar had been tried by the City of Westminster in the 1980's but their enterprise, involving the sale of several West London cemeteries to a developer for a nominal fee, had been nowhere near as successful. A similar subterfuge involving the sale of selected stocks of social housing to well-healed political supporters did succeed in the ruling Conservative administration retaining control of the Council during a difficult election but the project was subsequently declared unlawful leading to the downfall and disgrace of the person responsible who was, I am reliably informed by those who worked there at the time, a particularly unpleasant individual.

I did not venture in too far or for too long as I did not wish to intrude on the privacy of those who lived there but by Cairo standards, this was not a bad neighbourhood. Some parts had schools, shops and electricity and others even had piped water and sewers. It didn't seem to matter to the residents that they had a dead body in their front room.

Our next stop was the eleventh century citadel, which towered above Islamic Cairo and the Mohammed Ali Mosque, which lay within its walls. This was an inspirational Ottoman style Mosque reminiscent of Sinan's magnificent creations in Istanbul. Unfortunately, the tin sheeting which now covered its domes had conspired to disfigure and cheapen the overall effect. The mosque had been completed in 1848 but problems with its construction had led to the replacement of the domes during the 1930's with the tin sheeting being added as a precaution to protect against further deterioration.

I have always had a fascination for mosques but I can't remember when it first started. Since 1988 I have put together a collection of photographs from Turkey, Syria, Jordan, Spain, Bulgaria, and of course Egypt. Later I was to add many more from Pakistan, China, India, Malaysia, Indonesia, Thailand, Iran and Central Asia. At some time in the future, I was hoping to compile a book containing what I felt were my best efforts but, to date I consider my collection to be by no means complete.

If the outside of the Mohammed Ali Mosque was flawed, its interior was spectacular, with domes ornately decorated in green and gold, illuminated by a multitude of scintillating chandeliers and globe lights, while the glistening white marble tomb of Mohammed Ali lay within a bronze grille near the entrance. In spite of the interior lighting, I did not feel I could get a decent photograph without a tripod but I had not brought one with me and I left without taking a single picture.

The road which twisted its way down from the Citadel was surprisingly clear of vehicles but it flattered to deceive and we soon found ourselves in a slow-moving procession of traffic until we reached the Khan el Khalili bazaar, a veritable warren of alleyways containing souvenir stalls, jewellers, leather merchants as well as whole host of artisans' workshops, all aimed at separating gullible tourists from as much of their money as they could be persuaded to part with. It had been my intention to have a quiet walk around and to take a few photographs but this did not prove to be possible. As soon as I'd set foot in one of the main alleyways, I was grabbed by a shop-keeper, hustled into a souvenir shop and subjected to a master class in fast talking sales pitches until the perpetrator was compelled to pause for breath and I was able to tell him that I did not want to buy anything. My pronouncement was greeted with either disbelief or feigned anger. Some traders refused to accept that I could not be interested in what they had to sell while others turned plain hostile as though it was me who was wasting their time and not the other way around. In the end, I sat down in a tea shop with Jim, ordered two teas and a water pipe which Jim and I took turns to puff while we watched a continuous line of Cairenes and tourists perform a soft shoe shuffle past our table. Jim didn't say anything of course, but he must have been disappointed that I did not come here to shop like the package tourists and he asked me whether there was anywhere outside Cairo I was interested in going. I mentioned that I'd never been to Mount Sinai and his face lit up.

After I'd settled the bill in the cafe and we'd managed to extract our taxi from a morass of parked vehicles, Jim set off in the direction of Heliopolis where, he said, I could book an excursion to Mount Sinai. As we left the dusty streets and sand coloured buildings of Islamic Cairo behind us, I started to recognise our surroundings and well before we arrived at the travel agency, I knew it was going to be Sinai Desert Tours. We took the lift to the eighth floor and were met in the main office by another beautiful brown-eyed Egyptian lady, who proved to be extremely helpful.

In reply to my request she explained what was on offer, which was a three day, two night package involving two nights at the company's hotel in Na'ama Bay, the El Ghazala Gardens, an overnight ascent of Mount Sinai, a visit to St. Catherine's Monastery and transport there and back. The cost was something in the region of $150 US which was reasonable but I did not want to spend so much at the beginning of the trip as I might leave myself short at the end, so, much to Jim's chagrin, I thanked the lady and left. At this stage, I suspected that Jim had decided to cut his losses and find another visitor. Almost on cue, he suddenly invented a sick relative he had to go and visit and he suggested that he took me back to the hotel.

This suited me perfectly. I knew my way around now and there were places I wanted to return to without a taxi so that if I changed my mind and decided to take off somewhere else, I could do so without having to negotiate a price. Getting back early also meant that I could watch the football match between Ireland and Italy. While England's inability to qualify meant that I wasn't as interested in this world cup as I had been in the previous competition, it did not mean that I had no interest at all.

Failure to return to Na'ama Bay for want of spending a mere $150 proved to be a false economy as I might have been spared a rather unfortunate experience later in my trip. I might also have visited two sites in the Sinai that I missed the first time around and re-visited the sumptuous El Ghazala Gardens Hotel but it was not to be. Indeed if I ever decided to go to that part of the country in the future, I would find things much changed. In the early hours of the morning of 23 July 2005, an Islamic terror group rejoicing in the name of the Abdullah Azzam Brigades drove a truck packed with explosives into the foyer of the hotel and detonated it

Overlooking Na'ama Bay, Sharm-el-Sheikh.

killing 45 people. Shortly before that a bomb in a suitcase exploded outside the Movenpick Hotel and another truck bomb went off in the market taking the overall death toll to 88 people. Egypt had become a dangerous place to visit.

For the next few days, I visited most of the tourist spots including the Zoo and the Museum of Antiquities. I also made a return visit to the El Khalili Bazaar, without being harassed by belligerent shopkeepers but I was feeling like a change of scenery and booked a ticket on the overnight train to Aswan. This was due to leave on Friday night, two days from now so I had plenty of time to relax and chill out.

Adjacent Mosques of Sultan Hasan and Al Rifai below the Citadel, Cairo.

With two days left in this city, I decided to visit the area they called Islamic Cairo and walk approximately four kilometres from the foot of the Citadel, through the Bab Zweila to the Al Azhar Mosque. To call this Islamic Cairo was something of a misnomer since all of Cairo was Islamic but this was older, much older and went back to medieval times almost to the earliest days of Islam itself.

At 10 A.M. next morning, I jumped into a taxi a few blocks from Tahrir Square and promptly jumped out again when the driver set the flag drop at 60 Pounds. The whole trip should not have cost more than 35 so he was clearly cheating me. Other taxis I'd taken had set their flag drop at between 10 and 15 pounds and around here I would have no trouble finding one. This must have occurred to the driver, too, and after he agreed to set the drop at 15 pounds, I got back in again and we set off in a south easterly direction towards the old part of town.

I was set down at the base of the Citadel on the corner of Midan Saladin and the junction of Al Immam and Sayyida Aisha, paid the driver the 40 pounds on the meter and set off without tipping him. Midan Sala ad-Din, the square of Saladin was once a 12th century parade ground and had been laid out at the same time as the Citadel, but I soon moved on from there. Just along the road, I could already see the minarets of the Sultan Hassan and Riffai Mosques but in my haste, I did not see the motor cyclist who nearly hit me while I was crossing Al Immam and, judging by his reaction, he probably didn't see me either but that didn't stop the tirade of aggrieved invective he rained down upon me in Arabic.

I had seen these mosques on numerous occasions but for various reasons had been unable to visit them. They are highly photogenic and had featured in many magazine articles which had made me even more impatient to see what was inside their impressively high walls. I turned left into Sharia Al Qalaa, a narrow street which ran between both buildings and went straight to the Sultan Hassan Mosque. Believed to be one of the finest examples of Bahri Mameluk architecture in Cairo and known to be one of the largest mosques in the Islamic world, this edifice was commissioned in 1356 by the man after whom it was named and completed in 1363. Unfortunately, Sultan Hassan did not witness the opening of the mosque, having been assassinated several years beforehand. I entered a dark passageway which opened out into a quiet, peaceful courtyard, where I paused to take a few photographs.

It was with some regret that I was unable to do the same after I left this inspiring edifice, crossed the narrow Sharia Al Qalaa and entered the equally imposing Mosque of Al Rifai. Begun in 1869, though not completed until 1912, this mosque, with its towering walls rearing up like battlements gave the impression that it was even more significant than its neighbour. Within its walls were contained the final resting places of Khedive Ismail, who built the Suez canal, his three wives and his mother Khosiar Hanem. It was she who commissioned this vast mosque with the intention that it should become a mausoleum, dedicated to Egyptian royalty.

This immense structure was built on the site of the former burial place of Shaykh 'Ali al-Refa'I, a medieval Islamic saint and his tomb is now housed within the present mosque along with that of Yehia Al Ansary, a companion of the Islamic prophet , as well as those of many members of the Egyptian Royal family. In addition, there are the tombs of two former Shahs of Iran and the last two Kings of Egypt, Fouad and Farouk, neither of whom were particularly popular with the Egyptian people. Fouad was little more than a puppet for the occupying British while Farouk was not

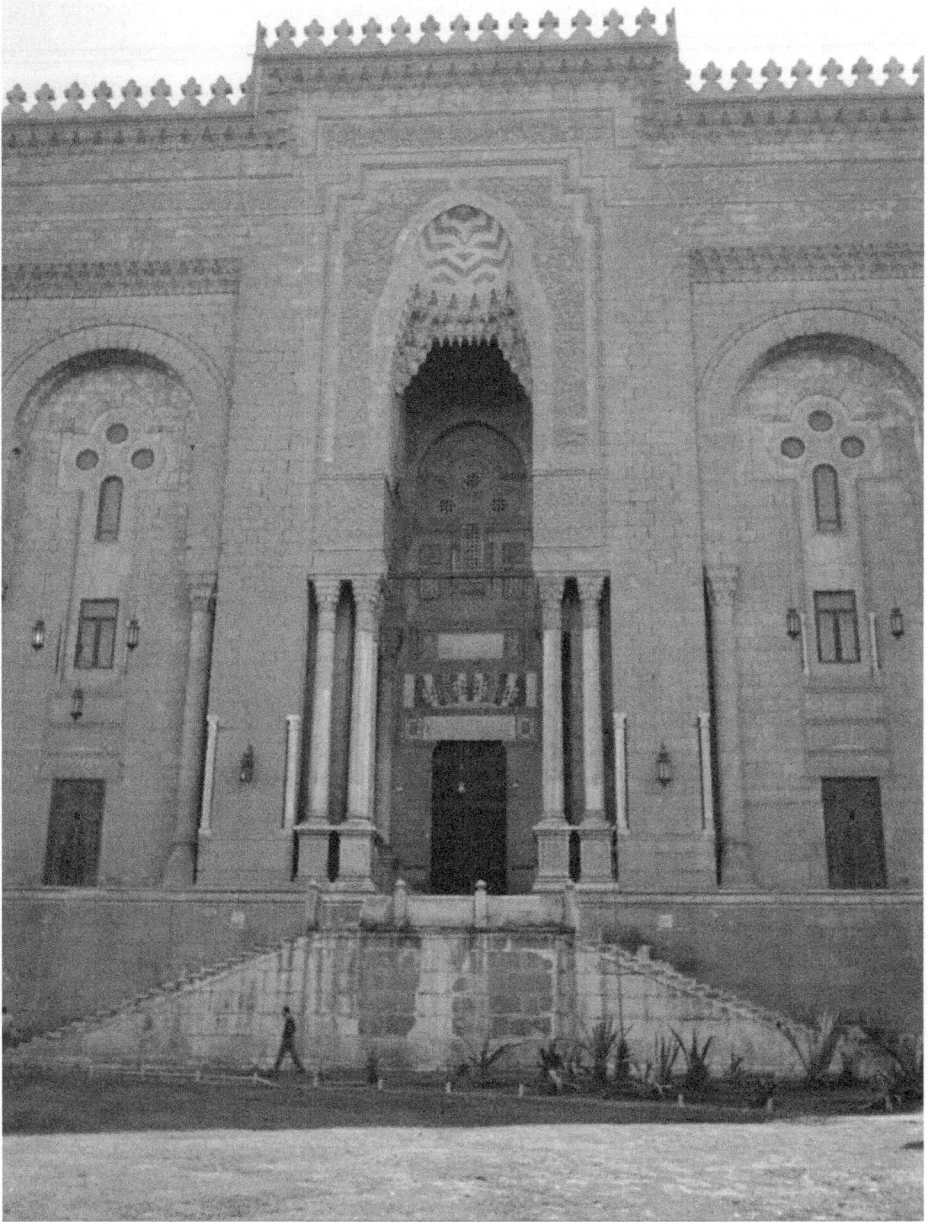

Rear view of Al Rifai Mosque.

very interested in ruling at all, preferring instead to gamble, drive fast cars and use his rank to coerce women of lesser status into his bed chamber.

To my immense annoyance, what should have been a spectacular blaze of light and colour proved to be nothing of the kind. Most of the lamps, large brass lanterns strategically suspended from the ceiling to enhance the appearance of the interior had been left off resulting in a shadowy, sepulchral gloom. There was a small aperture in the roof that let in some small shafts of light but this did not permit me to take any meaningful photographs and I cut short my visit.

Having collected my shoes from the rack near the door, I turned right and having reached the end of Sharia Al Qalaa, I was unsure how to proceed. I knew that the Bab Zweila was in a northerly direction from where I now stood and the most direct route was by way of the street they called Sharia al Tabana. They called it Ahmad Mahir Pasna and Darb Al Ahmar as well which was confusing, especially as the last name was also the name of the district through which it passed but it made no difference because none of them was anywhere near me. My guide book was next to useless since, while it contained all the main roads and those of interest to a traveller, not all of these were marked, particularly those which I currently sought. To add to my confusion, I was in a warren of narrow alleyways, not wide enough to be called streets and I was a little worried that I might inadvertently turn into somebody's front doorway.

I kept walking in roughly a northerly direction in the hope that I would eventually come across someone who knew the way and could point me in the right direction, preferably without demanding money for his help or appointing himself as my guide but this proved to be a forlorn hope. After about five minutes, the alleyway where I was walking opened out onto a wider road and as I approached a small group of Egyptian men to ask for directions, the nearest of them adopted a stance that I had already seen too often in this part of the world. Right arm outstretched, palm upwards "Baksheesh" he demanded without waiting for me to speak. His companions then put out their hands in a similar manner.

"La Shukran," (no thank you) I said to them and continued walking, grateful that they did not pursue me. Another group of Egyptians I encountered a little further down the road was more helpful and informed me that I was already in the street I was looking for. They called it Darb Al Ahmar and if I carried on the way I was going, I would eventually arrive at the Bab Zweila but I had a little way to go.

The Dar Al Ahmer itself had a colourful history, the name translating into "The Red Road," and had housed a thriving Islamic community since the 14th Century. Nowadays, its northern section towards which I was walking is called Ahmad Mahir Pasha and the southern part, Sharia At Tabana. In spite of the fact that it was late morning, there were fewer people around than I expected and most of them appeared to be heading in the same direction I was, which was encouraging but some of the others were a little worrying.

The street was lined on both sides with flat fronted buildings, small shops and what appeared to be workshops with Egyptian men, either in small groups or individually, sitting on the ground outside them, not doing very much of anything except keenly observing everyone who went past – a little too keenly for my liking. I had seen similar groups in other parts of the Middle East and North Africa, particularly in Morocco where they had been extremely predatory as if they had been looking for an opportunity to get into a man's pockets or a woman's knickers as indeed many of them were.

Suddenly, from out of nowhere a little boy no more than four years old appeared in front of me. There was a grim, angry expression on his face as though he was confronting something hateful even though the top of his head reached no higher than my belt buckle at which he was staring intently. He continued to stand his ground and when I took a sideways step, so did he, remaining steadfastly in my path. I then stepped back only for him to take a pace forward and when I stepped to the side, so did he implacably maintaining his position in front of me. I felt that all eyes were upon me particularly those of the men sitting at the roadside. I had read of a similar situation in Krakow, Poland, where a couple of local men had harassed a tourist in a similar manner, except that one stood in front of him and one immediately behind, effectively obstructing him at every turn. Presumably the tourist parted with money to escape, something I had no intention of doing.

I looked up and sure enough, the observers at the roadside were watching and waiting to see what I would do. Taking care not to make any contact with my diminutive adversary, I took half a step back before executing a quick slide shuffle and shimmy, changing direction as I did so and, in seconds, I had left everybody far behind me. It was the sort of manoeuvre that Mohammed Ali might have stolen from Willie Pastrano when they trained together and I am glad I remembered it as I was sure I would need it again.

I continued to walk more briskly than before, relieved to encounter growing numbers of people as I went. I could see the minarets of the Bab Zweila off to my right and quickened my pace even more. As I drew level with this inspiring structure, I became aware of a crowded street to my left, leading to the Street of the Tentmakers but I was now standing under the towers of the Bab Zuweila and its pull was irresistible.

Bab Zweila gate Islamic Cairo.

The Street of the Tent Makers is one of Cairo's oldest bazaars, leading to a food market with stalls packed with fruit and vegetables basking in the sharp aroma of herbs and spices. Food was being cooked on street side charcoal grills as Cairene families came to buy their weekend provisions. It was very tempting to break off and explore this pulsating host of humanity but I decided to leave it until my return from Aswan.

I paid the man at the Bab Zweila desk five pounds, climbed the stone steps and forsaking the minarets which looked a little claustrophobic, installed myself on the lower gate rooftop where I could take in the entire 360 degree view. The Bab Zweila is the southernmost of three medieval gates of the city commissioned sometime after 1087 by Vizier Badr ad-Din el-Gamali, the other two gates being the Bab-el-Futuh and Bab al-Nasr. The Bab Zweila is named after the al-Zawila tribe of Berbers, whose soldiers were once billeted nearby and the gate used to be the starting point for the faithful to begin their annual pilgrimage to Mecca. It was also the scene of many executions and a number of Emirs were hanged here including the last of the Mameluke sultans, Tumanbey. After the fall of Baghdad and Damascus in 1260, the Bab Zweila was the scene of the execution of four Mongol emissaries, who had been sent to demand the surrender of Cairo to Houlagu, the grandson of Ghengis Khan. Their heads were hung up on the gates and the Mongol advance was subsequently repulsed.

I am not sure how long I spent on the roof of the lower gate, gazing down upon a veritable forest of minarets, mausoleums, mosques, madrasas and crowded markets. I would have been far more comfortable up here with a chair, a table, a cup and saucer and a pot of Earl Grey but I had more chance of getting those in the market down below so I made my way downstairs onto Sharia al-Muizz li-Din Allah and another busy market similar to that of the Street of the Tentmakers opposite. There were vendors offering traditional Islamic and western clothes, household goods and what looked like sacks of raw cotton but no sign of a decent cup of tea. I did see a few young boys with trays of tea and I knew if I followed them they would undoubtedly lead me to a tea shop but, my recent experience in Darb Al Ahmar left me a little wary of pursuing this course of action. I carried on walking through the crowded market until I reached the junction with Al Muski where I opted to turn left into Sharia Gawhar al Quaid as the former was uncomfortably congested and this way seemed to be the easiest way to get to the Al Azhar mosque. Whether it was or not

I cannot say for certain but it was less congested and by now I had become selective as to which sights I wanted to see.

Reaching the junction with Al-Garmalyya, I could see the Midan Hussein – Square of Hussein – and the Sayyidna al-Hussein Mosque on the opposite side of the road. I'd like to have visited the mosque but entry to non-Muslims is forbidden. This is one of the holiest sites in the entire Middle East and contains the shrine in which the head of Ibn al Hussein, grandson of the Islamic prophet Mohammed is reputed to have been buried. The present building was completed in 1870 and supersedes a 12th Century mosque, which previously occupied the site. The exterior was disappointingly bland and I hoped for the sake of the faithful that the interior was more interesting.

The Al Azhar mosque, a little further down the road was certainly interesting. Dedicated in the year 972 AD, it is claimed to be the world's second oldest university behind that of Al Karaouine in Fes, Morocco. However, both of these claims have been widely contested by a multitude of scholars throughout the non-Islamic world on cultural grounds and the precise definition of what a university should be. Apparently, the Al Azhar's Muslim only admissions policy and its Islamic curriculum based on detailed study of the Koran and Islamic law, involving a great deal of learning by rote are considered by many international academics to be too exclusive, too narrow and too specialised for accreditation, particularly as the university's stated objectives remain the propagation of Islamic culture and the Arabic language. However, this conclusion may be unduly harsh as teaching is also provided for students in secular subjects and faculties of Medicine and Engineering were added in the early 1960s. In spite of reservations expressed by secular academics concerning its scholastic proficiency, the Al Azhar mosque is considered by Sunni Muslims to be the supreme school of Islamic law and jurisprudence in the entire Muslim world and its scholars are recognized to be the most influential and respected.

I passed through the magnificent 15th Century Barber's Gate, so named because this was where students used to have their heads shaved and proceeded straight through to the white facaded 10th Century courtyard, part of which was laid out with seating. When I asked one of the staff, I was told that some sort of gathering would be held here this evening and I was welcome to stay. I asked him whether I was allowed to climb one of the overlooking minarets and he virtually asked me to pick one.

The view into the courtyard was impressive and I stayed in the minaret for some considerable time before descending the winding stairway to the prayer hall, a vast expanse of pillars and arches separated by hardwood beams. When I checked my watch, I found it was already four O'Clock so I went out into the street and picked up a taxi to take me back to Tahrir Square.

The Ismalia House was a pretty easy-going place, people were in and out all the time and security around the reception area was somewhat laid back. People used to reach across the desk and take their keys while staff had either been distracted or were dealing with enquiries from other residents. It wouldn't have taken much for anyone to lean across the desk and take a key that wasn't theirs.

The following evening, I sat around talking to the Joseph and Bill, the Nigerian students and a couple of South African lads who had just been working on a Kibbutz in Israel and were trying to book a flight home at a price they could afford. Joseph said neither he nor Bill had any money so I treated them to their beer. The morning I was due to leave, Joseph knocked on my door and asked if he could borrow twenty pounds. There was no way I was going to get it back but I gave it to him anyway. Having done my good deed for the day, I went out, crossed the Tahrir Bridge to Gezira and headed for the Cairo Tower, a tall rotund monstrosity in concrete with a revolving bar on top, which provides panoramic views of the city when the weather is clear. It was getting hot already and the hazy cloud of dust and vehicle pollution suggested that visibility would not be at its best so I decided to give it a miss. Instead, my curiosity took me across the far bridge towards Dokki, where, for future reference, I decided to try and find the hotel I'd stayed in during my previous visit to Cairo.

As I approached an intersection, I was accosted by a respectable looking Egyptian in a suit who, I suspected, was either a tout for a souvenir or carpet shop or, worse, a gay looking for a partner. There seemed to be a lot of the latter in this part of the world but I was wrong on both counts. He owned a shop, which sold both souvenirs and carpets and he had a car nearby to take me there if I cared to go. This proved to be a stroke of luck since his shop turned out to be in the same block as the hotel and I spent a good half hour going through his stock. To his credit, he was not selling the usual low quality tourist tat and I was quite taken with some of the hand beaten metal plates he had on sale. I would have happily bought a few if I'd had enough money with me or if I'd had the means to take them with me on my travels. Unfortunately, I was leaving for Aswan that night and I did not know where I might be headed after that so carrying them around with me and keeping them safe was going to be a problem.

The problem was solved at a stroke. For a small surcharge to cover postage he said he would post them back for me and he would also accept payment by credit card so that I could save my cash. We jumped straight into the car and sped back to the Ismalia House where I quickly collected my Bank of Scotland Mastercard and returned just as speedily to the shop to complete the transaction. I ended up buying six gilded plates, most but not all of which bearing an impression of Nefertiti and I addressed them to myself care of my sister's house in Portsmouth. As the man put my Mastercard through his machine to complete the transaction, he left me with something valid to sign, but he split my card in half in achieving it. This would be very fortuitous later.

That evening, I made the short and relatively simple journey to Ramses station from the Midan Tahrir by Metro, the first time I had used this form of travel in Cairo. The underground train was jam packed with people but I was used to that. It was no worse than the Piccadilly or Victoria Lines at peak periods and a good deal better than some of the others. When I arrived at Ramses station, I found myself submerged in a sea of struggling humanity. Apart from other passengers, there were vendors, hustlers, touts and self-employed porters who wanted to carry my luggage. I would have liked them to carry my luggage, too, but I did not have very much change so, with such things as luggage trollies only available at airports, I was forced to haul a huge valise and a shoulder bag through this heaving mass of people unassisted.

It seemed the entire population of Cairo wanted to get on the overnight train to Aswan. I knew which platform the train was due to leave from because I'd checked that out when I bought my ticket but the train was so long, that when I got onto the platform, I couldn't figure out which end was which.

Also, my ticket was written out in Arabic so even if I did find out the direction the train should be facing, I still didn't know which carriage I would be occupying or which seat number I had been allocated, but I knew a man who did. A small amount of baksheesh paid to the nearest railway employee got me into the right carriage but he put me in the wrong seat so I had to pay out more baksheesh to someone else to get to the right one. I had decided to travel second class, not so much to save money, but because I had been advised at the hotel that there was not that much difference in quality, only price. As the train moved out slowly, I had hoped to see a spectacular view of Cairo by night but by then it was too dark to see very much of anything except tall shadows illuminated by street lights, so I settled into my slightly less than comfortable seat and fell into a fitful sleep frequently interrupted by tea vendors and less frequently by scheduled stops. One of these took place in the middle of the night at the troubled town of Assyut but I wasn't sufficiently awake to realise this.

RETURN TO ASWAN

We arrived in Aswan sometime after six next morning and the train was met by a pack of voracious touts, guides and hustlers. I decided to stay in my seat and let the other foreigners bear the brunt of the onslaught and by the time I had alighted, the crowd had moved away from the platform and the carriage cleaners were about to begin work. I started to make my way towards the exit but I did not get far.

"You look for hotel?" A young Egyptian in his late teens emerged from somewhere behind me and made to help me with my bags but I was already carrying both of them.

"It depends," I replied cautiously, "Whereabouts and how much?" The time I had spent talking to the other travellers at the Ismalia House taught me a lot about the hotels and the general street life in Aswan and I knew where to go, and, more important, where not to go. I knew that there were all sorts of cheap hotels for backpackers but I did not necessarily have to stay in one. If I wanted anything better, I could easily afford it and I was considering going back to the Cleopatra, a good class hotel where I could get a single room with en suite bathroom for around 20 US Dollars but I was prepared to listen to offers. There were supposed to be two hotels named after Bob Marley and both had been recommended to me. I'd written down a few others, too.

"This good hotel," he said predictably," My uncle is the owner." That was predictable, too.

"So, how far and how much?" I asked him

"Close to Kornesh," he said, which was good because that was where I wanted to be, "and ten pounds a room," he concluded which was the price of a bog standard flea-pit but I thought it might be worth a look.

"How do we get there?" I asked him.

"We have car, come," so I went. He had a battered old Citroen parked outside, which roared to life when he turned the key in the ignition and we headed off in the direction of the river at a blistering pace. If I didn't like the room, I could pay him for the lift but either way I would have no trouble finding somewhere at this time of year.

He took me to the Abu Shelib Hotel on the corner of Sharia Abbas Farid and Sharia Al Souk. It was less than 100 metres from the Corniche and just around the corner from the market so, all things considered it could not have been more convenient. My room had an en suite bathroom without hot water but at that time of year it made no difference, all the water was hot. For ten pounds a night, it was a bargain. In the small reception area, I noticed a few chairs and tables in front of a colour television, which, I was told, had been specially acquired for the world cup. There was a small restaurant, too, just off the reception area but because this was low season, they only served breakfast but there were plenty of other places nearby.

While I was at the Ismalia House, I'd been told all sorts of things about Aswan. About how persistent the hustlers were, how I'd never get a moments peace and I couldn't walk three steps down any road without getting harassed and how every single person I'd meet would be after me to give them money. They could have been describing anywhere in Morocco, Pakistan or India, but not Aswan. Here, I found exactly what I wanted to find and I spent a quiet week just hanging out talking to people, effortlessly exploring the town and taking the odd excursion or boat ride on the river. The only thing the people in the Ismalia House got right about Aswan was that at this time of the year the temperature would be ten degrees hotter than it was in Cairo.

After mid-day, it would get so hot that I could feel the heat from the pavement through the soles of my trainers. Anybody who wore sandals would have been very uncomfortable and anyone who went barefoot would have been badly burned. All the Egyptians just shut up shop and got out of the sun until five, which was the only sensible thing to do. After five, it was cooler, the town would slowly come to life again, the shops would reopen and people would gradually re-appear. The Souk would reverberate to the sound of traders touting their wares, the braying of donkies, and, later, the distorted wailing of the Muezzin summoning the faithful to prayer from an overworked PA system halfway up a minaret. Many, who had made a conscious decision to defer their devotions until after the last business transaction of the day, disregarded this while others, who were Christians or other denominations, did not subscribe anyway.

Between twelve and five, I occasionally took refuge on the covered terrace behind the Old Cataract Hotel, where I'd look out over the river and drink a few bottles of cold beer. At that time of the day, I had the whole place to myself as the guests generally took to their air-conditioned rooms. A flock of sparrows had taken refuge in the rafters, a cool place to hide from the blistering heat of the midday sun but they did not stay there for long. With every beer the waiter brought me, he also brought two or three little baskets of nibbles, either cheese crackers or salted peanuts and gradually, the birds would descend.

First of all, one would sit on the back of the chair next to me. He'd been given the job of seeing what I was likely to do and to ascertain whether it was safe for the others. When, after a few minutes it had decided that I was not a cat or any other predator that would cause it immediate pain, it hopped on to the edge of the table, paused for about three seconds before making a quick dash for the nearest basket from which it proceeded to liberate a small biscuit before flying off to safety to devour its prize only to be replaced immediately by two or three more of its compatriots. After about ten minutes, even the most timid among them must have realised that I was no threat to their safety and they all flew down from the rafters to help themselves to a piece of cheese cracker or a peanut

Every time I ordered a beer, they would retreat to the safety of the eaves until the waiter had gone, then the whole descent ritual would start again, first with one sparrow, then a couple more until gradually they were all over my table. These little birds soon came to regard me as just another piece of inanimate furniture, which consumed amber fluid from a glass and caused food to be brought for them. They perched on my shoulders and on my head while they steeled themselves for a quick swoop on the food baskets. For my part, I tried to keep my movements to a minimum, except for the inevitable trip to the toilet. Once I swept up my hand in an involuntary movement when one tiny sparrow, more adventurous than his fellows started to stick his beak into my left ear and another time I felt compelled to put my hand over my glass to protect it when another of them teetered unsteadily on the rim with his backside hovering ominously over my beer.

All in all, I found it a pleasant experience although I didn't realise just how many birds were climbing over me until one afternoon when a group of Australian hotel guests came down early from their siesta and walked into the conservatory. One of them, supposedly thinking she was witnessing a scene out of an Alfred Hitchcock drama let out a piercing scream causing the timid little creatures to scatter instantly and nothing I could do would bring them back again.

On the rare occasions when I did not spend the afternoon at the Old Cataract Hotel, I would go to the Cleopatra and sit in the air-conditioned reception area. On another afternoon, I caught the ferry, a replica of a pharonic barge, over to the north of Elephantine Island to the Aswan Oberoi Hotel. Arguably, this is the most expensive hotel in Aswan, yet from a distance, it resembles an airport control tower and looks so hideous, its architect must have had some sort of penis fetish. Once inside, it proved to be cool, luxurious and spacious but there were no guests. It was like booking into Hotel California.

I sat in the reception area with a glass of beer and watched while three people shuffled papers behind the reception desk and all sorts of waiters and flunkies were passing backwards and forwards, looking extremely busy. People were mopping floors, buffing brasses and polishing woodwork but there was no sign of any guests.

I finished my beer and went outside to walk around the grounds and it was the same thing here. They must have had a workforce comparable in size to that of Kew Gardens and they were digging, hoeing and watering everywhere I looked but there were no guests out here either. I was beginning to feel as though I'd intruded into some sort of institution where all the inmates were kept locked up. It was really disturbing out here, like being on the set of a "Halloween" movie so I made my way down to the landing and waited for the barge to take me back to the mainland before the knife wielding maniac in the ski mask put in an appearance.

Abu Simbel just after dawn.

The first day I arrived in Aswan and settled in at the hotel, I found that I could book excursions at reception. There were three visits I'd missed out on last time I'd been here and I was not going to do it again. The first one was to Abu Simbel and necessitated a 4 A.M. start. I went to bed early the night before and arranged to be called at 3.15. By that time, I was already in the shower but there was no call. I came down at 3.30 to find the night reception staff asleep on the floor. I was joined later by a young Englishman, also named Peter, and we waited patiently to see whether our transport would arrive or whether that, too, had been forgotten along with our morning call.

A large black taxi drew up outside at 4.15. The driver apologised for being a little late but he had gone to pick up two other clients first. Now he had us all on board, we set off at a sedate speed, presumably to take account of the heat of the desert and the age of his clapped out old Citroen. The reason we had to start so early was that Abu Simbel is approximately 280km south of Aswan and unless you arrive early in the morning, the whole facade is plunged into shadow and it is difficult to get a decent photograph. Also, as the morning goes on, plane-loads of package tourists start to arrive so that the interior of the temple becomes unbearably crowded making any attempt at photography futile. The attraction of the site is twofold. Firstly, there are four gigantic statues of Ramses II, which were originally carved out of a mountainside. There are also four similar statues in an adjacent edifice dedicated to his queen, Nefertiti. As if these statues were not sufficiently inspiring in themselves, there is an exhibition inside the temple complex showing how these magnificent structures were saved from total submersion in what is now Lake Nasser. I have to admit, I left there more in awe of what it took to move the temple than I was of the temple itself.

According to our driver, who doubled as a guide, UNESCO undertook this difficult and onerous salvage operation in the 1960's. The monuments were sawn by hand into over a thousand blocks weighing up to thirty tons each. Within two years, an artificial mountain had been created to match the original location and Abu Simbel was reassembled there, 180 feet above its former site. After I looked at the exhibition, I went back outside to take some more photographs and to take a closer look at the statues, and, allowing for the fact that they were the best part of two and a half thousand years old and every single one of them had been cut up into chunks and reassembled, I couldn't see any sign of a join. By 9.30

we had seen enough and we adjourned to one of the tea stands for break-fast as the first of the tourist coaches started to arrive.

A few days later, I went to see both Aswan Dams. This time I went alone by taxi from my hotel since both dams were reasonably close to Aswan so the trip was neither expensive, nor was it particularly long. The British built the original dam at the turn of the century and at that time it had been the biggest of its kind in the world. Although it stands 150 feet high, it is difficult to appreciate this from the top and, as there is no view to speak of, I did not stay long. I have to say that the High Dam was not much of a spectacle either. I have seen photographs of the Hoover Dam and it looks gigantic. By comparison, the Aswan High Dam looks quite ordinary, and standing on it is a most underwhelming experience.

Photography was strictly forbidden and security here was as tight as a drum but it was easy to understand why. If the dam were to burst, it would be a world-class disaster and Egypt would be submerged in a torrent of floodwater from here, all the way up through the delta to the Mediterranean coast. Numerous threats have been made against the dam since its completion, the most significant coming from the Israelis during the two wars and the Libyans in the early eighties so that the surrounding area is heavily fortified with anti aircraft weaponry and radar installations but none of this was visible from the road.

The driver lit up a cigarette while I looked back over Lake Nasser, conscious of the fact that I was standing on one of the earliest pawns in the deadly battle of wills that had been the Cold War. Originally, the fi-nance for the High Dam was to have been provided by the World Bank but when they went back on the deal, under pressure from the US Gov-ernment, the Egyptian president, Colonel Gamal Abdul Nasser turned to the Soviet Union for funding. He also nationalised the Suez Canal, which provoked an invasion by British, French and Israeli armed forces, an epi-sode in history that is forever engraved on my memory.

As a second year pupil at Portsmouth Grammar School, I can remem-ber looking out of my classroom window and watching a long procession of military hardware trundle down towards the Royal Naval Dockyard to be loaded onto transport ships and aircraft carriers. Over the previous few weeks, an invasion fleet had been assembled in Portsmouth Harbour and if anyone had needed to ask where it was going, the sand-coloured camouflage with which the tanks, armoured cars and Austin Champ jeeps had been painted provided an instant answer. The official story was that they were going to Cyprus and initially they were, but as far as we knew, there were no deserts there. Years later, I befriended a former officer in the Royal Marines who, as a young squaddie, had taken part in the landing at Port Said. Even today, he is convinced that the whole operation could have been mopped up in record time had the British and French Governments not caved in to American outrage and threats of Soviet intervention.

Although I did not find Aswan a particularly difficult place for hustlers, the riverside or corniche was an exception. This was low season and the felucca operators who did a brisk business around Christmas were now feeling the pinch. Any foreigner on the corniche was spotted a long way off and pestered mercilessly until he or she agreed to take a felucca ride. It wasn't just the felucca operators who were a nuisance, the shopkeepers, too, had a habit of jumping out in front of unwary visitors and dragging them into their souvenir shops where they would get the traditional hard sell before they managed to escape. However, unlike other places in North Africa, the Egyptian traders were polite and comparatively restrained.

After eating in one of the many floating restaurants which lined the river's edge, I tended to spend most evenings back at the Abu Shelib with Christian, a young German engineer who was in Aswan working on a Euro-funded project for the Egyptian Government. Like me, he was an avid football fan, but his national team were the current world cup holders and were there to defend it, unlike England who had played like geriatrics in all their qualifying games and never came close to reaching the finals. Although I pretended to make light of it, as far as English football supporters were concerned, our failure to qualify for the world cup finals was a humiliating national disaster. It was even more humiliating when compared to our performance in Italy in 1990 when we made the playoffs for third place. Each evening we were joined in the reception area of the Abu Shelib by Peter, our fellow resident and Gamel, a felucca captain who had named his craft "Baggio."

Gamel had a wife in England and while his spoken English was perfect, his written English was not and I used to write letters to her at his dictation. He told me he was trying to put together a felucca cruise to Edfu and I agreed to go with him. Peter, my fellow-traveller to Abu Simbel said he'd come, too, which left Gamel only three more people to recruit. He said he would need at least five passengers to make the journey viable and as soon as he signed them up, we would leave. Until then, it was really no hardship to stay in Aswan. Gamel had a brother who operated the "Baggio" in his absence and anytime I felt like a quick trip across to Elephantine Island or just up and down the stretch of river fronting the corniche, one of them would take me. This arrangement brought me an unexpected bonus in that the other felucca operators accepted that I was Gamel's customer and stopped harassing me.

Sometimes, in the early evening as I strolled down Sharia Abbas Farid on my way back to the Abu Shelib , I would see entire Egyptian families sitting in the street on chairs outside their homes with the television on the front doorstep, watching re-runs of the previous night's football. Invariably, they would ask me to join them but I would only stay a short while, as I was due to meet up with Gamel, Christian and Peter to watch the live game later. Inevitably, by the time the game had finished, much beer had been consumed and, after all the various key incidents had been re-run and analysed by the TV panel, it was well after twelve. I often wondered how Christian managed to get up for work every morning as I found myself sleeping in later and later, so much so that I was always too late for the boat trip to Philae island. In the end, I had to compromise.

Every other evening, a Son et Lumiere took place on Philae Island so as my opportunities for embarking on the day trip began to recede I opted for that instead. Just after dark, I took a taxi down to the Shallal motor boat dock on the edge of Lake Nasser to find that so few tourists had turned up for this particular performance, only one boat had been required and I'd just missed it. The rest of the boatmen were about to adjourn to a tea stand across the way to watch the football on a portable television. My taxi driver and I begged and pleaded with the other boatmen until one of them finally relented and said he'd take me providing I agreed to pay the price of a full boat, twenty pounds. It was a bargain but I did not want to appear too eager just in case he decided to renegotiate and double the price but I needn't have worried, that was double the price.

Philae Island is the site of the Temple of Isis, a magnificent Ptolemaic temple, which like Abu Simbel had been due for submersion under Lake Nasser and needed to be relocated. The massive structures had been the subject of another salvage operation by UNESCO during the 1970's, which moved them to higher ground on the island formerly known as Aglika Island.

Lake Nasser itself was quite a spectacle covering an area of 312 square miles. Once filled, the water surface of the lake caused the average

Taking the crops to market in a village on the Nile.

temperature in the region to reduce, while the Aswan High Dam has controlled the natural flooding of the Nile, which had previously been unpredictable and had sometimes led to disasters. Before the dam opened in 1971, the Nile used to flood annually, which was often something of a mixed blessing. Sometimes the water level would be too high and wash away farm crops leading to food shortages. Other times it would be too low, providing insufficient irrigation leading to crop failure. Two major plusses brought about by the dams are that the waters of the Nile have now been harnessed to provide hydro-electricity and passage down the river has improved considerably. Unfortunately, there have been unforeseen ecological difficulties. The rich topsoil that used to be carried down river by the annual flood surge is now trapped irretrievably within the confines of Lake Nasser, causing farmers to resort to the use of chemical fertilizers. To make matters worse, the flow of the Nile is no longer powerful enough to keep the Mediterranean salt water from forcing its way into the river, where it disrupts the natural habitat of many riverside animals and sterilises the soil in the area of the Northern Delta, causing the banks to become severely eroded.

I'd seen pictures of the Temple of Isis and it looked imposing and majestic but by the time my boat had tied up at the landing stage, it was dark and all I could see were shadowy silhouettes. When it started, the light show proved to be a workmanlike and efficient performance but they could have done without the soundtrack, which could have passed for an outtake from "Carry On Cleo." Any attempt at photography was out of the question, as I would have needed a tripod to take anything like a decent picture. The only trouble with this performance was that the lighting was turned down after each individual exhibit had been illuminated leaving visitors to stumble around the site in conditions of visibility, which varied from twilight to complete blackness.

I am not at my best in these situations.

Although there were only about a dozen or so other visitors that evening, those few that I avoided staggering into, I managed to fall over or step on and at the end of proceedings, they must have been very relieved to see that I was going back in a boat by myself. While I was staggering blindly from one location to the next, I managed to stub my toe twice on rocks before twisting my ankle and putting myself out of circulation for the whole of the following day but it was worth the experience, or so I thought at the time. I changed my mind the next day when I found that I was limping heavily and my attempt to walk along the corniche not only took me most of the morning, but I had to hobble sideways like a crab to make any progress at all. The locals were very curious and one or two of the children started to impersonate what they took to be my silly walk but I did become more mobile by evening when the football was due to start.

That night, after the game between Bulgaria and Germany, Gamel asked me if I wanted to go to a Nubian Wedding in his village on Sehel Island the following evening. Naturally, I accepted and asked if it would be OK if I took my cameras. I'd visited the villages on Elephantine Island

One of a pair of magnificent statues just past the West bank landing stage, Luxor.

several times and used up three rolls of film on its extrovert inhabitants, agreeing to post them their photographs when I returned home.

The next evening, looking resplendent in a brilliant white Djellabiya, Gamel came to pick me up from the Abu Shelib just after dark. It was a hot, humid evening as we set off in a taxi to the ferry landing four kilometres away where we were joined by a number of other guests on the small, wooden boat waiting to take the short crossing to Sehel Island. The lights from the island were sending gold and silver streaks across the water as the cheerful twittering of the daytime sparrows and egrets gave way to the long, mournful cries of the birds of the night. As we sat waiting for the boat to move, I could see thousands of small insects skimming across the surface of the water while I was aware of a number of others making a nuisance of themselves on the boat. I had taken the precaution of smothering myself in Deet extract and although I smelt like a chemical factory, I was confident that it would protect me from the unwanted attention of mosquitos as they came out to feed. They were not alone. Sinister rustling deep in the undergrowth indicated the presence of larger predators, whether rodent or reptilian I could not tell. The lights from the boat caught a black Kite as it swooped low over the surface of the water. Just then the engine suddenly burst into life and we began to move slowly towards our destination.

Before we reached the village, we had to cross two rocky, boulder-strewn hills where Gamel pointed out a series of Ptolemaic inscriptions that had been written on various rocks and stones. Exactly how they had been inscribed was something of a mystery since the lack of any indentation ruled out carving, neither did they appear to have been painted. It was possible that the words had been scorched into the rocks but there was no way of telling. When I asked Gamel, he did not know how they had been made, only that they were many centuries old. I found out later that these messages were either details of voyages that the various writers had made beyond the first cataract, which was just down the river from here, or prayers of thanksgiving following their safe return. I picked my way carefully as we went down the slope into the village as my ankle was still giving me trouble.

The village was a collection of single-storey buildings in rendered sandstone and mud brick, built as close against the hillside and as far away from the riverbank as it was possible for them to be. Some of the houses but by no means all of them had been painted white. Gamel took me to his home, a traditional mud brick building no different from the others and divided into several rooms. He introduced me to his mother a kindly woman who I guessed was a little younger than I was and to his eleven year old brother, who I'd not met before. They took me into a dining area where dinner had been prepared for us, a delicious vegetable stew on crushed grain reminiscent of cous-cous with brown unleavened bread. When we had finished our meal, Gamel told me that the wedding festivities would not start until around midnight so we moved to another room where there were cushions, seats, and, at the far end, a television set ensuring that we would not miss any football, even if it was only a repeat of an earlier game. Not every family in the village had a television set and before the game started, another of Gamel's brothers joined us along with a few of his neighbours. The Egyptians were football mad and were very patriotic in support of their national side but just like England, Egypt had failed to qualify for this competition so their supporters transferred their allegiances to other African sides. First, they backed the Cameroons, the most successful African side to compete in Italia 90 and after they had been eliminated, they transferred their loyalty to Nigeria's Super Eagles until they, too, fell by the wayside and, with no more African sides left in the competition, the local boys decided to support the eventual winners, Brazil.

After the football had finished and we had all shouted ourselves hoarse at the images on the screen, we made our way through the darkened village to the site of the festivities, a large clearing, which had been fenced off and divided into two improvised auditoria both brightly illuminated with arc lights that had clearly been erected specifically for this event. One area was empty and Gamel told me that this was set aside for socialising. It appeared that we would be getting live music as the second area contained a huge stage that looked like a tribute to Woodstock with a number of speaker and amplifier towers and a cluster of microphones. Gamel, like most young men from around here was a great fan of the late Bob Marley and he told me that a reggae band would be playing later. In between being introduced to most of the population of Sehel, all of whom seemed to be related, I was constantly being mobbed by children, who wanted their photographs taken but I had plenty of film and it was no hardship.

Gamel then led me towards a vast horde of ululating women and told me I was about to meet the bride but I couldn't see how. Like some sort of queen bee, she had concealed herself within this mass of friends and well – wishers and while I was being encouraged to push my way through to her, I was unable to do so since nobody was prepared to step aside. Luckily, help was at hand. One of the people I had met earlier turned out to be the bride's father and, with a wave of his arm he miraculously caused the throng to part and hustled me in front of a small stage lavishly decorated with multi-coloured drapes, where the bride sat in state, attended by a number of bridesmaids. Her face had been heavily made up in pale, pastel shades, which offset her burnished gold wedding dress, a stunning garment that had taken her family many months of intricate work to complete. Her father indicated that he wanted me to take photographs and I knew I would have no difficulty with the light as the stage was brightly lit. At first, the bride feigned shyness and modesty, presumably for the benefit of her friends and supporters but when I pretended to defer to her reticence and indicated that I was not going to take her picture after all she stopped pretending and posed for the camera like royalty. Ultimately, I sent Gamel a sizeable package of photographs when I got back to England and it probably took him a week to distribute them.

As the night went on, the crowd had swollen to several thousand strong, the men clad mostly in white djellabiyas, while the women wore traditional robes in a variety of bright colours to match the Islamic hijabs with which they covered their heads. I managed to miss the actual wedding ceremony in the crush but something must have been going on as the noise had become deafening. There was drumming, singing, ululation, dancing and, as Gamel had predicted earlier, there was Reggae as well, with a band from out of town turning in a creditable rendition of the old Eddie Grant classic, *"Livin' on the Frontline."* They played a lot of other stuff as well but that was the one I remembered, probably because it was so strange to hear a song so obviously written about South London being played at a wedding in Southern Egypt. Everyone I met made it their business to see that I had enough to eat and drink and when I asked if I could take their photograph, nobody refused me. It was three in the morning and there were so many people, but everyone was exuberant and nobody seemed to mind the crowds or the noise. Gamel had long since left me to my own devices. The ferry was running all night as part of the festivities as were the taxi's to and from Aswan on the opposite side of the river. When I wanted to leave, all I had to do was ask someone the way to the pier and the rest was easy.

I did not do a great deal the following day, apart from get up late and sit around most of the day drinking tea. My ankle was still swollen and I had a number of other bruises, too. I also had a headache, which in the absence of any alcohol the night before, I put down to the noise and lack of sleep. In spite of my ailments, I did manage to walk up the corniche as far as the post office and back but it was hot and I'd been up most of the previous night. At about 5 P.M., Gamel arrived at the hotel with another Egyptian, who he introduced as "Kangaroo". He, too, was a felucca captain and he was also trying to put together a trip up river. Gamel told me apologetically that he would be unable to take us to Edfu. He had telephoned his wife earlier and she had said she would be coming over in a week or so and obviously, he had arrangements to make, which was where "Kangaroo" came in. "Kangaroo," a close friend of Gamel's, had received his nick-name because he had so many Australian clients, and, in view of Gamel's recommendation, I agreed to go along with him as long as he did not leave before the World cup final.

WHY HOLD THE WORLD CUP ... THERE?

I tried to get enthusiastic about this world cup, I really did, but the most memorable aspect of it for me was the exotic location from which I watched it and the congenial company I shared while doing so. Apart from England's abysmal failure to qualify, the other thing that upset me about this particular world cup was that it was held in the USA, a failed British colony. Most of the population was blissfully ignorant – particularly about the world cup and the nature of the game that was being played. Apart from the irritating Ra! Ra! Razmataz and Disneyesque showboating, which assumed an identity of its own, and, in the process, trivialised a serious international sporting event, the Americans had no footballing tradition of their own, neither had they been any good at it on the rare occasions when they had condescended to play. Major League Soccer was established in the USA in 1993 and has grown slowly since then with the national side reaching the quarter-finals of the 2002 World Cup and being ranked tenth in the world by 2005. In 1994, they were not considered good enough to be also-rans but try telling them that. Try telling them anything. The rationale behind staging the World Cup in America was to sell the world's most popular game to the world's most insular population and to make a great deal of money in the process. I accept that their national side managed to beat England in a friendly during the run up to the competition but most people regarded the result as an aberration even though that particular England team was so bad, even Iceland could have beaten them.

From what I could glean from international newsreel coverage, the American sporting public had no interest at all in the event except to express a dogmatic, though irrational view that America would win the trophy because "*America always wins.*" That America went on to lose every game they played gave untold satisfaction to millions of serious followers of the sport throughout the real world, who'd suffered the indignity of having such groundless declarations of national superiority thrust at them through every organ of disinformation possessed by the jingoistic American media.

At this stage I must confess that I have never been to the USA and I am in no hurry to do so. Initially, I was put off by stories of drugs, violence and guns, but since such anti social behaviour has now crossed the Atlantic and the Indian Oceans, as well as the Mediterranean Sea and the North Sea, not to mention the White Sea, the Black Sea, the Irish Sea and the English Channel, they can no longer be used as an excuse. If I am really honest, I have actively boycotted our former colony because of the way the American establishment, its press and its politicians miss no opportunity to devalue our country and diminish its tremendous contribution to the modern world, both past and present. In spite of superficially embracing all things British, any so-called special relationship between our two countries is a myth. America has a long history of assisting anti-British movements throughout the world, the long-term funding and supply of arms to Irish republican terror movements and their refusal to extradite terror suspects being only the latest in a long series of such activities.

Additionally, the majority of the Americans I have met over the years have not been over-burdened with intelligence or common sense. This would probably explain why the likes of Spiro Agnew and Gerald Ford were elected Vice – President with Ford, once described as being unable to cross a road and fart at the same time without having an accident, eventually becoming President. I concede that it is a fundamental element of democracy that an electorate should be represented by one or more of its peers but I am dismayed that no American Presidential or Vice-Presidential candidate has ever been required to take any form of intelligence test, always assuming there was any intelligence in the cranial cavity capable of being tested.

Another thing that bothers me is that most adult Americans do not possess passports and are reluctant to leave their native land, preferring instead to remain marooned in the good old USA. Those Americans, who do travel, often give the impression that they have not left their homeland at all. For instance, whenever I ask one of them where they come from, he, or she – this is not a gender issue – will tell me the name of their city and the state in which the city lies. It does not occur to them that I might have asked them their country of origin. At this juncture, I used to ask them what part of Canada that was but I stopped doing it as it seemed to be unkind and the irony was lost on them anyway.

America appears to have more cranks and loonies per square foot than any other country on the planet, which goes a long way towards explaining why they were the first people to give to the world such priceless gifts as nuclear weapons, organised crime, recreational drug abuse, institutionalised racism, militant feminism, Coca Cola, Kentucky Fried Chicken, McDonalds and, in the space of eight years, two presidents called George Bush. It is hardly surprising, therefore, that America was discovered by accident, although discovered might not be a fitting word to use in the circumstances, since the people who were living there at the time had no idea it was missing. It is a historical fact, however, that when Columbus set out on his journey to America, he did not know where he was going. When he arrived, he did not know where he was. When he returned home, he did not know where he had been.

To add insult to injury, Americans claim to speak English. I agree that some of the early settlers might well have done so but what passes for English in that country now, a post-colonial dialect commonly known as Microsoft English (US) interspersed with African-American ghetto slang and a whole host of other incomprehensible noises, is ungrammatical, incorrectly spelt and when articulated, makes the speaker sound as though he or she is suffering from an incurable form of irritable vowel syndrome.

The two most popular forms of sport in America, and they go in their tens of thousands to watch both, either involves a bunch of Neanderthals dressed like Morris dancers playing a highly ritualistic form of Rounders called Baseball, or worse, what they call football, a sanitised version of Rugby League, indulged in by packs of giant, pumped-up robots in space suits. As for the beautiful game called Association Football and enjoyed by every nation in the civilised world, the Americans dismiss it out of hand, referring to it disdainfully as "Sakkur."

The match between Brazil and Italy promised to be a fitting climax to a competition, from which I felt unusually detached. Unfortunately, the two finalists seemed intent on boring their opponents into submission and in the process produced the worst final in living memory. I have to admit that there were times during that game when I wished I'd gone down to the pub only there wasn't a pub to go to. Gamel's hero Roberto Baggio was playing for Italy although he was carrying an injury and many felt that, in the final analysis, it was his lack of fitness that separated the teams. Be that as it may, by the time the whole non – event had ground its way down to the penalty shoot out, the only people still interested were Brazilians or Italians. In all, the game had been a bit of a let down but it suited my mood. Although I knew I had to move on, I did not want to trade the peace, tranquility and camaraderie I had found in Aswan for the noise and hassle I knew was waiting for me in Luxor.

AN INAUSPICIOUS RETURN TO LUXOR

There were four passengers on our felucca plus Kangaroo and his crewman, Ali. There was a young Swedish couple, Sven and Elsa and, of course, Peter from the Abu Shelib. There should have been another man, too, but he'd picked up a stomach bug and had to cry off at the last minute. I was wondering how that would affect the financial side of the trip but I decided to wait and see. We had been advised to buy at least ten litres of drinking water each but I bought a couple more just to be on the safe side. A felucca on the Nile in July was much, much hotter than the drafty old Sobek in December. The body of the boat had been boarded over to provide a deck so we could stretch out. It also enabled us to stow our baggage somewhere cool out of the sun.

This trip was completely different from the one I had taken on the Sobek, which used to chug away at a rate of knots. By way of contrast, there were times when our felucca appeared to be totally becalmed and we never seemed to move at all. What little breeze there was came from east to west making it necessary for us to tack into it, backwards and forwards across the river in languid zig zag patterns. None of this was any concern to us as we lay there, inert and apathetic in the heat, either watching one bank as it moved gradually away from us or waiting for the other to edge slowly towards us. Sometimes, there were people who waved to us from the bank. Other times they were driving camels, donkeys or buffaloes from the fields back to their villages. Occasionally, when I felt energetic, I took photographs, especially when we passed some sort of settlement, but most of the time, I just propped myself up on one elbow and watched the river banks, the lush vegetation and the people who lived there, glide slowly by. There was little shade and, although I tried hard to keep my films out of the heat, it was very difficult. In the oppressive humidity, even the birds had withdrawn their labour, packing the branches of the wilting vegetation and refusing to fly even short distances.

Eventually, we came to Kom Ombo, the temple of Haroeris and Sobek that had two of everything most temples have one of, except of course a pylon. We disembarked and strolled around the relics. There was nobody else here and we had the place to ourselves, except for a large friendly ginger cat, who was very approachable even though I had no food to give him. During the early part of the evening, Kangaroo moored up to the bank where, after their prayers, he and Ali would prepare the evening meal. This was a sort of vegetable stew with unleavened brown bread washed down by liberal supplies of mineral water. At first light, we all awoke to witness a spectacular blood red sunrise as Peter jumped fully clothed into the Nile, explaining afterwards that this was the nearest he was going to get to a shower and his clothes would soon dry out in the heat.

We spent another long, lethargic day hardly moving on the river followed by another warm but less than comfortable night wrapped in blankets on the bare boarded deck before we reached Edfu just after mid day. Our felucca journey was due to end here and we were to go on to Luxor by public bus. My misgivings about the funding of the journey proved to be well founded as Kangaroo explained with much embarrassment that as we were one person short, he and Ali would be out of pocket. I had no reason to disbelieve him but the Swedes were adamant that they were not going to pay any more and Peter did not look too happy either. Between all of us, the extra cost came to another sixty Egyptian pounds, about ten pounds sterling, so I told them all that I would pay and if they wished to contribute, they were welcome to do so. We had been well looked after on our voyage. I had enjoyed it immensely and I was not going to have it spoiled at the end for want of a pathetically small amount of money. Fortunately, the others felt the same way and contributed accordingly.

Our arrival in Luxor later that afternoon was chaotic. The bus station was a sea of shouting, screaming people in which we were slowly drowning. Our luggage had been stowed onto the roof of the beaten up old bus that had brought us here and now, one of us had to go up and pass it all down, case by case, pack by pack, to the less than steady hands of the others. Nobody was particularly willing to climb up, but, just as I was steeling myself to volunteer, two young teenagers saved me the trouble. As they approached us, the taller one addressed himself to me.

"I am looking for Mr. Peter, Mr. Peter, Mr. Sven and Miss Elsa," he said, and, when I told him he had found us, which wasn't difficult as we were the only non-Egyptians on the bus, he continued "We have come to bring you to our hotel. We get your luggage now." With that he demonstrated great agility by running up the metal ladder at the rear of the bus and indicated that I should follow him. When I reached the top of the ladder with my head protruding over the edge, he asked me to identify our bags so he could hand them down to his compatriot. When everything had been unloaded, including Sven's gigantic backpack, he explained that his uncle had telephoned to warn them of our arrival and they had come to meet us. I guessed that Kangaroo had phoned ahead knowing we were going to need somewhere to stay and decided to put some business in the way of his relatives. It was just as well we had paid him his money otherwise we would have been on our own, probably surrounded by touts and we could well have ended up in somewhat less than salubrious accommodation in a town that is far from tourist friendly. As it was, we had to walk to our destination, which took us about twenty minutes through the back streets, fully laden and I was struggling long before we arrived. They were taking us to La Fontana hotel, a newly opened low budget establishment on the edge of town some distance from the river, the sights and the hustlers. The hotel, though basic was clean and spacious. Ahmed, the proprietor welcomed us and allocated us rooms. Most of the rooms were twins but I was lucky enough to get a single. The reception area doubled as a restaurant so we decided that we'd eat in that evening. As La Fontana was a Muslim establishment, there was no beer, but none of us wanted to brave the Corniche just for alcohol, so we stayed where we were and drank fizzy orange.

The following day we each went our separate ways. I was never really an Egyptologist although I was impressed by the size and intricacy of the temples and by the fact that they were built by sheer sweat and sinew, I came to Egypt first and foremost for the Mosques but there were very few in Luxor that were of interest to me. I decided that I would give the Valley of the Kings a miss and that I would stay on the east bank. By mid day, I had been to five mosques, none of which was very notable. All the while, people were coming up to me in the street asking if I would like a guide or whether I wanted to go to a shop. It was all getting very tedious. I had also visited the Luxor Temple and was able to take all the photographs I wanted but the heat was blistering, my nerves were frazzled and I was in dire need of a long cold beer and somewhere comfortable to sit while I was drinking it

I walked up to the Winter Palace Hotel, only to find that it was closed for long overdue renovation so I went next door to the opulent New Winter Palace, sat down in the lobby and ordered a beer. When the waiter brought it, along with a small plate of crisps, I picked up my guidebook and turned the pages until I found somewhere that interested me. I decided that I would not stay here more than another day and would take a train to Alexandria before moving on to Port Said and Ismailyia. As I continued to read, I realised that, while it was low season here, it was probably high season on the Mediterranean coast and I was likely to need some financial back up so I reached into my shoulder bag for the black leather pouch that held my credit cards. I found it easily enough but something was wrong. I took out the two pieces of my broken Bank of Scotland Mastercard but that was all there was.

My two American Express cards and my Switch card were missing.

I sat there stunned. I could not believe what had happened and then I realised how serious it was. American Express cards were not like credit cards. The balance had to be settled in full every month and there was no upper limit on how much I could spend. In theory, whoever stole it could go into a shop, pretend to be me and buy whatever he or she wanted and I would have to foot the bill. I could lose everything I had, my savings, my retirement lump sum, even my flat. I sat there shivering, suddenly aware that the air conditioning was full on. It had been full on all the time but I had not been in shock then.

I finished my beer and went to the American Express office which was conveniently placed next door in a small entrance under the main staircase of the Old Winter Palace hotel but it was closed until 3 P.M.. My first priority was to get the cards cancelled. I needed to get word to my friends in Putney so I went back to the New Winter Palace and asked whether I could send a fax. A receptionist took me deep into the hotel, beyond the restaurant area to a desk, which claimed to deal with all forms of international communication. I was introduced to Marissa, a strikingly attractive young Christian woman who was very attentive. I explained what had happened and she gave me some hotel headed paper on which to write my fax. I wrote a brief account of what had happened and returned it to Marissa along with one of one of my friend's business cards. Marissa said she would keep any reply for me and I went back to the bar, ordered another beer and waited there, sipping it slowly until American Express opened.

I left the bar at 3 P.M. sharp and as I entered the American Express office, I was relieved to see there was no queue neither were there any other clients, just two heavily built, middle aged Egyptians sitting behind adjacent desks engaged in a serious conversation. If they had not been so obviously Egyptian in appearance, they might have been mistaken for the Welsh second row although their mannerisms reminded me of Laurel and Hardy, except that Laurel was just as big as Hardy and neither of them turned out to be very amusing. There was a cash desk with high glass surrounds at the end of the office but no-one was sitting there. I went up to the two men and waited but they ignored me. I tried the usual ways to attract their attention, like coughing, saying things like "excuse me please," but whatever it was they were discussing had to be really important. Maybe they were plotting to kill Mubarak, but I had troubles, too. I was a gold card-holder, or at least I had been until my discovery earlier on, and being the only customer in the office, I thought that I should be attended to. The two men obviously thought otherwise. In the end, I went around the two desks, stood between them so they couldn't ignore me and said.

"I have had my two American Express cards stolen." I was greeted with total indifference. Neither of them actually shrugged or said "So what?" or anything like that. In fact neither of them did or said anything. Maybe they were waiting for me to get out of their way but I was not going to.

"I want to report two cards stolen and I'd like them stopped." Still nothing. I might as well not have been there. "I want my cards cancelled… NOW!" I shouted at them.

I was likely to lose everything I owned and I'd had enough of their indifference. Their behaviour was straight out of the Victor Meldrew charm school, insolent and provocative. I felt like grabbing each of them by the scruff of the neck and kicking their fat backsides all the way down the corniche but I thought I'd give diplomacy one last try. I produced the Amex emergency number in Brighton and handed it to the man nearest to me.

"Would you telephone this number for me, please?"

"Who will pay for the call?" He asked. I couldn't believe this. I'd handed him an Amex headed sheet with the number written in quarter inch high figures with the words "Emergency Number-Freephone " printed above it in letters the same size.

"American Express will pay." I said," It's part of the service." He refused to acknowledge this. I told him that if he failed to get me the number I would make an official complaint about him to his employers. He appeared to consider this threat to his livelihood for a minute or so and then in a sullen and resentful manner he slowly dialled the number. As soon as he had a reply he handed me the receiver. It was the Amex emergency desk in Brighton. The operator at the other end wanted to put me on hold but I asked him not to. He had been unaware that I had been calling from Egypt and did not know what to do next. I gave him the number of the Luxor office and asked him to get the relevant person to call me straight back, which seemed to be a sensible thing to do. Before anyone could say anything else, we were interrupted by a heavily accented woman's voice asking who was going to pay for the call. I told her that American Express would pay and, in the absence of anything to the contrary from the other end of the line, I assumed that would be all right but the two buffoons opposite me had other ideas.

"You pay for the call." Laurel snapped. By now, I was having a great deal of trouble keeping my temper but I tried.

"The call is part of the service," I said, "I am a Gold Card holder."

"Show me your Gold Card." interjected Hardy irritably.

"I can't," I replied, "It's been stolen. I came here to report the theft." They both shrugged indifferently.

"So you pay for the call." said Hardy triumphantly.

"They will be calling me back from Brighton soon," I said, "After I have spoken to them I'll hand them back to you and you can sort out the cost of the call between you."

"We won't let you speak to them until you pay us for the call." said Hardy slyly. I told him not to be so stupid. I also told him that I would be sending a written account of what had happened here to American Express head office. He did not seem very interested.

The phone rang. I beat Laurel to it and picked up the receiver first. It was the call from Brighton as I knew it would be. I explained what had happened as far as I was able. I still had no idea how the cards had been stolen, when or from where. He asked me if I needed money but I told him I was OK and I just wanted the cards to be cancelled before I lost everything. He told me not to worry and assured me that the most I would lose would be a nominal charge of about twenty pounds per card. After we'd completed the formalities, cancelled both cards and arranged for a new Green Card to be left for me at the office in Cairo, I mentioned how I had been treated by the two clerks here and their insistence that I hand over cash for the cost of my phone call, which according to all the literature that I had been given by American Express, was part of the service. He asked to speak to one of the people I considered responsible and I passed the receiver to Hardy who had been hovering over me all the time trying to look menacing.

I don't know what was being said as Hardy just stood there impassively listening to the voice on the other end of the line. If he was getting a rollicking, he didn't give any outward indication to that effect but when he came off the phone, his sullen attitude had not improved.

"You go to Police and report theft." He grunted angrily. I was going to ask him for directions but I decided to consult the map in my guidebook instead and found the place quite easily in a nearby shopping precinct. Unlike Laurel and Hardy, the Police were very courteous and helpful but the man I needed to see wasn't on duty and would not be back until 7 P.M.. As it was now only 3.30 P.M., I decided to go back to the New Winter Palace to get something to eat. Afterwards, I went to see Marissa at the Telecommunications Desk but there were no faxes for me. I went for a walk along the river but it was hard going. I was being hassled at every step by self-styled guides, people selling boat rides, taxi drivers and men driving horse-drawn caleches.

There were a lot of horse drawn caleches in Luxor and I felt sorry for the horses that pulled them. Actually, I felt sorry for any domestic animal in Egypt and for many of the people, too. Animals are not treated well here. In Europe, and especially in the UK, any person who treated an animal as badly as they are treated in Egypt could expect to be prosecuted for cruelty. But in Egypt, there are many poor people and their poverty does not allow them the luxury of western values. They are too busy trying to stay alive to become bogged down in arguments concerning ethics or morals. Such things are for the Mullahs or the priests. There are few pets here. Animals are beasts of burden and they must earn their keep.

I noticed that the physical condition of the horses pulling caleches varied considerably. While some of them were clearly well-fed with healthy, glossy coats, there were others who were seriously mal-nourished and whose bones protruded pitifully from their sagging flesh. I remember when I was here before in high season, it was quite common for a horse to collapse between the shafts of a caleche. Camels were treated badly, too, but the creatures, which suffered most, were the donkeys. These poor little beasts were frequently overburdened to the extent that their harnesses tore deep gashes in their flesh, and, because these wounds were never given the chance to heal, they would putrify in the searing heat, attracting flies and other insects.

While the plight of these wretched creatures seems hopeless, an organisation operating in Egypt called the Brooke Hospital Foundation takes pity on these pathetic bundles of bones and offers free veterinary care to the working animals of poor people. The Brooke Hospital Foundation was set up by Dorothy Brooke in 1934 and since then, its staff has treated hundreds of suffering animals a day and saved others from many years of grinding labour. Those that are too ill or too old to return to work are given a brief period of rest, relaxation and care before being put down humanely – for many the only act of kindness they ever receive at the hands of humans.

I first came across this organisation in Jordan operating a veterinary surgery outside the ruins of Petra. Many young Jordanians earn a living here carrying tourists on horseback from the site entrance, through the Siq, a narrow gorge some 2 kilometres in length, to the ancient ruins. During the time they have been operating there, the veterinarians at the Brooke hospital have taught the horsemen to respect and care for their animals demonstrating clearly that a robust, well-fed creature would be able to work harder and earn more money than one that is underfed and ill-treated. They would also remain in good health and live longer. Before the hospital was set up, the young men would race their horses through the siq at breakneck speed, which often resulted in serious injuries and fatalities to both horses and riders. They have now been persuaded to stop this dangerous practice and instead, they take part in organised races on open ground five kilometres away.

While I visited the Brooke Hospital at Petra, I never managed to track down any of their hospitals in Egypt but I was told that they have establishments in Alexandria, Aswan, Cairo and Luxor, and, based on what I saw, there is a crying need for more. Donkeys are renowned for their longevity but in Egypt, they have an average life expectancy of just four years.

I went back to the Police station at 7 P.M. as I had been told but there was still no sign of the man I needed to see but his deputy was there, the local equivalent of a Detective Sergeant and he offered me tea. At 7.30, the main man arrived and got straight down to business. He was a large gentleman in his forties with a pleasant smile but piercing brown eyes that did not miss a thing. He spoke excellent English and asked me to explain in detail the exact circumstances surrounding my loss. I did this as far as I could and he asked me to write out a statement so he could get it translated into Arabic. After I had completed this, he asked me where I had been in Egypt and the hotels at which I had stayed. He didn't seem too interested in the Abu Shelib, but when I told him I had been staying at the Ismalia House while I was in Cairo, he started asking questions, lots of them. He wanted to know who else had been staying there, who I'd spoken to and what I had been doing. I must admit, I wasn't able to tell him very much and he didn't appear to be too happy with my answers. He went on to ask about what I'd been doing in England before I came out to Egypt, how much money I had and whether I had any debts. I reassured him that I had ample savings but I still had misgivings about my potential losses in spite of what I had been told by American Express.

After I had been there for two hours, I suddenly remembered Marissa at the New Winter Palace and suggested that we contact her to see if any faxes had come in for me. He dialled the number without looking it up and after speaking to what was probably the switchboard operator, he was put through to Marissa. He handed me the telephone and she told me she had received nothing for me. I thanked her for her trouble and handed the receiver back to the Policeman. Instead of putting it straight down as I expected, he started talking to her in Arabic and did so for a long time. He then replaced the handset offering no explanation. He told me that would be all for now but that I should go back to American Express the following day to see if they could tell me if the cards had been used and then return here the next evening.

I made my way back to the Fontana on foot and told everyone of my misfortune when I arrived. Everybody was very sympathetic, Ahmed made me tea and we all sat around discussing what had happened. To change the subject, I expressed misgivings as to the safety of my films in the heat on board Kangaroo's felucca and the consensus was that they might well have been damaged. Ahmed gave them to Mohammed, one of the youngsters who had brought us here originally and he agreed to get them processed for me. He brought them back the next evening, and, while the damage could have been far worse, I found that the heat had affected about twenty per cent of my pictures. Fortunately, all the wedding photographs seemed to be intact.

Next day, I was in no hurry to go out as I was beginning to feel very vulnerable on the streets. It had been a long time since I had felt like this. In Cairo, the street people had been persistent but polite. In Aswan, apart from the corniche, there was nowhere near as much pressure but here, they were positively voracious and unrelenting. In the late 70's and 80's I made several visits to Morocco but I stopped going there because of the constant aggravation to which I was being subjected. The touts, guides and hustlers were extremely loud, aggressive and easily inclined to violence. Towards the end of the 1980's the level of violent street crime had intensified to such a degree that the Foreign Office issued warnings to anyone who intended to visit Morocco so I gave up any thoughts of going back. More recently, a profound change in local attitudes has resulted in a revival of the ailing Moroccan tourist industry and by 2005, it had once more become a prime destination for European tourists. The people working the streets of Luxor had some way to go before they emulated their 1980's Moroccan counterparts but in my present state of mind, they were too much for me.

I had breakfast and sat around the hotel until early afternoon by which time I had started to feel stir crazy. I knew that American Express would not be open until 3 P.M. so I decided to go down to the New Winter Palace to see if my friends had sent me a fax. By now, paranoia was setting in and I was wondering whether they had received the fax I'd sent them the day before. As I approached the international telecommunications desk, I thought I saw Marissa glaring at me and as I came closer, I could see that I was right. She was cold and scrupulously polite. Nothing at all like the friendly young woman I'd spoken to yesterday. As far as she was concerned, I'd suddenly developed plague.

She told me that there were no faxes for me and when I asked if I could send another, she angrily pushed a pen and paper across the counter towards me. I could see no point in asking what was wrong but I suspected that it might have been something the Policeman had said. I continued as though nothing untoward had happened, completed the transaction and left. I went to the main lobby area, ordered a beer and made it last until I was due to return to American Express.

I was dreading another encounter with Laurel and Hardy. These two surly brutes were by far the worst American Express employees I had ever encountered. There were two other clerks in the office this afternoon as well as my two adversaries but the newcomers were busy with paperwork and paid me no attention whatever. Hardy was sitting at the cash desk behind the glass panelling while Laurel motioned me over to where he was sitting. He gave me a form to complete and after I had returned it to him, I asked him if there had been any news of my cards.

"You have used the card!" boomed Hardy from behind the glass. I swivelled round on the chair to face him and told him that neither of the cards had been used before I had brought them to this country and that I had not used them while I was here.

"The card has been used!" he exploded again as if it had been his personal property. I shrugged and told him that I had not used it.

"You have used the card!" he repeated aggressively. I am not sure what he thought he would achieve by this approach, but if he was trying to provoke me, he was about to succeed. I started to explain again that the card had not been used before it had been stolen when he proceeded to shout.

"The card has been used. You have used it." He'd pushed me too far and I lost my temper completely, springing to my feet intent on finding a way into his glass case so that I could beat him to a pulp but I couldn't get to him. Laurel tried to intervene and I turned on him instead. He looked at me with a mixture of fear and disbelief as I moved towards him and he retreated to the comparative safety of his workstation, carefully keeping his desk between us. I managed to regain something approaching composure but I was still very angry when the telephone rang. It was the Brighton office for me and Laurel was so relieved by the interruption that he forgot to harass me for the cost of the call. The man in Brighton confirmed that the cards had been stolen and that one of them had been used quite extensively. He said the local staff would provide me with the details. I repeated my complaint about Laurel and Hardy, adding the latest incident to my catalogue of gloom and I asked whether anything could be done about them. The man said he would make representations to the Luxor office, which was the sort of coded message they used to trot out at the London Borough of Wavering when they meant that nothing would be done.

When I asked Hardy for details of the transactions made against my stolen card he told me that it was none of my business and that I should ask the Police. I went back to the New Winter Palace for something to eat and another beer and sat there until it was time for me to meet the Police at seven. I was angry upset and confused. I had been robbed and instead of receiving sympathy and help, I had been treated like a leper, a criminal and then it dawned on me.

They thought I had sold my American Express Cards.

With all the visitors, back-packers, waifs and strays who converged on a high profile tourist centre like Luxor, the Police must get a lot of cases of credit card fraud. Looking at my situation from their point of view, I could see how easy it was to jump to that sort of conclusion. Unfortunately, from my point of view, I was in enough trouble just by being robbed but if the Police could substantiate their theory that I'd sold my cards, I could end up in jail.

My interview at the Police Station was much more relaxed this time and much less formal. I assumed that my inquisitor had checked out everything I had told him the day before and found that it all tallied. Even so, I'd like to have known what he had told Marissa. I asked him if he knew whether either card had been used and he handed me a sheet of paper setting out handwritten details in English of all the transactions that had taken place so far. The Gold Card had not yet surfaced but someone had shopped until they had dropped with the Green one with a list of purchases that totalled in excess of $5000. Looking at the dates, I saw that seven days had elapsed between the time I had left Cairo and the date on which the card had first been used. Also, as far as I could ascertain, all the transactions had taken place in Cairo. I guessed that whoever had stolen my cards must have sold them to an intermediary who had sold them on again to someone who was able to pass himself off as me. I handed the list back to the Policeman.

"How did they manage to spend all that?" I asked him

"They were in the gold shops in Cairo," he replied.

"Do you think you will catch them?" He looked at me and shrugged

"Maybe," he said finally, "Maybe not." and I knew that meant "No"

He had lost interest in the case. As far as he was concerned, a tourist had been careless with his cards and they had been stolen. The thief subsequently generated $5000 worth of business for Cairo shops on the strength of it and the only real loser was American Express, an international finance house, which could easily afford the loss. OK so I was £40 out of pocket as well but why should he care about that? Why should he care about any of it? If the truth were told, all he was ever going to do was arrest me for complicity and if he'd thought there had been a case, I would have been locked up yesterday.

"What are you going to do now?" he asked me

"I have to go back to Cairo as soon as I can and get the first available flight home." I told him. "I was hoping to go on to Alexandria but not now."

"Where will you stay in Cairo?" He asked. It seemed an innocent enough question but what if he wanted to keep tabs on me? I hadn't done anything wrong so why did it matter? If I ended up in Cairo with a Policeman for a minder then that was OK by me.

"I'm not sure where I'll stay." I said and that was the truth. "Maybe I'll stay at the Marwa Palace for a few nights." I told him, eventually.

"Do not go back to the other place." He warned

"Do you think that was where my cards were taken?" I asked. He nodded, took out a pipe and proceeded to fill it slowly. It seemed unusual to see an Egyptian smoking a pipe, well, not a pipe like that anyway. As he lit up, he signalled that the interview was at an end and that I was free to leave. I thanked him for his help, we shook hands and I left.

I took a taxi back to the Fontana and the driver charged me about three times the normal fare but I didn't care. I just wanted to be out of Luxor as quickly as possible. It is likely that I could go back to Egypt one day, but, if I live to be a hundred, I will never again set foot in Luxor. The next morning, Peter and I boarded the mid morning train for Cairo and neither of us expressed a word of regret that we were leaving.

CAIRO, ONE LAST TIME

It took me a week before I could confirm a return flight to London with Air France, which gave me plenty of time to explore Islamic Cairo. It also gave me back my enthusiasm for Egypt, which my experiences in Luxor had caused to wane. At Peter's suggestion, I stayed at the Pensione Roma on top of a weathered concrete high-rise on the Sharia Mohammed Farid about ten minutes walk from the Midan Tahrir. The Proprietor appeared brusque with a stern and forbidding exterior but she made my stay there a comfortable one. She also made sure what remained of my valuables were securely locked away so that nothing untoward could happen to them.

I spent my last few days in Cairo visiting Islamic sites and trying to find places used by the British during World War Two but that had been a long time ago and this city had moved on since then. I did find Groppi's, a nondescript coffee house on Midan Talaat Harb, once used extensively by British other ranks. It was another one of those establishments that reminded me of an old ouzo bar in 1970's Athens but that was OK. I used to like those places. I also found Garden Groppi's a few blocks away. It was reputed to be grand in its day but now it was grubby and showing its age. I put much of that down to the time of year. It was now mid July and the dry, dusty air was laced with a toxic haze of petrol fumes so that what should have been a cool quiet haven for middle-class Cairenes in a busy metropolis became no more than an arid paved patio whose shrivelled, defoliated trees gave little or no shade from the scorching, mid summer heat.

It took some effort for me to find what remained of the once opulent Continental Savoy Hotel, which occupied a whole block on the Sharia El Gumhorriya. When I finally found it, I had to check with my guidebook just to make sure I was in the right place but there was no mistake. It was still standing and not quite derelict but it was clearly disused and had been totally abandoned to the ghosts of its grandiose past. I reached the vestibule by means of a narrow dark and dusty arcade. At the far end, I found that an attempt had been made to board up the entrance but I had little difficulty getting in but when I did, I wondered whether it had been worth the effort just to witness a study in neglect and decay. At least the structure of the building seemed sound but a great deal of money would need to be spent to restore it to anything like its former glory.

My assumption that terrorist attacks had been curtailed during low season proved to be a shade optimistic and, four weeks after I left Cairo, Gama'a al-Islamiya gunmen attacked a bus carrying tourists in southern Egypt, killing a young boy from Spain. A month later armed terrorists shot and killed three Germans and two Egyptians in Hurghada but by then, I'd set off on another journey, which lasted many months and took me through Russia, China, Central Asia, Pakistan and Nepal until I reached India.

BIBLIOGRAPHY AND REFERENCES

BULGARIA

A Short History of Modern Bulgaria. R.J.Crampton

A Peace to End All Peace David Fromkin

EGYPT

"Misr" The Arab Republic of Egypt – Parts One, Two and Three – Fr Bill Turnbull W.F.

Mr. Mohamed Arabi: The "Bird Man" of Aswan – Susan L.Wilson

Chronology of Attacks on Tourist targets in Egypt – Reuters Ltd and US Dive travel
   network

Egypt History – http://www.egyptfcus.cm/Modern.htm

Egypt History: The British Occupation-7 January 2003
   http://www.egyptfcus.cm/british.htm.

World: Middle East Bin Laden "Behind Luxor Massacre"
   http://news.bbc.c.uk/1hi/world/middle_est/343/207.stm

Gema'a islamiyah – Vanguard online – http://www.vngu.rdnlinef9.c.uk/0803.htm

The Wahhabi Myth Al-Ikhwan Al Muslimun (The Muslim Brotherhood)
   http://www.thewahhabimyth.com.ikhwan.htm

World: Tourists massacred at temple – BBC News
   http://news.bbc.cuk/1/hi/world/32179.stm

AFRICANET Egypt – History

Egypt: Hostage taking and intimidation by Security Forces: Human Rights Watch
   Report Vol.7No.1 January 1995

Egypt During the War 1939-45
  http://lcweb2.loc.gov/egi-bin/query2/r?frd/cstdy:@field(DICIDego0040)

Egypt: Military Ally or Liability, The Egyptian Army 1936-1942 – Steve Rothwell Egypt 30 April 2004

See Egypt: British Occupation (1882-1952) 30 April 2004

Egypt 8th March-28th August 1801 North/South Gloucestershire Regiments – 1st June 2004 http://history.farmersboys.com/Postings/Egypt/egypt.htm

The British Empire: Egypt http://www.britishempire.co.uk/maproom/egypt/htm

The Campaign in Egypt 1801-1802 http://www.graham.day.dsipipex.com/naI8.htm

HUNGARY

Political Strikes: The state of Trades Unionism in Britain Peter Hain

Spycatcher Peter Wright

Friends in High Places Jeremy Paxman

The Labour Government: 1964 to 1970 Harold Wilson

Gerry Healy: A Revolutionary Life: Corrinna Lotz and Paul Feldman

A SHORT HISTORY OF ANTI BRITISH EGYPT

Empire: The History of the British Empire Trevor Lloyd

Empire: How Britain made the Modern World Niall Ferguson

A Fighting Retreat: The British Empire 1947 – 97 Robin Neillands

The Rise and fall of the British Empire: Lawrence James

El Alamein: Field Marshall Lord Carver

White Knees Brown Knees: Douglas J.Findlay

Egypt: On the Threshhold of Revolution 1945-52 – Library of Congress Country Studies – December 1990 http://countrystudies.us/egypt/31.htm

Napoleon Bonaparte (Napoleon1) (1769-1821) – BBC

Napoleon' s Battle of the Pyramids 21st July 1798
  http://www.napoleon-prints.com/pyramids.htm

Broadside. Battle of the Nile http://www.nelsonsnavy.co.uk/broadside1.html

Napoleon Bonaparte 1769 -1821

Napoleon in the Holy Land – Nathan Schur – Greenhill Books

The Ottoman Empire – Excerpt scanned from B.R.514 Geographical Handbook Series PALESTINE AND TRANSJORDAN, December 1943 naval Intelligence Division (of the Admiralty)

Egypt (1945-1956) – James Robinson.

The Trials and Tribulations of the Suez Canal – Chad Clark 23 November 2001

SUEZ CANAL ZONE EMERGENCY – BRITAINS SMALL WARS

All of the following reports have been posted on the Britains Small Wars website and appear there. For this reason, only the title of the report and its author have been listed.

The Anglo-Egyptian Alliance Treaty 1936: Summary by John Marrs and Richard Woolley

The Suez Canal Zone – A short History 1950 – 1954: Summary of the relevant section of the Memoirs of General Lord Robertson of Oakridge by David Williamson. Summary by John Marrs.

The Royal Air Force in the Canal Zone: Rabbi Burns, Hamish Campbell, John Grant.

The Navy's Here: Derek Harper

The Balloon is going up: John Marrs

Torture and Mutilation (From the Library of Congress "Egypt on the threshold of Revolution 1945–1952" summary by John Marrs.

Bodies Found in the Sweet-water Canal: Extract from the Red Beret – Egypt 24th November 1951 – D.Atkinson, John Marrs

Suez Canal Zone Driving – Its Many Dangers: Richard Woolley

Trouble in Ismailia: Cpl James Collender, Royal Dragoons

Seven Hours of Hell – The Ismailia Riots as told by the wife of a serviceman – Mrs Win Masters

The Ismailia Riots – "The Lancs and the Tanks go into action." Report from the Gallipoli Gazette summarized by John Marrs.

Riots and Bed Bugs – The Arashia Riots, A soldier's wife remembers. Report of Mrs. Marian Williams posted by John Marrs and Richard Woolley.

Policing in Hell – Former RMP Thomas B. Walker.

Women who served in the Canal Zone – John Marrs

Egyptian Propaganda – John Marrs

Newspaper Reports between April 1952 and December 1953 – John Marrs and the Award Alliance Group

The Paras in the Canal Zone – Sergeant Terry Lawton and John Marrs

The Poachers Take on Egyptian Terrorists – a summary by John Marrs and Richard Woolley of information provided by Captain John Lee and Captain J.P. Richards

Shots in the Dark: Arthur Major and Richard Woolley

A Tribute to Sister Anthony (Bridget Anne Timbers) 1900-1952: Tony Tolan, Richard Woolley, John Dodd and John Marrs

Incident Information – Some Statistics and a Sitrep: Statistics concerning incidents during part of the Suez Emergency – October 1951 to July 1954 – John Marrs and Richard Woolley

Canal Zone Casualties – Egypt/Suez Canal Zone, Post WWll Dead (Emergency 1951 – 1954) War Grave Commission Facts – John Marrs and the Award Alliance Group.

Was it War? – Egypt Terrorist Activities, Parliamentary Debate 29th January 1952 – Tom Radford, John Marrs and Richard Woolley

Honour at Last – Tony Tolan

Report to the Committee on the Grant of Honours, Decorations and Medals. Suez Canal Zone 1951-1954.: Richard Woolley and John Marrs

Made in the USA
Las Vegas, NV
31 May 2021